CULTURE**SHOCK!**

A Survival Guide to Customs and Etiquette

BELGIUM

Mark Elliott

Marshall Cavendish
Editions

This edition published in 2006 and reprinted in 2009 by:
Marshall Cavendish Corporation
99 White Plains Road
Tarrytown, NY 10591-9001
www.marshallcavendish.us

Other Marshall Cavendish Offices:
Marshall Cavendish International (Asia) Private Limited. 1 New Industrial
Road, Singapore 536196 ▪ Marshall Cavendish Ltd. 32–38 Saffron Hill, London
EC1N 8FH, UK ▪ Marshall Cavendish International (Thailand) Co Ltd. 253 Asoke,
12th Flr, Sukhumvit 21 Road, Klongtoey Nua, Wattana, Bangkok 10110, Thailand
▪ Marshall Cavendish (Malaysia) Sdn Bhd, Times Subang, Lot 46, Subang Hi-Tech
Industrial Park, Batu Tiga, 40000 Shah Alam, Selangor Darul Ehsan, Malaysia

Marshall Cavendish is a trademark of Times Publishing Limited

ISBN 10: 0-7614-2487-3
ISBN 13: 978-0-7614-2487-1

Please contact the publisher for the Library of Congress catalog number

Printed in Singapore by Times Graphics Pte Ltd

Photo Credits:
All photos by the author except pages 40–41, 132–133 (alt.TYPE/REUTERS);
pages 35, 36–37, 55, 116, 151 (Photolibrary); page 123 (Dani Systermans);
pages 105, 163, 164, 186, 192, 231 (Jo Systermans).
▪ Cover photo: Photolibrary

All illustrations by TRIGG

ABOUT THE SERIES

Culture shock is a state of disorientation that can come over anyone who has been thrust into unknown surroundings, away from one's comfort zone. *CultureShock!* is a series of trusted and reputed guides which has, for decades, been helping expatriates and long-term visitors to cushion the impact of culture shock whenever they move to a new country.

Written by people who have lived in the country and experienced culture shock themselves, the authors share all the information necessary for anyone to cope with these feelings of disorientation more effectively. The guides are written in a style that is easy to read and covers a range of topics that will arm readers with enough advice, hints and tips to make their lives as normal as possible again.

Each book is structured in the same manner. It begins with the first impressions that visitors will have of that city or country. To understand a culture, one must first understand the people—where they came from, who they are, the values and traditions they live by, as well as their customs and etiquette. This is covered in the first half of the book.

Then on with the practical aspects—how to settle in with the greatest of ease. Authors walk readers through topics such as how to find accommodation, get the utilities and telecommunications up and running, enrol the children in school and keep in the pink of health. But that's not all. Once the essentials are out of the way, venture out and try the food, enjoy more of the culture and travel to other areas. Then be immersed in the language of the country before discovering more about the business side of things.

To round off, snippets of basic information are offered before readers are 'tested' on customs and etiquette of the country. Useful words and phrases, a comprehensive resource guide and list of books for further research are also included for easy reference.

CONTENTS

NOTE

ON PLACE NAMES AND FOREIGN WORDS

In a trilingual country like Belgium, there are alternative words for almost everything, including place names. In general, this book uses the names appropriate to the area of origin: i.e. Flemish names in Flanders and French names in Wallonia. Important exceptions are the names of the following cities:

- Brussels (should be Brussel/Bruxelles)
- Bruges (Brugge)
- Antwerp (Antwerpen)
- Ostend (Oostende)

For those I have used the familiar English forms. An extensive list of French-Flemish variants is given in the Glossary.

At even the most banal local carnivals, you can expect to be showered with 'Carnival Snow'—mini circles of recycled old paper thrown from bags or fired by air-powered 'cannons' from passing floats. This paper 'dandruff' is liable to afflict your coats for weeks after.

ACKNOWLEDGEMENTS

Thirty thousand thank you's to Dani Systermans without whom I wouldn't have come to Belgium in the first place and certainly couldn't have written this book. Her inspiration, support and kindness (in not making me eat those Brussels sprouts) are beyond measure. Unending thanks too to my unbeatable family across the Channel, to Wieland de Hoon for his patience and beer stamina, to Kris, Beverly, Marc, Dominique, Stella & Pierre, Deedee, Carine, Karine, the staff at Waterloo OTSI, and dozens of other people who have helped me experience and enjoy this country so much more. May your chips never want for mayonnaise.

DEDICATION

To the memory of
Jo Systermans (Hermont),
who sadly didn't live long enough to see it published.

MAP OF BELGIUM

NORTH SEA

NETHERLANDS

FLANDERS

GERMANY

•BRUSSELS
BELGIUM

WALLONIA

FRANCE

LUXEMBOURG

FIRST IMPRESSIONS

CHAPTER 1

'Belgium—Officially Not Boring'
—headline on a British travel website

UNLIKE MANY OF THE MORE OBVIOUSLY EXOTIC COUNTRIES covered by books in this series, Belgium is a place that carefully shields visitors from the most immediate forms of culture shock. On the surface things seem very straightforward. The people are practical, multilingual and obliging. As an English speaker, you'll be able to get by without learning the languages and without leaving the comfortable confines of a multinational expatriate environment. Then three years later, you discover that your apparently level-headed neighbour sneaks out to carnivals dressed in a barrel costume, boggle-eyed mask, and tarantula hat to throw oranges at passers-by. Or that his smart university student daughter spends unashamed hours reading comic books. That his wife drinks beer flavoured with raspberries. That they all rave about holidays on one of Europe's most rainy, concrete blighted beaches. Belgium takes a perverse pleasure in its 'boring' image. It's an image which it almost seems to foster, perhaps, to make it seem ideally suited as the capital of Europe. But underneath, the culture is a unique, complex and intriguing blend: proud but not nationalistic, friendly but reserved, accommodating yet obstinate. And practical in its approach to almost any issue. This book helps you uncover the real Belgium, and to help you make the most of your time amongst Europe's most underestimated people.

My First Impressions of Belgium

Before coming to live here, like so many other foreigners, the limit of my knowledge of Belgium was a series of stereotypes: the quaint canals of Bruges, the wickedly strong beers, the dull flat views seen in transit from Belgian motorways, the melt-in-the-mouth wonder of Belgian chocolates, Tintin and Hercule Poirot.... I'd met many interesting and inspiring Belgians while travelling in exotic distant lands yet had never stopped to doubt all the derogatory images: Belgium the grey, Belgium the wet, Belgium the boring.

But when one of those travelling Belgians became my wife, it was time to learn more. Being British, the first shock was discovering the need to have an ID card. To get an ID card ,one needs an address. But to get an address, one needs to have an ID card. Fortunately, thanks to my wife, the address was no problem, but this catch-22 was a great eye-opener to the Kafka-esque surrealism that makes Belgium so simultaneously frustrating yet intriguing. My wife's job in a multi-national company seemed to fit with Belgium's 'centre of Europe', open-minded persona. In her office were both French- and Flemish-speaking Belgians along with a South African, a Macedonian, a Turk, a Czech, a Moroccan, a German, a Russian and a Nigerian. Most were at least trilingual, and between them they spoke a dozen or more languages. So when new American bosses decided that their staff should take a training course on 'diversity', there was general astonishment at the idea's sheer irrelevance... especially when the course tutor proved to speak only a single language!

(Continued on the next page)

(Continued from previous page)

But it didn't take long for me to realise that Belgium's multicultural open-ness was not quite as deep as it looked. I quickly learnt that the term 'foreigner' didn't mean someone from another country. In fact, it was used as a negative term for Turkish and Moroccan residents who otherwise-liberal Belgians seemed to eye with little-disguised racism. Meanwhile, although the nation had recently been united in grief over the death of popular King Baudouin/Boudewijn, the Francophone-Flemish divide quickly became apparent when we visited Leuven. There, to my surprise, my bilingual wife chose to address the Flemish waitress in English. Just to be safe! In Leuven, she told me, her poorly-accented Flemish might give her away as being French-speaking; so better pretend to be a tourist.

Over a decade later, the newspapers suggest that the linguistic tensions have grown ever worse. Yet our friends are an equal mix of French and Flemish speakers, most of whom sneer at the divisiveness of radicals that threaten to divide the country. Meanwhile, the superb food, the hidden delight of Belgium's festivals and the sheer convenience of living in the 'heart of Europe' are enormous plusses. And the people, though reserved and not overflowingly hospitable, are uninvasively friendly once one works on gaining their trust. And their practical-mindedness, cynical humour and general taste for the good life means that one really couldn't call life here 'boring'. Not in the slightest.

WHAT IS BELGIUM?

Belgium is a miraculous compromise. Utterly artificial, it is a fusion of linguistically incompatible peoples thrust together by religio-historical chance, and sealed by a masterpiece of 19th century cartographic bravado. Over 2,000 years ago, an ill-defined entity called Belgica had been spotted lurking at the violent northern edge of the Roman Empire. But thereafter no such thing as Belgium existed up until 1830 (except for a very brief period after the 1789 Brabançonne Revolution). Once created, no one really expected the little nation to last out the decade. But survive it has, thanks to its remarkable capacity for compromise, practicality and fudging: characteristics that still fundamentally shape the Belgian mindset.

Belgium can be roughly divided along linguistic lines. The northern half (Flanders or Vlaanderen) is a flat, richly agricultural land whose population mostly speaks Flemish (Vlaams), a language very similar to the Dutch of neighbouring

Trop is te Veel. 'Enough is enough.' Few phrases are more Belgian. Combining words of French and Flemish, it is commonly used to express mild (sometimes humorous) exasperation rather than any genuine resolve to make a concerted stand. And what could be more appropriate in Belgium than to have stickers complaining about taxes—in this case the VAT (TVA/BTW) on food?

Holland. In the southern half (Wallonia or Wallonie), people mostly speak a variant type of French (Français) and collection of yokel French dialects known collectively as Walloon, though there are also small pockets of German-speaking people living in and around Eupen. To complete the picture, add Brussels. That historically Flemish city is increasingly Francophone, nominally bilingual, and heartily multicultural: a great choice for the 'capital of Europe'.

The very survival of Belgium relies on the compromise between its communities. As you will see, the regions and various factions in society are often openly antagonistic toward one another, but underneath all that, the people maintain a practical 'let's get on with it' spirit. This compromise is the essence of Belgian culture, along with a deadpan, self-effacing humour. While crises blow by and politicians wrangle, ordinary Belgians quietly tuck into some of Europe's finest food and best beer with a chuckle and a 'so what' shrug.

LAND AND HISTORY

CHAPTER 2

'With the great North Sea, as the last empty space,
Just the void of the dunes to arrest its advance...
With a sky so low that a canal gets lost in it...
With a sky of such grey that you have to forgive it...
This flat country of mine.'
—Jacques Brel

THERE'S NO MORE EVOCATIVE DESCRIPTION of Belgian geography than Jacques Brel's poignantly bittersweet song 'Le Plat Pays' ('The Flat Country'). Portraying a country that is at once dreary yet loveable, this is self-effacing Belgian modesty at its best. One line's untranslatably poetic description of the country's 'cathedrals as its only mountains' is almost true. Northern Belgium is indeed home to the fertile, pan-flat, drained marshland of Flanders and some of Europe's widest expanses of sand along the North Sea coast. But the centre of the country is decorated with plenty of gently rolling contours. And the relief climaxes in the heavily forested Ardennes of the south-east. Describing these as 'mountains' is really a little over optimistic, though some have tried to do so. In fact, millions of years of erosion by the elements and Dutch caravanners have worn these former peaks down ino mere 'hills'. Even at their highest point, the Belgian Ardennes only reach a modest 694 m (2,277 ft) above sea level. This is the Signal de Botrange, an extremely undramatic minor incline. Nonetheless, it still manages to draw local tourists on the few weekends a year when there's enough snow for a bit of skiing.

WEATHER
The weather has a crucial bearing on national character. In Belgium, the grey skies, low clouds and drizzling rain seem to nourish the stoical national character of home lovers.

"Look—an undulation!" Belgium isn't entirely flat.

Of course, there can be days or even weeks of splendid summer sunshine accompanied by the buzzing of lawn mowers and hedge cutters. But more memorable are the thick fogs in spring and autumn. Belgian winters are typically cold but not unbearable. You can expect two or three heavy snowfalls during a typical Brussels winter, after which the city looks briefly magnificent and the Brussels Ring road becomes even more of a death trap than ever. In the Ardennes, there is usually enough snow to allow a few weekends of cross-country skiing.

REGIONALISM

Since 1980, the kingdom of Belgium has been divided into a federation of three regions: Wallonia, Flanders and Brussels-Capital. The controversial Lambermont Agreement of 2001 transferred more power than ever to the regions and made Brussels more equivalent with the other two federal regions, though certain Flemish groups fear that this will mean that Flanders is always opposed two-to-one in federal

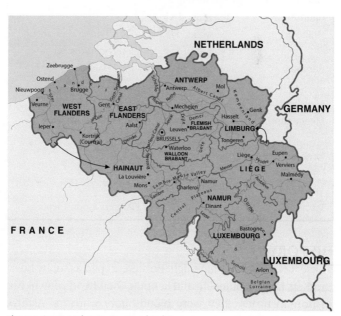

The provinces and main towns of Belgium.

disputes. Already the nation's two main regions, Wallonia and Flanders, are so autonomous that they occasionally appear to forget that they are part of a single, federal Belgium. 'Flanders—at the heart of Europe' shouts a series of posters and advertisements trying to attract business and tourism to the region which gave the world many of its greatest painters during the Middle Ages. The regional identity of French-speaking Wallonia is less defined and Francophones are more likely than the Flemish to be proud of the sobriquet Belgian. Be careful of what you call them, however. Canadians are not American. Scots are not English. And Walloons are most self-consciously not French. (*For more on regionalism, see* Chapter 4:.Socialising and Fitting In, *pages 55.*)

Geographical Areas	
Ardennes	south-easterly hill country
Borinage	mining zone of southern Wallonia
Fagnes	hill country stretching from Couvin to the Hautes Fagnes in eastern Wallonia
Famenne	central Wallonia
Gaume	area around Virton
Houtland	'the wooded land' around Tienen even though it's now almost completely deforested
Kempen	flat heathlands of eastern Flanders. Called Campine in French
Maasland	far eastern Flanders on the Dutch border
Meetjesland	meaning 'land of the little meadows' (the area around Eeklo)
Pays de Herve	cheese country east of Liège
Pajottenland	south-west of Brussels
Waasland	area around St Niklaas
Westhoek	far western Belgian Flanders around Ieper

HISTORY

These days, Belgian men might be stereotyped as tubby beer-drinkers living a quiet life and keeping their heads down. But in Roman times, they were bloodthirsty warriors. Asterix in Belgium features fearless tribes of 'brave Belgae'—and

that's not supposed to be a sarcastic swipe. For several years around 50 BC, a Belgian Asterix by the name of Ambiorix really did lead the Belgae tribe and proved a great nuisance to the Roman legions around Tongeren. "Of all the people of war, the Belgians are the bravest," Julius Caesar is supposed to have said. Of course Caesar's comments were aimed less at flattering the illiterate Belgian fighters and their chip-frying descendants than at explaining away a couple of unexpected, if short-term, military setbacks for the Roman legions. But today, the quote launches history lessons for Belgian school kids, much as Alfred's burnt cakes do for Brits.

Seeds of the Language Divide

The Belgae were a sizeable group of Gallo-Celtic warrior clans consisting of the Morini in Flanders, the Nervii in Brabant, the Atuatuci in Namur, the Eburones in Limburg, and several others, around half a million in total. They arrived in the 2nd century BC armed with iron weapons and equipped with seaworthy boats. The clans developed forges to improve their ironwork using coal from Hainaut, and the coins which they made are thought to have been traded as far afield as Greece.

In a protracted series of harsh battles between 57–52 BC, the Romans conquered the Belgae; the Nervii were defeated near Cambrai and once the Atuatuci of Namur were crushed, the other clans surrendered. 'Belgica' became a Roman province and the fertile plains of Wallonia proved suitable for agricultural development. But the Romans decided not to bother with the impenetrable forest and swamp of northern Belgium.

The area neglected by the Romans caught the fancy of Norse-Germanic Viking tribes who besieged the coasts with as many as 12 full-scale raids between AD 795 and 1098. By the 12th century, some of these tribes had decided to stay put and were comfortably settled in what is now Flanders.

Thus Flanders developed a Germanic language, while Wallonia separately adopted Romanic Latin, and eventually, French. Exactly what happened to the legendary Belgae tribe is not clearly recorded but quite unwittingly, they were to give their name to present-day Belgium some 19 centuries later.

Early Unrest

From the middle of the 3rd century AD, the Roman Empire was reeling from a series of Gothic raids. At its northern flank, Belgica became increasingly dominated by the Germanic Franks. By the end of the 4th century, Tournai, once the area's most important Roman town, started to develop into a Frankish royal city. Childeric I, the king of Gaul and father of Clovis, established his capital here while Charlemagne, the great Gallic empire builder, came from just across today's border at Aix-la-Chapelle (now Aachen, Germany). Charlemagne dragged Belgica into the French-Gallic empire. Cheeky Belgians might argue that in fact, he dragged France into a greater Belgium. To Francophone kids, Charlemagne's better known for having 'invented school'. This is a 'fact' celebrated in a well-known France Gall song.

From the end of Charlemagne's era (AD 814), even Flanders had theoretically become a vassal of the French. However, Flanders was still separated from Wallonia by thick forests and remained largely autonomous; increasingly so as towns such as Bruges, Gent and Ieper developed into bustling international trade and textile centres in the 13th century.

Belgium in The Da Vinci Code

Dan Brown's talking-point thriller, *The Da Vinci Code* has three key Belgian moments. However, with the same geographical carelessness that the author allows a character to follow a non-existent railway line from Andorra, Brown blatantly places Orval Abbey 'in France near Stenay, in the Ardennes'. Orval is indeed in the Ardennes. And it is near Stenay in France. However, as any beer drinker will attest, Orval Abbey and its famous brewery are now across the border in Belgium. So too is Bouillion, from which Godefroy (Godfrey), the leader of the first crusade hailed. Much of the public intrigue over the Da Vinci code rests on whether Godefroy was, as claimed, in a Merovingian bloodline which could be very controversially traced back to the offspring of Jesus and Mary Magdalene. A third Belgian reference is the copy of Da Vinci's last supper by an unknown 16th century in the abbey at Tongerlo. That certainly does exist as you'll see at the website:

http://www.tongerlo.org/da_vinci/davinci_index.htm.

The 'Low Countries'

The 'Low Countries' region—encompassing today's Belgium, Netherlands and Luxembourg—formed a patchwork of medieval duchies, counties and principalities with shifting alliances that slowly coalesced under the leadership of the French dukes of Burgundy. The exact boundaries vary through history but, at times, stretched as far as Lille, Gravelines and Cambrai in today's France, notably including Artois, the district centred on Arras.

This was not a nation state—such a concept didn't appear in Europe until relatively recently. The French-speaking overlords simply administered a jigsaw of disconnected territorial fragments and expanded their rule by conquests or tactical marriages. Initially, that hardly mattered to most of the population. For the peasant majority, medieval life was simply a battle for day-to-day survival. So long as their traditions were not threatened and taxes not increased, relatively few cared or even noticed who their rulers were (not so different from Belgium today, one might cynically venture).

But as Flanders quietly developed into a major textile and trade centre, more and more people moved into towns. By the 14th century, Bruges was one of the richest towns in Europe with some of the continent's best-educated citizens. And educated people do the unthinkable—like questioning the divine rights of their feudal lords. Organised into guilds (somewhat like trade unions), the Flemish townsfolk were prepared to fight for civic liberties and privileges that set them apart from peasants. These tussles occasionally boiled over into full-scale uprisings. This is what happened in 1302 when Bruges guildsmen refused to pay a new round of taxes. Pieter de Coninck led the townsfolk in rooting out Francophones by the administration of a very basic Flemish language test: bad pronunciation of the Flemish phrase *schild en vriend* ('shield and friend') was punished with the sword. The rebellion spread, and the French responded by sending in a dazzling army of heavily armoured knights. But the warriors were tricked into the Groeninghekouter marsh near Kortrijk and simply got stuck in the mud.

This 'Battle of the Golden Spurs' was unthinkably humiliatingly for the noble knights whose defeat at the hands of mere commoners undermined their chivalric myth of natural superiority. The battle remains a tremendous emotional landmark for Flemish nationalists. Although the French were soon back in control, the towns did manage to assert their rights, symbolic recognition of which eventually came to be enshrined in the Joyeuses Entrées (ceremonial visits by the future monarch to every part of his realm). New monarchs still present themselves to each town, as the present crown prince, Philippe, and his bride Mathilde did in 1999.

Burgundians and Austrians

Despite a nod to the French kings, local power in Belgium coalesced in the hands of the Dukes of Burgundy as the 14th and 15th centuries progressed. The Burgundians had held Flanders since 1384. With strong-armed rule and Machiavellian political manoeuvres that add a sarcastic twist to his popular name, Philip the Good (1419–1467) managed to piece together a large, virtually coherent domain on the edge of the French empire. Initially, he made a cheeky alliance with England against his supposed French overlords, capturing Joan of Arc whom he handed to the English for a bonfire party. But once France had agreed to release Burgundy and Flanders from vassal status, Philip switched sides and fought beside France against his former English allies. Brabant, Limburg and Antwerp were inherited, Namur was bought and Hainaut (packaged with Holland and Zeeland since 1299) was won by subterfuge. This gave Philip most of present-day Belgium. The main gap in his collection was Liège, a neutral, religious enclave that remained an independent Prince-Bishopric until 1794! (Liège was finally taken by revolutionary France; Walter Scott's *Quentin Durward* is a historical fiction recounting those events.)

Philip also managed to tighten his grip on the prosperous new towns, reeling in hard won civic privileges but simultaneously improving their economic performance. By the time he married Isabella of Portugal, he was rich and powerful enough to indulge in his passion for reading and to become a major patron of the arts.

Philip's son, Charles the Bold, married the King of England's sister and set about a series of wars planning to build an ever bigger Burgundian duchy into a kingdom in its own right. When Charles was killed in battle, his daughter and heir-apparent, Mary, was kidnapped by fed-up Flemish citizens and released only when she agreed to grant again the civic rights that had been eroded over previous decades. Mary went on to marry the Holy Roman Emperor, Maximillian, who became sole ruler when Mary fell off her horse and died. Suddenly, the Low Countries became part of the vast Hapsburg empire, ruled initially from Austria. And later from Spain. And later still from Austria once again…

Spanish Rule

Maximillian's grandson Charles V (Charles Quint/Kaiser Karel) was born in Gent in 1500. Arguably the greatest Belgian ever, he was certainly one of the most powerful men ever to rule in Europe. He reigned over vast inherited domains 'on which the sun never set' including Austria (which he later gave to his brother), Burgundy, the Low Countries, the Holy Roman Empire, Spain and Spain's fabulously wealthy American conquests.

With Bruges' fortunes fading following the silting of its river estuary, Charles V encouraged the growth of Antwerp which became one of the most important cities in the 16th century world. The Antwerp Beurs (stock market) opened in 1531 and was soon turning over around a million pounds sterling per day. Antwerp also became a great cultural centre for painters, writers and thinkers. Even William Shakespeare studied here. It was a cosmopolitan community, a medieval Manhattan, the greatest trading port of the Western world.

Throughout the Low Countries, a high level of education and the development of new printing processes meant that locals were increasingly literate. For the first time, people could read the Bible for themselves. And this led to trouble. Suddenly, ordinary people began to realise that the priests of the often corrupt Catholic Church weren't really following 'God's Way' in the way the Bible proposed. Far from it. Many had turned salvation into a profitable business by selling redemption as a commodity. Lutheran and later Calvinist Protestantism spread rapidly across northern Europe. Despite the Edict of Blood which threatened protestants with the death sentence for heresy, future-Belgium became rapidly 'infected' with Protestantism while Charles V's attention was more focused on Spain.

The first Belgian Protestants to be burnt at the stake were two Augustinian monks who were roasted in Antwerp in 1523. But the city soon realised that killing nonconformists was very bad for business. After all, many of the heretics were rich traders. These signs of tolerance did not sit too well with the staunchly Catholic monarchy. But initial attempts to introduce a Spanish-style inquisition were strenuously resisted by the towns, who considered that an infringement of their traditional civic rights. However, sparks really started to fly once Charles abdicated in 1555.

Charles V's son, Phillip II was not a compromise-prone Belgian. He had been brought up in Spain with all the ruthless heretic-burning zeal of a good contemporary Hispanic. In the liberal-minded Low Countries, this was to prove a severe problem. When Phillip II succeeded his father in 1556, he was a bit surprised to find that in the Low Countries, people didn't always do what they were told. It was the start of a major conflict.

The Dutch Revolts

In 1566, an extraordinary fever of civilian outrage at the rigid and heavy taxing system imposed by the Spanish swept through the Low Countries. A year later, this uprising was ruthlessly put down by King Philip's commander, the Duke of Alva. Yet taxes had to be raised again to fund the garrisons of Spanish troops who stayed on to keep the peace. This fed the public's discontent and a second revolt erupted on April Fool's Day in 1572. Failed grain harvests, plague and an English trade boycott had generally made everyone more miserable than ever. Dutch rebels managed to capture large caches of armaments which the king had shipped to the coast for an abortive invasion of England. And Spain reacted cautiously. It was also carefully watching the Franco-Belgian border in case the Protestant Huguenot leaders in Paris should use the opportunity to strike east. After the Huguenot leaders were massacred en masse in France, however, support for the Belgian rebels collapsed. With the pressure reduced, Alva set about a vicious retribution in Belgium. His troops swiftly retook the region and sacked Mechelen to supplement their poor wages. But they failed to take Holland, where the leader of the rebels, William of Orange, had retreated. William was able to defend that area by opening the dykes and watercourses; this flooded low-lying fields so that Alva's men simply couldn't march across them.

The war became a stalemate. Again Spain was having trouble paying its troops and, in 1576, a mutiny of the unpaid Spanish garrison virtually destroyed Antwerp. In the Union of Arras in January 1579, many of the Belgian counties decided to cut their losses and say 'sorry' to Spain, returning to Philip's empire. At the same time, however, the Dutch United Provinces declared themselves outside such jurisdiction in what was effectively the world's first declaration of independence: the Union of Utrecht. Neither Dutch nor Spanish signatories would have realised at the time that they were setting the first stage in the eventual foundation of a new nation: the Netherlands. And that what was left of the 'Spanish Low Countries' would eventually be moulded into Belgium.

17th Century Decline

The Dutch revolts proved to be an unmitigated economic disaster for proto-Belgium. The primary concern of the Spanish regime was to re-Catholicise the population. Those Protestants who survived the reinforced inquisition under the Spanish fled to Holland or England, draining the land of many of its skilled workers. Flanders and Brabant, once at the forefront of Europe, were now forgotten provinces of a distant, conservative Hapsburg empire ruled from Spain (and later Austria). The once great city of Antwerp withered: 6 per cent of its population had been massacred in the mutiny of 1576 and its trade role had been undermined by decades of war. Trade with the Indies, which had brought in much revenue for Antwerp, moved steadily away to Amsterdam and Rotterdam, especially after 1580 when the Dutch started taking for themselves many of Portugal's colonies. The port of Antwerp was closed to legitimate international trade following the revolts. Many of the unemployed Flemish seamen turned to piracy in order to make ends meet.

What remained of artistic life in Belgium took a sharp turn toward the conservative. The sparkling intellectual world that had encouraged humanitarian thinkers like Erasmus and Thomas More gave way to a retrograde obsession with religion. Artists like Rubens thrived on painting vast Italian-influenced Baroque canvases glorifying the daunting, overpowering Catholic mainstream. The opulence of his work was a deliberate contrast to the discredited austerity of Calvinism and to the horrific doomsday surrealism of Bosch and Breughel, which had prevailed a few years previously. Rubens himself was saddened by the state of his once great Antwerp which he described as 'languishing like a consumptive body' and, in between masterpieces, he acted as diplomat to try and improve relations between Spain and England in hope of a cure for the city. But to no avail. The war, that had rumbled on between Catholic and Protestant Europe since the Dutch revolts, lasted 80 years. It was finally concluded in the 1648 Peace of Westphalia (Peace of Münster). But this was anything but good for Antwerp. In a nod to the Dutch, the treaty closed the River Schelde to shipping and thereby killed off Antwerp's last trickle of lifeblood, trade.

Austrian Rule & The Brabançonne Revolution

Carlos (Charles) II, the last Spanish Hapsburg emperor, died childless in 1700. In his will, he left his realms to Philip d'Anjou, the grandson of the French king Louis XIV. Louis gleefully prepared to take control of the Spanish Netherlands (i.e. Belgium) but Holland and England were having none of it. A further expanded France would have been too much of a threat and the affair sparked off the War of Spanish Succession. For a decade or so, the English Duke of Marlborough skirmished with French troops across Belgium with key battles at Tienen, Ramillies, Oudenaarde and Malplaquet. Finally, in 1713, France reluctantly signed the Treaty of Utrecht which gave Belgium to the Austrian Hapsburg empire.

By the late 18th century, the artificial division between Dutch and Flemish cultures had solidified into real differences. Although later Austrian rulers proved relatively enlightened, Emperor Joseph II, a reformist, nearly caused a war with Holland when he tried to re-open Antwerp to international trade. His liberal attempts to legalise Protestant forms of worship were not only futile (by this stage, there was barely a Protestant left in Belgium to welcome the move) but actually resulted in the 1789 rebellion referred to today as the Brabançonne Revolution. The 'Revolution' led briefly to the creation of the independent United Belgian States and is still celebrated in the Belgian national anthem. However, this new independence was crushed within a year by the Austrian Hapsburgs.

The French Barge In

The Austrians didn't last long. In 1789, France had also had a revolution and France's new republican, anti-religious zeal seemed unstoppable. In 1792, a French revolutionary army led by General Dumouriez marched into the Austrian Low Countries and defeated the Hapsburg army at the battle of Jemappes. By 1794, the French had taken control of the whole of Belgium. The main result was the desecration and dispossession of the abbeys, in line with the anti-religious beliefs of the revolutionaries. Even today some monastic masterpieces like that of Villers-la-Ville, still remain in ruins from those years!

By 1799, Napoleon had come to power. He demanded that the Dutch allow an end to the blockade of the River Schelde. This was to allow the renovation of the port of Antwerp, which he described as a 'pistol pointed at the heart of Britain'. But Napoleon never got to fire that pistol. After the French attack on Russia and their subsequent ignominious retreat from Moscow in 1812, the Low

Countries were once more in revolt. Napoleon's last-ditch attempt at a comeback in 1815 was a remarkable feat of mobilisation considering he'd been in exile a few months earlier. However, his reign came to a definitive end when he famously underestimated Wellington's multinational armies at Waterloo, just south of Brussels.

Dutch Rule

In 1815, the Kingdom of the Netherlands was created by the Congress of Vienna in the aftermath of Waterloo. The Netherlands was a buffer state that lumped together the former United Provinces (today's Netherlands) and the Austrian Netherlands (today's Belgium). The new king William I declared Dutch the official language and set out to secularise the schools. This did not go down well at all with the French-speaking population in the south. In July 1830, revolutionary fervour was again rising in France, and Brussels caught the wave a month later. One of history's most unlikely rebellions began as high-spirited concert-goers poured out of a performance of Auber's opera *La Muette de Portici* singing along to the patriotic French aria 'Amour Sacré de la Patrie' ('Sacred Love of Patriotism'). Given the circumstance, the Dutch did not recognise the rebellion, thinking it a joke. The troops stayed in their barracks. But before they knew it, the rebellion was spiralling out of control across the country.

Much to their bemusement, the Belgians suddenly found themselves with their very own state. A republican national constitution was rapidly formulated. But by the conservative norms of the day, it seemed dangerously liberal. To give it a suitable veneer of respectability, the authors decided to graft on a figurehead monarchy. The kingdom of Belgium was born.

Independence: An Inauspicious Start

Scouts went fishing around the courts of Europe, looking for a suitable king. After a few rejections, they settled for the pompous Leopold Saxe-Coburg as a politically appropriate (i.e. non-French, non-Dutch) compromise. Leopold had been 'unemployed' since the untimely death of his wife Princess Charlotte, heir apparent of England. Having lost his hopes of becoming British consort and still keen to start a dynasty, he'd already been shopping for thrones around Europe. Having rejected Greece as a bit too risky, he finally decided to make the best of it with Belgium. That was quite a feat at first, as the country was considered a joke by most outsiders. Few believed the country would last more than a decade. But Leopold was single-mindedly determined to give it a go despite the country's distinct lack of national spirit. Belgium's survival was first threatened just a year after independence by Dutch invasion, and later by several attempts of foreign powers to conquer or divide it. But through careful manoeuvring, Leopold managed to maintain the little country. And by 1848, Belgium was strong enough to survive at a time when the majority of the European monarchies were tumbling or being shaken by revolutions.

Industrialisation and Growth

Leopold's unexpected success was helped by his careful maintenance of political neutrality, and by the gradual industrialisation of Wallonia. However, the biggest boost to the economy came from his son Leopold II's outrageous colonisation of Congo. With Machiavellian cunning, Leopold II managed to obtain sponsorship to fund a private venture to the vast African region, a project that he initially dressed up as a religiously-motivated humanitarian mission. In fact, Leopold took over the Congo as his personal garden exploiting its vast sources of raw materials and using the population as virtual slaves. The enterprise was an extremely profitable business and Leopold gained vast personal wealth. However, even by the callous standards of the day, the treatment of the Congolese was so unmitigatedly exploitative that in 1908, a shamed Belgian government felt it had to take over the colony to repair the nation's dreadful reputation for colonial cruelty. But by this stage, Leopold II had already invested large sums of Congo-made money in the development of Belgium. Brussels, in particular, was transformed from a relatively humble provincial town into a grand, fashionable Art Nouveau metropolis.

War

All progress came grinding to a halt in World War I. German troops poured across the border assuming that Belgium, being a neutral party, would not put up a fight. Though quickly overwhelmed, the plucky Belgians skirmished valiantly under their 'Soldier King' Albert, who equally valiantly insisted on participating in the frontline action. They managed to hold out just long enough. Belgian valour allowed the Allies time to shore up the western front. The fields of Flanders became a mousse of blood and mud and the historic town of Ieper (Ypres, since rebuilt) was pounded to ruins. Nonetheless, Albert refused to leave Belgian soil. Using a trick from the Dutch Revolt, he positioned his troops at De Panne in far western Flanders, then he blew holes in the dykes between his position and that of the advancing Germans. The intervening area was flooded and remained impassable for the rest of the war.

Belgium had an even harder time in World War II. Heavily bombed by both sides, the country was invaded by Nazi Germany which not only decimated the Jewish community but also fomented tensions between the Francophone and the previously marginalised Flemish-speaking population. (*See* Chapter 8: Language, *page 219*.) King Leopold III proved much less statesmanlike than Albert I in World War I. Publicly suspected of collaborating, he was finally forced to abdicate in 1950.

Recent History

Post-war Belgium has quietly done a very good job of making itself prosperous again, despite constantly teetering on the edge of a break-up along linguistic lines. Since 1963, the linguistic communities of the French, Flemish and German speakers have been officially recognised. Belgium was also divided into regions in 1980 and has been a federal state since 1993, but it is still Belgium. Despite grave recessions in the heavy industries of Wallonia, the economy remains reasonably vibrant, thanks in part to the numerous international organisations which are based here—notably the Supreme Headquarters Allied Powers Europe (SHAPE) in Mons, and NATO (since 1977) plus the gargantuan EU bureaucracy in Brussels.

Broad-strokes Historical Eras	
Belgae	from approximately 1500 BC
Roman	from 52 BC
Frankish	AD 5th century
Norse-Germanic Vikings	AD 9th century
Flemish golden era under nominal French suzerainty	AD 12th century
Battle of the Golden Spurs	AD 1302
Burgundian dynasty	from AD 1419
Spanish/Hapsburg rule	from AD 1482
Spread of Protestantism	from AD 1520s
Dutch revolts	AD 1560s
Split with Netherlands	AD 1579
Austrian Rule	from AD 1701
Brabançonne Revolution	AD 1789
French Invasion	AD 1792
French rule	from AD 1795
Dutch rule	from AD 1814
Independence	AD 1830
World War I	AD 1914-1918
World War II	AD 1939-1945
Federalisation	AD 1995

THE BELGIAN PEOPLE

CHAPTER 3

'There are no Belgians,
never have been any, never will be any.'
—Talleyrand
19th century French statesman and diplomat

YOU MIGHT THINK OF BELGIUM (Flanders and Wallonia) as a traditional, married couple who have long ago realised they're incompatible. They do the dishes together without talking, but keep up public appearances for the sake of the children.

Just below the surface, Belgium appears to be an unstable, heterogeneous society. But contrary to popular belief, there is a deeper sense of Belgian-ness which transcends the antagonistic linguistic divisions, regional individualities and social strata. This is manifested in the self-deprecating sense of humour, the practicality and the ability to compromise. Mutual distrust between the linguistic groups is real enough but is rarely as strong as the shared Belgian disdain of foreigners. And despite an apparent lack of patriotism, there is a great, understated national pride in the success of famous Belgians and all things Belgian.

CHARACTERISTICS
Self-image
How does a Belgian sum up his or her own national characteristics? "Ah ...we're the country of great individualism," claimed one local journalist, "We have Magritte, Tintin, Jacques Brel..." Sadly of late, he admits, the image has been somewhat tainted by some pretty unpleasant brushes with crime, food contamination and paedophilia. So is Belgium really a nest of evil, rotten to

the core? For the neighbouring Dutch, that is just what they have always imagined of Belgium. But the Belgian answer is that everybody's got the same troubles; Belgians are just more open about their failures. "It's a national masochism," explained the journalist over half a dozen beers. But it hurts deeply those who try to maintain the façade of the little rainy paradise.

Basic Social Divisions
Belgium's social divisions are drawn along the lines of language (predominantly Flemish or French) and of socio-political class. Religion (*covered later in this chapter, page 49*) is rarely a great issue as such a large majority of people are nominally Christian. And Christian is assumed to imply Catholic unless otherwise qualified. But beware—in Belgium the term 'Catholic' is also commonly used as a social label. Almost every institution—from political parties, to trade unions, to hospitals, to universities—tends to be divided into one of three broad social categories: Catholic (conservative, snobby and rich), Liberal (also well off, and also Catholic but more discreet about it!) and Socialist (poorer or more radical).

Patriotism
Pure Belgian nationalists are about as common as Martini-sipping mullahs in Mecca. But this doesn't preclude a strong national pride. My Belgian wife loves Belgium. She thinks it's one of the best countries in the world. She likes the compact convenience, the standard of living, the social system, the health service, and the ease of going anywhere else from here. These are archetypal Belgian choices—calm, logical and based on rational benefits. When it comes to more traditional measures of nationalism, she falls flat. Once, I asked her to sing the national anthem. Standing to attention, chin in the air she started as though singing for a packed stadium:

'Oh cherished Belgium, sainted land of our fathers
Our soul and our hearts are... are... are...'

The stiff pose vanished and she collapsed, laughing, "I don't even know the words!" Worse, she has twice humiliated herself by mixing up the Belgian and German flags, saying, "Well they look much alike, don't they?"

Flemish Nationalism is another thing altogether (*discussed in* Chapter 4: Socialising and Fitting In, *page 57*). But Belgian patriotism, if it exists at all, rests gently on shared values of practical mindedness and liberal good sense. Perhaps it's the shared self-mocking temperament that comes from being a small country, yet a country which manages to make its little mark on the world despite all the odds.

Making a Mark

A great example of this feeling came before the US-led invasion of Iraq in 2003. Belgians simply didn't believe that Saddam Hussein had 'Weapons of Mass Destruction' (WMDs) that could hit Europe in 45 minutes. Belgian politicians fought with surprising vigour to prevent this claim being used as an excuse to attack Iraq. For its efforts, Belgium was derided in the global press as 'France's Chihuahua'. The French reference didn't go down well. But overall, there was a certain inverse pride at the chihuahua image. Here was a little, defenceless Belgium snapping away with little teeth in the name of (what most locals perceived to be) fair play. They seemed sure to lose but were hanging on anyway, just as in World War I! Some locals criticised their politicians for uncharacteristically putting principles before financial common sense (in the face of a potential American backlash, there were rumours that Belgium would be punished by removing the NATO headquarters to a more pro-coalition country like Poland). However, most locals savoured Belgium's plucky little stand, especially when the invasion proved that Saddam never had the famous WMDs after all.

Commericalism versus Humanity

If you've been in bustling Bruges vainly looking for a hotel room on a rainy night, you might remember Belgium with less than glowing warmth. And if you've peeped into the tacky Brussels souvenir shops decked with inferior lace, you might be tempted to think that the Belgian tourist industry is cold-heartedly commercial. But remember that Bruges sees so many millions of weekenders from every corner of Northern Europe that service is bound to slip occasionally. The reality almost everywhere else is that few businesses seem to squeeze for maximum proffits. Stylish cafés are spacious enough to allow customers to sit down even on Saturday nights. Small shops close at lunchtime to give the staff a break. Almost every little town and village has a tourist office producing sheaves of listings, historical information, walking ideas, beautiful maps and colourful brochures. Yet one suspects many do so because that's what they're meant to do. These same offices often seem surprised and intrigued to find that anyone actually comes. The same goes for rural museums that seem to exist based on love and enthusiasm rather than economics. But that doesn't mean they'll stay open late if it's time to go home and cook the potatoes.

Belgian Humour

Belgians don't like to take Belgium too seriously. And those Belgians who do so are suitably vilified. The Flemish David Letterman, Rob Vanoudenhoven, cheekily kicked off a TV interview with the chief minister of Flanders, saying, "So you're 'Minister President' of the region?! That sounds a bit pompous and pretentious doesn't it?" One of his XII *Werken van Vanoudenhoven* shows launched a tongue-in-cheek 'I love Wallonia' campaign amusingly seeking out Walloon mediocrity. Meanwhile, a regular Sunday night pseudo-documentary *À la Flamande* gently pokes fun at Flemish eccentrics by giving them the chance to demonstrate a gamut of weird hobbies to a TV camera. Best of all, it's a programme made by the Flemish themselves, proving that the humour is not sectarian. Top Francophone comedian François Pirette is similarly ruthless in mocking Walloon foibles. He deliciously plays up the 'lazy' stereotype of French-speaking Belgians and his website homepage (http://www.pirette.be) recently displayed a simple road sign 'Slow Down Men At Work'. No commas.

Belgian Stories

"Oh that's a Belgian story," my wife declares every time we hear a new, nonsensical news story that, she claims, could never happen elsewhere. Take two stories on a typical day in October 1999.

Headline news was of a 12-year-old boy who had broken into the Brussels tram museum and driven off in one of their streetcars. An interview with a tram driver revealed a certain respect for the child who must have researched rather carefully to have been able to operate the vehicle. Oh, and by the way, the parents will be billed for all the disruption caused.

Later in the day was a stranger story still. In the village of Frameries, an audacious gang of thieves had stolen the roof from the local school. "Yes," said the bemused headmaster, "I too assumed it was a joke when somebody called me." But sure enough, a gang had, with unimaginable daring, removed all the galvanised strips from the roof. Despite making all kinds of noise, nobody had raised an alarm and they'd made off with some thousands of francs worth of scrap metal. The reporter summed up deliciously that the school's staff had not planned to extend their open-door policy to an open-roof one.

Jokes

The most obvious form of Belgian joke pokes fun at the 'other' linguistic community like Polak jokes in the US, Irish jokes in the UK, or Kerryman jokes in Ireland. Take the following conversation...

"I've got a good joke about the Walloons."

"Watch it, I am Walloon!"

"Don't worry, I can tell it three times!"

(If told by a Francophone, simply replace the word 'Walloon' with 'Flemish'.)

But it's not just Flemish-Walloon differences that are the butt of mutual ribbing. There are similar regional jokes based on local stereotypes. Thus a Fleming from Gent might make the following dig at someone from Limburg:

"Name one Third World colony in Belgium."

Answer: "Limbabwe!"

Similarly, Namurites are thought of as slow amongst Belgian Francophones. A much-repeated joke relates three old men sitting on a roadside bench in Namur. A red sports cars squeals past. For five minutes nobody moves, then one says, "Hey. Nice Ferrari." Ten minutes later, it goes by again. After a long silence, the second man says, "But it's a Porsche!" Eventually, the car passes once more and a few minutes later, the third man gets to his feet. Grumpily he mutters, "If you two don't stop arguing, I'm going home!"

Belgian jokes don't have to be sectarian. The following is a national classic:

A Belgian driver approaches a low bridge in a four-meter truck. "Watch out," says his mate, "the sign says 'max height three metres'."

"No problem," says the driver. "There aren't any cops."

Either linguistic group recognises themselves in this gag where the character's stupidity is egged on by that age-old Belgian passion: beating the law.

The other great element of Belgian humour is the ironic 'laugh or else you'll cry' observation. A common butt is the Carrefour Leonard (*see* Chapter 5: Settling In, *page 95*), an infamous intersection on the Brussels Ring road where tailbacks, traffic jams and appalling accidents have become a daily matter of course. Rather than complain, Belgians wheel out the black humour:

'This week, it seems that the world's population has reached six billion. But science remains incapable of explaining why they all meet at the Carrefour Leonard every morning.'

Similarly self-mocking was Jean-Claude Defossé's classic *Travaux Inutiles* TV show and 'guidebook'. Literally translated as 'Useless Constructions', it was a hard-hitting yet humorous catalogue of Belgium's shockingly large collection of apparently pointless public works: bridges with no access roads, buildings built but never furnished, etc.

Going Too Far?

While they're very happy to joke at their own expense and about other areas of the country, Belgians' tendency to extend such jokes to racial minorities can often appear overtly racist. Belgium was given the dubious privilege of being rated the EU's most racist country following a report by the European Monitoring Centre on Racism and Xenophobia. One in four Belgians polled admitted, with unguarded candor, that they were 'intolerant' toward minority groups.

As it is in many countries, humour is often a political tool in Belgium. The classic example is Noël Godin, who is widely known as the *entarteur* (pie thrower). It is his self-proclaimed mission to splat the faces of any celebrity he considers pretentious, narcissistic or snobbish. And do it again later if they don't have the sense of humour to laugh it off. Microsoft's Bill Gates was one of his many victims. While few of his fellow Belgians would go as far, Godin's actions are seen as bringing a certain sense of moral justice, a victory for the little person against authority. The Belgian chihuahua strikes again!

Superstitions

Belgians share many of the superstitions common across Western Europe. Bad luck can be brought upon oneself by walking under ladders, breaking a mirror, opening umbrellas indoors, and having black cats cross one's path. If you happen to have a dead relative in the house, don't invite people to pay their last respects on a Sunday.

Like most Westerners, Belgians traditionally consider horseshoes to be lucky symbols, and will touch wood, cross fingers or perhaps throw salt over their shoulders to prevent good fortune from souring. Some Belgians think a sure-fire way to win the lottery (or at least to ensure a healthy income) is to cook pancakes on Shrove Tuesday while holding a coin in one's hand. The numbers 7 and 13 can be lucky or unlucky according to the context. Some of the curious facial hair on show in Marollian cafés may be related to the old superstition that sideburns are a magnet for good fortune, although nowadays the idea has been largely forgotten.

Gossip

Belgians love to gossip. Despite being publicly proud that their country doesn't have a tabloid press, many will voraciously flick through the pages of *Gala*, *People*, or *Paris Match* for the latest dirt on anyone in the limelight. Celebrity affairs are lapped up with glee. But Belgian gossip is fueled by interest rather than a tendency to judge. So when King Albert was found to have fathered a child with another woman, the affair neither evoked horror nor brought down the monarchy. The issue died down within a week or so.

WOMEN'S ISSUES

In practical ways, Belgium is outwardly egalitarian across the genders. Married women have never been expected to change their surnames (although children take the father's surname). At work, there's legal provision for prenatal and maternity leave, laws against sexual harassment, etc. However, there are still plenty of working wives willing (and expected) to come home and cook the potatoes for their beer-swilling men. Generally, Belgians are tolerant of what might be termed sexism elsewhere. "I bet that's a woman driving," my wife would say about a badly driven car. Women have only had the right to vote since 1948. But now, female politicians are well represented, and although only four out of the 20 cabinet ministers and commissioners are women, two of these are amongst the four 'deputy prime ministers'.

Miss Belgique/Miss Belgie/Miss Belgium
The first recorded beauty contest was held in Spa in August 1888. This tradition perhaps explains why one of the country's biggest annual televisual events is Miss Belgium. Even if you find such shows nauseating, they're interesting for the display of national unity—all candidates are expected to chat in both French and Flemish. And usually English too.

ATTITUDES TO MEDICINE

There's an undoubted hypochondriac streak in the national character. Rustle around in most Belgian homes and you'll find a cupboard comprehensively stashed with pills and medicaments. When queried, the Belgian would say,

"I don't like taking pills but, hey, why suffer?" This attitude is reflected in the apparent profitability of the pharmacy trade. Till recently, some even offer loyalty bonuses of up to 10 per cent. Not bad for people on 100 per cent insurance schemes who, having claimed back their medicine fees, could then get this bonus as cash in pocket.

Normally a pretty modest bunch, the Belgians are rather proud of their health care system. And justifiably so since it is one of the best in the world—cheaper than in the United States and much quicker and more flexible than in the UK. Recent laughs at the expense of the British medical system included a cartoon showing a patient in an English hospital receiving a transfusion of dogs' urine. The caption reads: 'Whoops, sorry. At least it's free.'

THE MONARCHY

In a 1999 opinion poll, 70 per cent of Belgians thought that their country would have split without the monarchy. And with a radiantly popular new crown princess (Mathilde) who has already dutifully produced an heir, the royal line looks set to continue.

Lascivious Leopold II (1835–1909) funded his grand Brussels-development projects by ruthlessly exploiting the people of the Congo.

As in any country, the popularity of the monarchy has fluctuated wildly with individual personalities and press attitudes to them. The first two kings, Leopold I and II, were hardly anybody's first-choice candidates but brought the country riches. Warrior king Albert I, whose helmeted statue adorns most Belgian towns, was well-loved for his World War I efforts. He died in a tragic accident while rock-climbing near Dinant, to great national consternation.

During World War II, Leopold III remained in Nazi-occupied Brussels. Initially, the king was perceived as a lonely, prisoner figure still mourning his fairytale bride (the super-popular Queen Astrid who'd died in a mysterious car accident). Public sympathy vanished, however, when he unexpectedly remarried in 1941. People started openly questioning his ambiguous relationship with the Nazis. Captured or collaborating? What about the birthday greeting he sent Hitler? Towards the end of the war, Leopold was moved to Austria by the retreating Germans and temporarily replaced by his brother Charles as regent. On his return, he was virtually forced to hand over the throne to his son Baudouin, to avoid the abolition of the monarchy once and for all.

Rebuilding the Brussels Royal Palace took 14 years and must have cost a fortune to the Dutch royals for whom the job was finally completed in 1829. Imagine their annoyance when, just a year later, Belgium broke away and they lost the place to upstart Belgian king Leopold I. Like much of Brussels, the palace was re-designed by Leopold II but monarchs haven't lived here since Leopold III moved out to Laeken in 1935. Today, it hosts a museum but is also the residence of Crown Prince Philippe.

Baudouin is usually remembered as irreproachably good, if a teeny bit dull. Locals suspect that he would have preferred to have been a priest than a king. Distant but fatherly and overwhelmingly respected, he and the national football team managed to keep the country together against an increasingly acrimonious squabble among the linguistic communities in the 1970s and 1980s. Baudouin gained further respect over his handling of the 1990 abortion legalisation bill. This was a law which his Catholic conscience would not allow him to approve, but which, as the leader of a modern European nation, he felt he could not impede either. So, in a very Belgian compromise, he abdicated for the day, leaving his brother to sign it.

Baudouin's early death in 1993 caused a shock wave on a scale similar to the mass hysteria following the death of Princess Di. Many Belgians have admitted to crying on hearing the news. The funeral was a moment of national reflection and caused a rare upwelling of Belgian national togetherness as Flemings and Walloons stood together amidst the flowers strewn on the grounds of the royal palace.

The present king, Albert II, is the brother of the childless Baudouin. He is well liked, notwithstanding the salacious revelation that a London-based papier-mâché sculptress by the name of Delphine Boël is, in fact, Albert's illegitimate love child. While the news caused great interest amongst the gossip-loving public, there was no hint of a popularity backlash. It is well known that during much of the 1970s and 1980s, Albert and his wife Paola led different lives. This was never considered consequential as it had always been assumed that Albert's son Philippe would take over rather than his father. But Baudouin's early death caught Phillipe as yet unmarried, and a reluctant Albert took on the job to give his son a little more wooing time. Phillipe appears to have managed with a degree of success that few expected in finding, marrying and rapidly impregnating the radiant Mathilde d'Udekem d'Acoz.

Present Attitudes to the Monarchy

There's a general feeling that Francophones are more pro-monarchist than the Flemish, many of whom reportedly see the monarchy as an anachronism, meaningless within a unified Europe. But both the Flemish and the Francophones seem to prefer the idea of a king to that of an elected president. And both communities were evenly split on the question of whether the approximately € 10,000,000 annual cost of supporting the monarchy is worth the money (0.17 per cent of tax revenues).

Other Belgian Royals

Impress your Belgian friends with your knowledge of the lesser members of the royal clan. For example, there are two queens (Paola, the king's wife, plus Fabiola, widow of King Baudouin). Or that should Philippe suddenly disappear, it would be his sister, Princess Astrid, that becomes queen, rather than Philippe's brother Laurent.

The 'male takes precedence rule' that still stands in the UK was dropped in Belgium in favour of a strict age order. A breakthrough for women's equality? Perhaps. But some Belgian jokers claim that it was more a case of averting the then 'worrying possibility' that chubby Prince Laurent could become king. Although Laurent is a better public speaker than most of his family, his penchant for surrounding himself with fast cars and beauty queens had created a less than regal image. His friendship with Princess Stephanie of Monaco, considered a 'royal bimbo', hadn't helped either. Although quietly admired for not giving a damn, Laurent had long been harshly teased as the family dunce. There was long debate amongst the public over a military parade in which Laurent, against all protocol, saluted the army dogs. Was it because he didn't know better, because he hadn't learnt the rules, or that he's an animal lover? In 2003, the 'Prince of Dogs'' marriage resulted in a sudden surge in his popularity. In obvious contrast to the stiffness of his brother, he appeared human and in touch, not least for his choice of a 'biker priest' to read the sermon.

Belgium's Crown Prince Philippe with his wife, Princess Mathilde, and his three children, Prince Gabriel (left), Princess Elisabeth (right) and Prince Emmanuel (in arms).

Princess Lilian de Réthy, the second wife of Leopold III, had always been a controversial figure. For years after her husband's death, she had been kept hidden away on a generous government pension at the château at Argenteuil (up a forest track reached by a perilously dangerous turn off the Brussels Ring). When she died in 2002, a most unedifying public spat began as her offspring attempted to have the castle made into a museum, while the royals tried to get back their share of the family silver!

Marie José, daughter of Belgian king Albert I, became queen of Italy on 6 May 1946 when her husband Prince Umberto took over from his discredited father, King Victor Emmanuel. Just her luck. A month later, the Italian monarchy was abolished. Known thereafter as the May queen (she was out by June!), she lived on fairly incognito in Switzerland until her death in 2001 aged 94.

Joséphine-Charlotte, sister of the late King Baudouin, lives the Belgian dream—she moved to Luxembourg. And in style, too. She married Luxembourg's Prince Jean in 1953. After 36 years as Grand Duke and Duchess, they abdicated in 2000, retiring in favour of their dashing son Henri and his Cuban-born wife Maria Theresa.

THE BELGIAN HOME

Belgians love their homes and many feel a real need to keep up with the Smets. Hedges should be clipped and lawns regularly mowed, but never, of course, on a Sunday. That's not a religious prohibition but one of noise reduction for those who wish to snooze in their own gardens. Or, perhaps, listen in on their neighbours' conversations.

Where They Live

When Belgians buy a home they tend to stay there for years. Or forever. Buying and selling your way up the property ladder, as happens in the UK, doesn't make sense in Belgium. That's because fees, charges and taxes on house purchases can add some 20–25 per cent to the actual selling price. You'd need a pretty hefty rise in property values to offset such charges. So the result is that homeowners are stuck.

This partly explains why so many people in Belgium have long commuting distances: if your job moves, you can't afford to move home. Another result was that for years, the property market stayed remarkably stable. All that has changed in the last decade, however. With poorly performing share markets and the lowest interest rates for decades, investors have decided that property wasn't such a bad deal after all. And the result has been a sudden property boom which has caught many locals off balance. Although prices have risen less than in the UK, for Belgium the 71 per cent rise in values since 1997 remains almost unprecedented and has had a knock-on effect on the rental market.

The majority of Belgians who rent an apartment or house, typically do so on renewable three-, six-, or nine-year contracts that leave tenants feeling secure enough to decorate and furnish from scratch. Certain towns, such as Leuven, have big student populations and a supply of reasonably priced basic apartments known as *kots*. But on the whole, school leavers seek further education in universities close to their parental homes and commute. Thus, there is relatively little in the way of student accommodation.

Building Their Own

US-style condominiums or British-style luxury housing estates are relatively rare in Belgium. People want to design their own home. According to the popular local saying, there's a 'brick in every Belgian belly'. Yet, although almost every Belgian seems to dream of having his or her own home built to order rather than buying someone else's, few seem to have much imagination when it comes to designing one. Some of the greatest 20th century architects were Belgian, including art-nouveau geniuses Victor Horta and Paul Hankar. Yet these days, home designs are usually remarkably staid and stolid, and rarely seem to justify all the effort. Whitewashed brick homes in pseudo-farmhouse-style are particularly popular in the suburbs, with heavy wooden shutters and a flower box or two. Leave the bricks un-whitened if you like the idea of your neighbours passing by with a quiet tut.

After 1995, there was a brief boom in self-building, thanks to a new tax relief law that brought value-added tax (VAT) on materials for self-built homes down from 21 per cent to 12 per cent. However, the supply of available land with planning permission was limited, leading to soaring land prices and a rapid return to the status quo. Now, there are better tax breaks available for the renovation of old houses.

A tradition amongst house builders is to put a branch or a potted plant at the apex of the roofing beams once the frame is completed. This symbolises the new life arriving with the building's construction. If you want to do this in mid-winter when real saplings are leafless, you can buy an artificial version from DIY shops to keep up appearances.

Home Décor

Naturally everyone has their own way to decorate a house. Unlike neighbouring Holland where you can look straight into almost anyone's front room, Belgian houses often maintain their privacy with net curtains. Stereotypically nosy neighbours lurk behind them, rustling amongst the leaves of ornamental sanseveria plants trying to watch unseen what's going on on the street below. Mrs Bucket from the UK TV series *Keeping up Appearances* would feel right at home.

Young people with newer homes are less likely to endure or encourage the gloomy, shuttered interiors that seem to be popular with the older generation. Older homes are likely to have religious symbols (a crucifix or a Madonna statuette) tucked away in bedrooms, a penchant the younger generation consider spooky. Lurking in more than a few households are obsessive kitsch-collectors and garden gnome aficionados. TV channels delight in seeking out such citizens and allowing them to show off their prize possessions, much to the embarrassment of their friends and relations.

The Postbox

Outside the city centres, few Belgians receive mail through a slot in the door. Instead, like American suburban homes, the norm is a separate postbox at the end of the drive or

LA MBERT
DAVAUX

Like garden gnomes, postboxes allow suburban Belgian
famillies to exhibit individuality, taste and refinement.

front garden. The three most typical, no-nonsense designs are the simple bread bin-style boxes, hollow brick gateposts, or metal pentagons. However, more than a few Belgians have decided that postboxes represent important fashion statements. The much copied trend in nouveau riche suburbs is to buy super-heavy monoliths in filigree cast iron somewhat reminiscent of half-sized Victorian Royal Mail boxes. Occasionally, these are even painted red and sometimes confuse passing British tourists into depositing a letter or two. The design has the further advantage of being unmistakably expensive in as understated a way as could be. However, they are also a tempting target for any thieves with suitable lifting equipment.

House owners wishing to convey a more trendy, youthful image invest in shiny aluminium tubelike postboxes. Americans will be bemused to know that what is fundamentally the standard mailbox in the United States is a fashion item here.

Things get worse. Belgian postmen have to drop letters into mini-windmills, gnome mushrooms, animal mouths, carriages, barrels, nymphs, and little model houses. For those with a love of kitsch, a survey of the postboxes along the suburban roads and avenues can enliven even the dullest day in an unpromising town.

LAW AND ORDER
The law is there to be broken. Rules are not taken as morally important and if a Belgian can get away with something, he or she will try. This would probably be the same in most countries but in Belgium, the fact is that people can get away with things. Tax avoidance is the 'national sport' and there's an almost total disregard for most traffic rules. Curiously, however, people are very careful where they park their cars. Traffic wardens do patrol with the steady ruthlessness of urban tigers. And those little tow-away symbols outside garage doors are not just for decoration.

To get an idea of the otherwise liberal attitude of the traffic police, listen to the daily radio announcements which list where speed traps will be placed that day. A traffic policeman interviewed in a local magazine was quoted as saying, "We have to make sure traffic runs smoothly. If someone does something seriously illegal, then we write down the licence plate. But otherwise, we're not very strict."

That's fine. But serious crime is also rising. Arsonists regularly take on the insurance industry in blatant fashion. Security van drivers delivering cash to banks got so fed up with being robbed en route that they went on strike. TV news shows chuckle at occasional outrageous criminal attempts to rip cash machines from the walls of banks and shops using tow trucks, excavators and winches. But burglary is becoming so common that people are feeling palpably more insecure. And the biggest perceived danger is carjacking—theft of your vehicle at gun point at a red light or outside your home in your own garage! Don't put up a fight and you shouldn't get hurt. The most popular targets are generally company vehicles. On average, 104 cars get stolen per day and even members of parliament have been victims of carjacking—one minister twice! It all sounds pretty bad, but may boil down to the fact that in a small country, more of the crimes reach the news. In a bigger country like the UK, national news is less likely to cover every burnt warehouse.

Police are so understaffed that in February 2003, the commune of St-Genesius Rode (just south of Brussels) took the unprecedented step of hiring private security guards to mount patrols. Nonetheless, despite the lacklustre policing, Belgium is pretty safe. In 1999, the number of crimes committed in Brussels came to a total of 98,259 reported cases, of which only approximately 11 per cent were violent. There's little reason to fear the streets of Brussels even as you stumble home drunk at 5:00 am.

HERITAGE
A term 'Brusselisation' has been coined to mean the turning of a beautiful, historic city into one of bland mediocrity through poorly considered renovation and rebuilding.

Actually, despite the huge scars of the EU district and other ill-conceived 'improvements', Brussels is still remarkably attractive and has around 80 sites and 270 monuments under protection. But that number is relatively low compared with other European capitals. Compared to the UK, where almost any demolition requires years of enquiry, the rules by which the worth of old buildings are assessed seem relatively lax in Belgium. The public is generally cynical, believing that big money will inevitably sideline public consultations, so rarely puts up much of a fight when historic buildings are threatened.

However, this doesn't mean that the Belgian people aren't proud or interested in their heritage. Far from it. Heritage Days in Brussels, Wallonia and Flanders open the doors to hundreds of interesting sites every year according to an annual theme. On such days, access is granted to public buildings that are normally closed to the general public. These might include dramatic Art Nouveau commune halls, austere national and European parliament buildings or demure 1950s schools. The 1999 Brussels Heritage Days brought around 150,000 visitors to the city. The city took the opportunity to declare protected the grandiose 19th century Palais de Justice—the biggest 19th century building in all Europe. The general public reaction was one of horrified disbelief. Although unpopular when it was built (its builder Joseph Poelaert was disdainfully dubbed the *skieven architekt* or the twisted architect), it is now a great landmark. Everyone had assumed that it had been protected for years. If the Palais de Justice wasn't on the list, what is?

Belgians love their forests and the mildly attractive landscapes which survive in some corners of the country. These spots of nature are a favourite with dog-walking weekenders, joggers and cyclists. But this love rarely translates into a mass movement to protect threatened areas. As they have with their cities, pragmatic Belgians quickly accept the inevitability of destruction that is a by-product of further development.

RELIGION
Catholic Majority

The vast majority of the population, whether Francophone or Flemish, consider themselves at least nominally Roman Catholic. You'll notice plenty of little Madonna and saint figures in niches and grottoes if you keep your eyes open.

When the Low Countries were divided after the Dutch Revolt, Holland escaped from Spain's barbed Catholic grip. But despite the initially strong resistance, the inquisition was allowed to get its teeth deep into the Belgian soul. By the end of the 19th century, religious differences with the Dutch had grown too wide to allow a permanent reunion of the Low Countries. This proved a key factor in the very creation of Belgium.

While Catholicism remains deeply rooted, as with all things Belgian, religion is rarely allowed to stand in the way of practicality. Unlike more conservative Catholics in countries like Ireland, few Belgians seem hopelessly mired in guilt or overshadowed by papal dogma. One devout septuagenarian believer candidly told me that she discounted former Pope John Paul II as an embarrassingly senile old man not worth taking seriously.

Divorce may not be entirely straightforward, but it's a fact of life. Birth control has long been accepted as normal and sensible. Abortion was legalised in 1990, gay marriage in 2003 and in the little village of Dave, Belgium's first married Catholic priest took to the pulpit in June 2005.

Nonetheless, however relaxed the form of Catholicism practised, religious 'tourism' is still an important activity. Pilgrims have been visiting Scherpenheuvel near Diest since the 14th century when a miraculous statuette of the Virgin appeared, stuck to a tree. These days, pilgrims converge here the first Sunday of November. More peculiarly, superstitious drivers come year round to have their new cars blessed by a priest! For those without the time or money to go to the real thing, Belgium has its own mini Lourdes at the hamlet of Banneux where the young Mariette Beco reputedly saw eight visions of the Virgin Mary in 1933. The village has since attracted over 400,000 of the faithful who come during the healing season (May–October). Quite coincidentally, many of the shops and souvenir stalls just happen to be run by the Beco family. At Lourdes itself, there are a remarkable number of bars stocked with Belgian beer, ideal for rotund Belgian pilgrims to relax with after a hard day's prayer.

'Looking Catholic'

Belgian friends use the term 'Catholic' as a social label. Pointing to a group of people with the comment, "Don't they look Catholic, eh?" doesn't mean that a gaggle of nuns is waddling past. Instead it means, "Hey, they look classical, well-dressed and expensively educated (i.e. snobby)." Practically speaking, the Catholic look means pastel colours and pearls for women, Berber jackets for men, and well over 2.2 kids in tow.

Other Christian Groups

In Belgium, the term 'Christian' is generally equated unquestioningly with Catholicism unless otherwise indicated. Nonetheless, there are a sprinkling of other denominations, in many cases foreigners and descendants of immigrants. The meetings of several such groups are announced weekly in *The Bulletin*.

Belgians are a tolerant, relatively self-contented people. Few seem to share the insecurities that seem to make cults and 'new churches' so popular elsewhere. Mormon missionaries tell me that Belgium is considered a tough posting. Even to a group of people who must be congenitally accustomed to having doors slammed in their faces, Belgians stand out as being unusually disinterested in their brand of salvation.

The Forgotten Muslims

Belgium has a small but growing Muslim minority, which is verging on a majority in one or two inner city communes (e.g. St-Josse in Brussels which in 1995 recorded 39 per cent of its inhabitants to be of Muslim Turkish and North African descent). Although many are second- or third-generation immigrants, they're still considered 'foreigners' by the majority of society. And in a cultural sense, the Islamic population will always remain foreigners, not just due to a thick streak of xenophobia in the otherwise courteous Belgian soul, but also because good Muslims don't drink alcohol. And how can one be a true Belgian without a beer?!!

Enlightened first attempts in 1968 to involve immigrant groups in local decision-making brought to the forefront importantly sensitive suggestions such as the setting aside of special areas for Muslim burials in municipal cemeteries. However, this idea was not acted upon and only reappeared in the media spotlight in the late 1990s when the body of Loubna Ben Aissa, the Moroccan victim of a paedophile, had to be repatriated to North Africa due to the lack of Islamic burial space in Belgium.

The Jewish Community

The flowing black robes and hair curls of traditionally dressed Hasidic men make Antwerp's modest Jewish community particularly visible, especially around Pelikaanstraat and the diamond district. Yet, in reality, the less obvious Jewish population of Brussels is around the same size— some 15,000–20,000.

A small group of Ashkenazi Jews who settled in Brabant in the early Middle Ages was largely exterminated by locals who blamed them for poisoning the well water to kill the Christians. This, the locals believed, triggered the onset of the plague in the 14th century. Despite the persecution, the repression of Jews in Spain led to another wave of immigration in the 15th century. Although Spain theoretically controlled the Low Countries at the time, cities like Antwerp initially protected the refugees. Most later continued to non-Catholic Holland where there was less threat of inquisitional attacks, but a small nucleus of less than 40 families lived on in Antwerp against the odds.

Conditions improved after the French Revolution and Belgian independence. Shortly after 1831, the state recognised the Consistoire Central Israélite de Belgique (which brings together Orthodox and secular Jewish organisations) as the official representative body for the Belgian Jewry. The Jewish community grew rapidly, the diamond industry finding jobs for thousands of refugees from the 1880s pogroms in Central Europe. Numbers rose even faster in the years immediately before World War II. In 1940, Belgium itself was invaded by the Nazis, and while many fled further afield, roughly half the Jewish population perished. More information is available at:

- http://amyisrael.co.il/europe/belgium/index.htm
- http://www.trabel.com/antwerp/Jewishantwerp.htm

SOCIALISING AND FITTING IN

CHAPTER 4

'Belgium's the toughest posting I've ever had.
The people are just too content.'
—Mormon missionary after a whole day
of doors slamming in his face

BELGIANS LOVE LIFE AND APPRECIATE GENTLE PLEASURES but don't see any great need to show off the fact. They are generally humorous and curious, but are much less outgoingly hospitable than people from Asian or Mediterranean cultures. Nor do they rush to form surface-friendships in the American fashion. Relationships tend to take a long time to build but are stronger as a result. It would be rather unusual if not rude to 'drop in' unannounced at a friend's house, especially without bringing at least a token gift. Even after years of good relationships, neighbours are more likely to chat across the garden fence than to invite one another in to each other's homes, though obviously much depends on the individuals. Children tend to encourage closer neighbourly relations.

As in any nation, it's helpful to learn the local languages to get better acquainted with the locals (*see* Chapter 8: Language, *page 216*). However, in Belgium, the linguistic division makes this a little more complicated. Indeed it's often better to speak English than to use the 'wrong' local language (i.e. French in Flanders, Flemish in Wallonia). Trying to get a handle on the arcane politics of this extraordinarily complex nation isn't so easy, but at least you'll earn yourself a beer or two for being sensitive to the linguistic tensions that frequently leave Belgium on the brink of splitting in two. Some of these issues are explained later within this chapter.

At Belgium's wonderful terrace cafés, it's not just the tourists who nurse a drink and watch the world go by.

You'll also gain respect and a deeper insight if you familiarise yourself with cultural issues, trends and folkloric events (*see* Chapter 7: Culture, Sport and Travel, *page 156*) and having conversations will be easier once you have a basic knowledge of major sports, music and TV stars (including those from France when talking to Francophone Belgians). Although Belgians aren't outwardly patriotic, it might impress some of your local friends to show that you know at least a few famous Belgians (or famous Flemings if talking to a Flemish nationalist). If, like many foreigners, you thought that Hercule Poirot was the only such star, take a look at the 'Famous Belgians' section of Chapter 10 (*page 253*). There's lots more fun to be had by diving into the local cafés and wallowing in the humour of Belgium's extraordinary characters and regional idiosyncracies.

REGIONAL DIFFERENCES AND STEREOTYPES

British citizens from Scotland are far more likely to call themselves 'Scots' than to say they're 'Brits'. Yet the English will happily, even carelessly, use the terms 'English' and 'British' interchangeably.

In Belgium, the semantics reveal a similar division of identities. Many people from Flanders see themselves primarily as Flemish. However, virtually all Francophones, even from rural Wallonia, simply consider themselves Belgian.

But either is likely to have an even stronger regional identity. Asked where he or she comes from, a proud Fleming would more likely say 'Antwerp' or 'Gent' than 'Flanders'. Francophone areas also have very pronounced regional images. It's fun to be aware of the stereotypes associated with each town or district, though naturally these are potentially dangerous over-generalisations.

Some Over-generalisations

- Aalst — unrefined, ugly accent
- Antwerp — permissive; 'going to Antwerp?' said with a wink between men, might suggest a night of seedy debauchery. Also famed for a superiority complex. 'Going to *stad*' (town) refers to Antwerp as though no other town existed.
- Bruges — civilised, conservatively Catholic, staid
- Charleroi — poor, industrial, full of Italians, cheerful but short-tempered
- Gent — raunchy and radical (compared to Bruges). Stubborn and independent minded 'noose-wearers' (*stroppen-dragers*).
- Hasselt — snobby, superior (but for no obvious reason)
- Kortrijk — traditional, strongly Catholic, snobby show-offs (but genuinely wealthy)
- Leuven — radical and staunchly Flemish
- Limburg — ponderous, slow
- Mechelen — rich, narrow-minded 'moon extinguishers' (*Maneblussers* from a fable in which the townsfolk were tricked into believing that their town hall was on fire—it was simply illuminated by reflected moonlight).
- Mons — traditional, staid
- Namur — backward, boring
- Ostend — worldly wise, persuasive

BELGIUM: IS IT ABOUT TO SPLIT?

Unity (or disunity) is a constant issue in Belgium. Daniel de Bruycker described his Belgium as 'the only country that wonders if it even exists'. There are occasional waves of intercommunal handholding—like on the death of King Baudouin or in the wake of the terrible paedophile cases in the late 1990s. But like in Canada, the spectre of a possible separation is always there, waved like a bully's club by nationalist groups to get political concessions.

The country's social fragmentaion means that nobody is making much attempt to re-bind the fractured country. Politics is very locally focused and the country's regions often act as though they were independent (*see* Chapter 10: Fast Facts, *page 246*). Political parties, unions and even universities and hospitals tend to divide by language and by class (Catholic, liberal and socialist). Yet somehow, everyone manages to compromise just enough to get along. How very Belgian. But for how long?

Flemish Nationalism

In the 15th century, Flanders was an economic powerhouse and one of the richest areas of Europe. By the 19th century, however, it had lost chunks to the Netherlands and France and had become something of an agricultural backwater. With the development of the new state of Belgium, the upper echelons of Flemish society took to speaking French, possibly due to the backlash against the imposition of Nederlands during Dutch rule. French was the language of power spoken by the nobility, by government institutions, the army, secondary schools, universities and even the law courts. However, the more plebeian Flemings became relegated by language to virtually second class citizens. Economically, Wallonia became a great centre of industry while Flanders floundered.

The increasing use of French had dire consequences. In World War I, Flemish soldiers were executed for not obeying the orders of Francophone officers because they couldn't understand what had been said. And court cases against Flemish defendants were often unintelligible to

Flemings being tried. After the shock of World War I, the Flemish literary movement steadily became more politicised. Originally championed by writers like Guido Gezelle in the 19th century, the movement stood up for non-French speakers styling themselves after Christian pacifists. However, things were seen differently after World War II. When German tanks rolled into Belgium, their pacifist leanings as well the hope for political gain, encouraged Flemish Nationalist groups to collaborate heavily with the invaders. This proved initially effective but masked the divide-and-rule motive the Germans had in mind. The 'liberators' rapidly lost their appeal. But the damage was done. The Flemish nationalist movement became tarnished with a pro-Nazi image. Politically sidelined from the democratic mainstream, it became something of an embarrassment to liberal Flemings.

Today, much in Belgium has changed. The linguistic communities now enjoy equal language rights. Flanders has a great deal of autonomy in the present federal structure, and its economy is now prospering while that of Wallonia is moribund. But the nationalist cause has not died. Founded in 1977, the right-wing Vlaams Blok (now Vlaams Belang) nationalist political group has recently been gathering an ever-increasing slice of the vote. And in what sounds like a comical farce (but is actually a serious political statement), large numbers of Flemings gather once a year to cycle around the periphery of Brussels. This event is known as De Gordel (The Girdle), and is a symbolic reminder that Brussels is surrounded. By Flanders.

Walloon Nationalism
What?! While there are a right-wing Francophones in Belgium, few (if any) have ever envisaged an independent Wallonia in their wildest dreams. Admittedly during the 1950s, it was the French-speaking community which was on the verge of insurrection over the Royal Question (how to remove 'collaborator' King Leopold III). But there is no Francophone equivalent to the Flemish nationalist movement. The nearest you'll find to extremists are the handful of spoilsports who

occasionally throw thumbtacks on the route of De Gordel to puncture Flemish tires.

Even if independence made economic sense, an independent Wallonia would probably remain unpopular. For most Walloons, the French are more despised than the Flemish. And an isolated Wallonia might end up as a mere forgotten adjunct to France. Visit somewhere like Roubaix near Lille to picture the nightmarish scenario. Most Walloons simply scoff at any talk of nationalism: "We're Belgians and that's it."

Communes with Secondary Language Rights

On a day-to-day level, Flanders and Wallonia effectively operate as entirely separate countries. Each has its own TV network, its own political parties and parliament, its own newspapers, etc. In fact, a Walloon hears more about France than about Flanders; and a Fleming, more about anywhere in the world other than about Wallonia. But on the periphery of Brussels, there are a few special flash points. Six communes which are politically within Flanders have relatively large populations (even majorities) of Francophones. These communes were granted *à facilité* language rights in the 1960s, i.e. the recognition that much of the community was Francophone and 'needed time to learn Flemish'. It is here that intercommunal friction tends to flare. From the Flemish point of view, it's incomprehensible why even after several decades, so few Francophones have learnt the official language of the commune. And the Flemish feel humiliated at not being able to use their own language in the daily transactions conducted in their own towns. Francophones argue that many French communes are equally swamped with non-Francophones (mainly non-Belgians) and that, anyway, it goes against the grain of democracy to force the majority of a population to speak a minority language.

At least one commune tried to introduce a Flemish language examination, which residents had to pass before buying and owning land in the town. This, however, broke EU guidelines on discrimination. The controversial Peeters

Circular in the late 1990s brought this issue to a head again. It pointed out that all residents had had enough time to learn Flemish by now and should start receiving all official communication in Flemish. This has since been ruled out too but the issue caused plenty of bad blood. To this day, tension plagues the flashpoint communities. Francophone friends in Overijse have had their doorsteps paint-bombed and find that letters addressed in French occasionally go astray. OK, so it's hardly Baghdad. The nearest Tak Aktie Komitee (TAK) radicals came to 'terrorism' was glue-jamming the locks of some Francophone schools.

In April 2002, the Council of Europe agreed to classify Francophone and Flemish populations within one another's communes as recognised 'local minorities', and thus deserving of certain linguistic rights. As we go to press, the discussion of the voting rights in the Brussels-Halle-Vilvoorde capital arrondisement is the latest itch for politicians to scratch on the open sore of linguistic enmities. (*Please see page 252 for more on this.*)

BELGIUM AND THE EU

Belgium is at the heart of the EU. It was an original member and in its heterogenous, multilingual nature, it is almost a Europe in miniature. With the Eurocracy and EU parliament in Brussels, the nation is more keenly aware than any other that the EU is doing something, though many aren't entirely sure quite what. For years that wasn't really a problem. What mattered was the general forward motion which was bringing European nations ever closer together and ever further from warlike hostility; after all, wars had destroyed little Belgium twice in the 20th century. As a country that's not particularly patriotic, Belgium was happy to remove border controls following the Schengen agreement. Its people hardly grumbled about adopting the common Euro currency (till they saw the prices rise).

And the idea of a United States of Europe has long been seen as a natural and desirable progression, not as a terrifying spectre as British Euro-sceptics consider the idea. However, enthusiasm for Europe has been waning in recent years. Philosophically, the idea of a European Union relies on moving slowly enough that countries become economically aligned. But that requires time, money and goodwill. These days, economies are struggling. Yet at the same time, the EU has been rapidly expanding. Too rapidly for many tastes. Plans to extend membership to Romania and Turkey are considered by many pro-Europeans to be an almost deliberate attempt to prevent the EU developing as an effective political counterweight to the US and China. Tellingly, the biggest champions of Turkish membership are the most anti-European nations. Meanwhile, the small but visible arrival of Albanian mafiosi and East European gypsy groups has been commonly blamed for rising petty crime adding to the undercurrent of racism that lurks in many Belgians.

VIEW OF FOREIGNERS

As of 2004, 8.4 per cent of the legally registered population was non-Belgian, with the figure in Brussels over 25 per cent. In reality, the biggest groups are of Italian (180,000, especially around Charleroi), French (115,000) and Dutch (100,000) origin. However, when talking disparagingly about 'foreigners', the majority of Belgians are probably referring to Turks (41,000) and Moroccans (85,000). With barely disguised racism, many Belgians see these groups as social security swindlers sending money to extended families abroad. The North Africans in particular are held responsible for most of the country's petty crime. The increasing rise of anti-immigration right wing parties is curiously most pronounced in Flanders even though that is the area where the population of 'foreigners' is smallest (5 per cent). Figures exclude illegal immigrants (estimated at around 100,000) and those who have recently become naturalised Belgian citizens (around 8,000 Moroccans and 6,000 Turks per year since 2000).

On the positive side, Turkish, Greek and North African shops and restaurants are popular because they are cheaper, more creative and open longer hours than many Belgian equivalents. Especially in Francophone Belgium, Turkish and North African shopkeepers are considered unusually friendly, in part because they insist on the using the familiar forms of the French language (*see* Chapter 8: Language, *page 223*). This is a curious paradox because such cutesy parlance would be thought cheeky or downright impudent coming from a local.

The attitude to the relatively small community of Congolese is slightly patronising but generally positive. They are usually thought of as law-abiding, generally well-educated, honorary Belgians.

Images of Other Countries

The following is a list of stereotypical ideas Belgians have of certain other countries and their people:

- UK
  - positive: masters of orderly queuing, atmospheric country pubs
  - negative: high cost of living, terrible health service
- US
  - positive: hospitable, efficient service
  - negative: plastic smiles, arrogant yet ignorant
- Dutch
  - positive: liberal, broad-minded, clean
  - negative: tight-fisted
- French
  - positive: cheap wine, lovely country
  - negative: uptight, temperamental
- Germany
  - positive: hardworking, straightforward
  - negative: dull, conformist

SOCIAL INSTITUTIONS AND CUSTOMS

On both sides of the linguistic divide, Catholicism has been a defining feature of the culture for centuries (*see* Chapter 3: The Belgian People, *page 49*) Yet despite deep roots, it is seen from an objective angle and remains open to mockery. This is typical of the level-headed practicality and self-deprecating sense of humour that are such prominent aspects of the national character. There is a similar curious ambivalence to many other social institutions including marriage and the family.

Family

In general, Belgians do not come from especially tight-knit families. But family ties are extremely strong, nonetheless. As with all Belgian attitudes, the genuine love and care family members shower on one another is tempered with a very sensible dose of practicality. My wife, for example, spent years of her life fussing over her grandmother to keep her happy, healthy and independent. But she'd have no qualms about popping her into a nursing home if she needed to.

Common to many countries with a Christian background, most children have a godmother (*marraine/meter*) and a godfather (*parrain/peter*) whose role is theoretically to ensure that the child has a good Catholic upbringing and respects an acceptable moral code. These days, however, the godparents' main task is to provide a few presents and to be a free babysitter on call. Anyone could, in principle, be a godparent, but the diplomatic Belgian norm is to choose one grandparent from either side of the family.

Marriage

Until recently, marriage was relatively unpopular. This was not just an echo of a pan-Occidental latter-day trend, but also a reaction to the odd fiscal quirk that a married couple was taxed less favourably than as two individuals, at least until retirement. In Belgium, when it comes to a tussle between religion and the national sport of tax evasion, it is fiscal fighting which sounds more appealing. October 2000 tax reforms, however, removed the worst tax disincentives for marriage by treating each partner as an individual for certain calculations, and equalising tax exempt values between married and single people.

Inheritance tax continues for now to favour spouses and direct linear relations (parents-children) at 3–27 per cent compared to 10–50 per cent for cohabitants.

MARRIAGE USED TO BE UNPOPULAR BECAUSE OF A FISCAL QUIRK. THAT'S YOUR FATHER'S EXCUSE.

TRIGG.

When people do tie the knot, betrothal is a quasi-legal contract and traditionally, marriage should follow within six weeks of the official engagement announcement. In reality, it's only the royals who are bound to this conventional time scale. On the wedding day, the first stop for the couple and their witnesses is an office at the commune's town hall. It is there that the legally important civil procedures are conducted, even for those who choose to continue to church for a traditional ceremony.

Separation of Assets

If you're planning to get married in Belgium, very seriously consider going to a notary to make a separation of assets' contract. This means that anything owned by one or the other partner before the wedding remains that individual's property should the couple ever split. Similarly, it ensures that any debts run up by one spouse are not the legal responsibility of the other. Without such a contract, all property and debts will be legally considered shared by the act of marriage. For more information see:

http://www.notaire.be.

Divorce

Divorce is a minefield of regulations and traps, some of which appear to be very differently interpreted by the different tribunals who oversee such break-ups. Divorce by mutual consent is possible after 18 months of marriage but requires both partners to make several personal appearances before these tribunals over a period of several months. If either partner misses a session, the whole procedure returns to square one.

The concept of one partner being at fault is very much alive when it comes to adjudicating divorces. To prove 'fault' in cases of adultery requires solid police evidence which can be hard to gather. Yes, that really can mean having private detectives laying in wait to spy on unfaithful spouses. If a couple has been legally separated for five years, one partner may use the length of separation as grounds for divorce. But in this case, the initiator of the proceedings is considered to be 'at fault' and thus may in the future become responsible for alimony payments.

Having a pre-marriage separation of assets' contract (see above) ensures that a couple's personal bank accounts are not considered legally pooled in the case of divorce. However, whatever contract you might have made at the time of the wedding between yourselves, it's not possible to firewall yourself against potential alimony claims.

Death and Funerals

If you want to have your remains buried in a cemetery, there's an important choice of type. Short-term free plots in the commune's cemetery are recycled twice a decade. So if you don't want to have your memorial stone evicted after five years, it's necessary to be interred in a concession, which is a special longer term site where, upon the payment of a suitable rent, the site can be maintained for up to 50 years. There are also rules for the disposal of the ashes of those cremated. Under Belgian law, you are not allowed to sprinkle your ashes at sea—if you desire a maritime end, your *cendres* may be disposed of in a special soluble urn. All funeral and cremation arrangements are handled through Pompes Funèbres/Begrafenisondeming funeral homes.

Organ Donation

In Belgium, the assumption is that when you die, you'd want to donate your precious organs to medicine. Should you specifically chose otherwise, make that clear with a declaration lodged at the commune.

If you're a resident in Belgium, it's likely that Belgian law would apply upon your untimely death, so it's highly advisable to make a will that corresponds to the curious local particularities. Most surprisingly, perhaps, is that if there's no will, your spouse won't automatically get any of your inheritance. There are several other details that need to be carefully taken into consideration too—you're highly advised to get advice from a notary. Their advice is free, though it's advisable to leave a copy lodged with your notary, a service which will cost around € 100 (a one-off fee regardless of how many times you subsequently change the will).

When deciding on how to leave your amassed fortune, there is a fairly complex table of death taxes to bear in mind.

The exact percentage varies depending on your relationship to the recipient, the sum left and whether you're resident in Flanders, Wallonia or Brussels (and for how long!). See why you need that notary?!! One thing to be aware of is the enormous tax disincentive of leaving money to anyone other than a direct relation (spouse, child or parent). For example, in Wallonia, leaving € 100,000 to my wife would cost € 7,000 in tax. To my brother, it would cost € 35,000. To a friend (or to charity), I'd pay € 90,000 tax. That's right, only 10 per cent would actually reach the people intended.

Whatever you actually write in your will, a certain percentage of your bequest is legally bound to go to your children or grandchildren if you have any, and possibly your parents. If the will contradicts this rule, those concerned could legally challenge the will. Again, it's worth checking the exact details with a notary. See http://www.notaire.be in French.

SEX AND PROSTITUTION
Visitors over the centuries have remarked on the sanguine savvy of Belgian women. Sir William Temple found local girls in the 17th century quite ready to use sex to their advantage but noted that their passions 'seem to run lower and cooler here than in other contreys where I have converst'. The Spanish entourage of Philip II visiting in 1549 came to similar conclusions that women here were 'naturally cold' and free from the lusty passions that confound girls in more Mediterranean climes.

Lusty or otherwise, Belgium is certainly not a prudish place. Catholic or not, it takes its liberal lead from the Netherlands. I was astounded to find that established companies took their employees and business guests to places like Brussels' Chez Flo—a rather raunchy transvestite cabaret. But why not! The oldest profession is very visible around Brussels' North Station, with plenty of the red-light flesh windows more typically associated with Amsterdam. And locally, Antwerp has a sin city image, appropriate for Europe's second biggest port. Even in rural areas you'll notice windowless nightclubs dotted along the three-lane 'national roads'. The names of such nightclubs, like Pussy Galore or Love Shack, are as unsubtle as their drinks are exorbitant.

TV news announced, without a snigger, the creation of a school for prostitutes as part of a scheme aimed at improving working conditions. There are limits, however. Payoke, Antwerp's centre for prostitutes, had to fire its co-ordinator in 1999 when it was revealed that proposed 'training courses' practised at least five acts that would be considered criminal offences.

When the police do crack down on prostitution, it is generally to liberate captive foreign women. True to the Belgian sense of humour, a sweep of Brussels brothels in 1999 was code-named 'Operation Moore' after Demi Moore, star of the film *Striptease*.

HOMOSEXUALITY

Attitudes to homosexuality are generally open and unjudgemental. Homosexuals are quietly accepted as a part of society. One government minister, suspected of having been a paedophile, later revealed that his gay partner was not a minor. The relief at the revelation that he was 'only' a normal gay, proved to be a boost to his popularity. Even in the Church, the gay priest Rudy Borremans continued to serve his flock despite several reprimands for breaking the vow of celibacy. He was finally suspended when he was deemed to have pushed things too far with a book on the difficulties of being homosexual in the Church.

Many cities have official gay meeting places and associations. In June 2003, Belgium became the second nation (after the Netherlands) to allow full, same-sex marriages, and in late 2005, the lower house of parliament voted to allow same-sex couples to adopt children.

ROBBING THE CRADLE

While Belgium probably has no more paedophiles than anywhere else, recent scandals have put the issue into the public eye. But it's not for the first time! In between running Congo as a personal allotment and glorifying Brussels with grandiose imperial buildings, King Leopold II

(1835–1909) had an insatiable libido to fuel. At the turn of the 20th century, though approaching 70 years old, he was spending much of his time with a teenage prostitute by the name of Caroline Lacroix, who would later be the mother of two of his illegitimate royal children. Leopold had also been named amongst the clients of a London madam, Mrs Jeffries, who was indicted for procuring prepubescent sex slaves. He never denied it.

A century after Leopold, the bad name he brought upon his country remains. During the mid-1990s, you'd see hundreds of little flyers all over Belgium on which were printed the innocent faces of missing children. Unlike the ever changing mugshots on American milk cartons, these faces were always the same few. The kids, it appeared, had been kidnapped, raped and some then murdered; worst of all was the fear (albeit unsubstantiated) that there was a high-powered paedophile ring to which the children had been provided like items on a takeaway menu. The chief suspect was Marc Dutroux, a convicted rapist who'd been allowed out of jail despite warnings to the authorities from his own mother! The slack attitude of the police and their blundering horrified the public. Apparently, when the police had visited Dutroux's house months before he finally surrendered, they simply asked if there was a secret chamber with some kids in it. "No," said Doutroux. "Fair enough," said the cops. And off they went. Some of the missing kids had indeed been hidden in such a chamber at the time and later died there. Dutroux finally admitted to kidnapping some of the missing children. But one of the girls, Loubna Ben Aissa, remained long unaccounted for. When she was eventually found dead, killed by an altogether different sex offender, people really started to doubt their own society—were government ministers involved? why was the police so apathetic? This was the era of the White Marches. For much of 1997, people took to the streets every weekend, dressed in the colour of innocence. Answers were demanded, but few given. White Marches eventually fizzled out, but they did lead to the development of a well-publicised Child Focus hotline (tel: 110) which very rapidly mobilises search squads and co-ordinates poster campaigns if children are reported missing.

Convicting Dutroux took the courts the best part of a decade during which there was a farcical debacle with the nation's most guarded man managing to escape while ostensibly checking legal documents. He was rapidly re-captured, however, and finally found legally guilty in 2004. The nation scratched its head, pondering the vast cost of the legal processes. Dutroux's ex-wife Michelle Martin also got 30 years in jail for complicity. This had an unexpected effect. Frightened by the severity of Martin's sentence, a certain Monique Olivier decided that it was time to confess the appalling crimes of her own husband, a certain Michel Fourniret who made Dutroux look like an angel. Fourniret appears to have 'hunted' (raping then systematically killing) virgins right across Europe. Most shockingly, he'd been jailed in France for raping children; yet by simply moving across the border into Belgium, he'd had no trouble getting a job in a local school. Once again, Belgium started to doubt the security of its systems. And so it starts again.

NATURISM

At travel fairs, I am often surprised to see the many stands related to naturism. Yes, naturism as in public nudity. My wife, however, was more surprised at my reaction. "We're not prudes," she reminded me and named a couple of friends and cousins who, as it transpired, were themselves naturists.

If you like the idea of throwing off all your clothes with a group of equally unself-conscious people, you'll be pleased to know that a Belgian nudist beach finally opened in Bredene in summer 2001, and that there are, in fact, no less than 17 naturist associations in Belgium. Most have swimming pools, saunas, and gym facilities and some organise open-air sporting activities, although perhaps not during the winter. For more information, contact FBN (http://www.naturisme.be). The International Naturist Federation (http://www.inf-fni.org) is based in Antwerp.

PETS

Belgians don't quite share the same protective mania Brits have for animals. Relatively few harp on about animal rights. And almost no one has the slightest qualm about wearing fur. But that doesn't mean Belgians don't love their pets. Quite the contrary. Even in family restaurants, you can often find a playful puppy sculking under one of the tables. In the streets, you're not likely to be worried by strays, but Belgian dog owners are infamously casual about educating their darlings on the topic of doggy defecation. As a result, city pavements are notoriously full of *crottes/hondenpoep*.

Belgium has bred some of the world's finest sheep-dogs. There are four main Belgian types, but think twice before buying a short-haired Malinois. Loveable as the pups might look, the fierce, grown dogs can be unpredictable and are best left to the police work to which they're generally better suited.

SETTLING IN

CHAPTER 5

' "Wow—I didn't know Antwerp had such a
beautiful palace," said an American looking
through photos in the tourist office.
"It hasn't," replied the Belgian beside him.
"That's the train station!"
—Overheard conversation

FORMALITIES

The strain of moving to a new place is always pretty intense. Even though many Belgians do speak great English, the language as well as the cultural barriers don't make things any easier. The first thing you'll need is a good impartial source of advice.

Fortunately there's plenty of help to be had. The wonderful Community Help Service offers advice in English to anyone who needs it. They have an office at rue St Georges 102, Box 20, 1050 Brussels (tel: (02) 647-6780) and operate a 24-hour information and crisis line (tel: (02) 648-4014) where you can seek help with any problem. There's also the weekly English-language weekly *The Bulletin* which lists meetings of expatriate societies and associations. It also produces the extremely helpful *Newcomer* supplement twice a year (free for subscribers). The latter has all the latest details on housing, paperwork, schools, etc. There is also a very helpful website aimed directly at English-speaking expatriates in Belgium at http://www.xpats.com.

Residency Documents

To get a residence permit or identification card you need to locate the *maison communale/gemeentehuis* of the commune you are residing in to register as a commune resident. Technically, you have to do this within eight days of arrival. Take along your passport plus some photos and money to pay the local tax. You may also be asked for a copy of your lease or accommodation arrangements. Ironically, the latter may require you to have an identity card to start with! Non-EU citizens will need a residence visa and a work permit. The visa must be applied for before arrival and the employer in Belgium needs to append the work permit to a copy of the employment contract. The employer must also confirm that there is no local labour to fill the post.

Once you have registered with the commune, you should receive a temporary residence permit which will allow you to stay for three months. You can extend your stay to five years if you can prove that you have filed an application for self-employment registration or that you've got a job. Evidence of previous social security payments is also expected and you may need a medical certificate, passport, photos and verification that you haven't got a criminal record.

The website http://www.newintown.be is designed to help new arrivals with details on all the paperwork for immigrant workers, refugees and asylum seekers. As yet it's a little clunky and many of the multiple language options are not yet operational.

Professional Card

If you want to start your own business, you need a professional card. You can apply for one through the Belgian embassy where your visa application is lodged, or in the commune where you live. You can approach the Ministry of Economic Affairs, and it is also worth contacting the relevant regional governments:

- Brussels   tel: (02) 204-2111
- Flanders   tel: (02) 507-4367
- Wallonia   tel: (081) 333-700

The professional card will only be granted to businesses in a very specific field of economic activity. These businesses may also be subject to acceptance within a relevant, usually strictly regulated, professional body (e.g. Kamer van Ambachten & Neringen/Chambre des Métiers & Négoces) organised on a provincial basis. The best source of information is the curiously named Ministry of Middle Classes (http://mineco. fgov.be/homepull_en.htm, tel: 0800-120-33).

Visas and Permits

Information on visas is available from:

- Ministry of Home Affairs, Alien's Office
  Tel: (02) 206-1300
  Website: http://www.dofi.fgov.be

- Foreign Affairs Ministry
  Tel: (02) 501-8111
  Website: http://www.diplomatie.be/en/travel/visa/default.asp
  For more details on the 'Schengen' visa which allows common entry to many Western European countries see:
  http://www.eurovisa.info
  For full details of work permits (in French) consult:
  http://meta.fgov.be/pc/pce/pcee/frcee07.htm

FINDING A HOME
Where to Live

Most expatriates tend to be based in Brussels, and in the suburban towns and villages around the city. Areas like Uccle are expat magnets with their good housing and plethora of shopping and upmarket dining options. Richer locals migrate toward places like Tervuren, Kraainem or Woluwe-St-Pierre. Thanks to its range of large supermarkets and fast food places, Waterloo is sometimes said to be the most 'Americanised' satellite town. It certainly has a cosmopolitan feel with English widely spoken and a good balance of services, but is rather a long way from central Brussels and the transport facilities leave much to be desired.

Apartments in certain city communes can be surprisingly affordable. Many of these communes have exaggeratedly negative images and are thus unpopular with wealthier locals looking for accommodation. St-Gilles is recovering from such a bad reputation and is becoming trendy again, but Anderlecht and Schaarbeek are often thought of as no-go ethnic ghettos (which is, of course, a great exaggeration).

The 19 communes that constitute the Brussels-Capital region are officially bilingual (French and Flemish). But if you stay beyond the city limits, your choice of address will affect the language you need to learn, especially if you are sending your children to local schools. If you are considering communes such as Overijse with their *à facilité* language rights, it's worth at least being aware of the linguistic tensions (*see* Chapter 10: Fast Facts, *page 250*). If you want to get by only in English, Waterloo or Uccle are probably the most comfortable choices. But also amongst the most expensive.

What Type of Accommodation?

Especially in Brussels, there is a reasonable choice of Aparthotels (short-term, apartment-style hotels) for those making relatively brief business sojourns. For longer stays, the main choice is between a house in the suburbs or an apartment in town. Unlike in the UK, there are very few house-sharing arrangements where cheap rooms in a house are rented out. This is partly because rental fees are usually lower than those in London and because Belgian law holds anybody registered at an address liable for the debts of co-occupants. In other words, if your flatmate runs up a huge bill, the bailiffs could confiscate your property to pay for it, unless you have absolute proof that the items are your own. The rare house-sharing opportunities that are available are advertised in *The Bulletin* or at http://www.xpats.be.

Beware of Extras

Apartments are generally cheaper than houses for obvious reasons, but whether you rent or buy, beware that apartments may have very substantial extra maintenance charges for heating, lighting and the renovation of communal areas and elevators. If you are considering staying in the inner areas of the cities, check whether parking is available and if so, whether there's a separate charge.

Renting versus Buying

Most Belgians themselves rent. Or if they buy, they stay put for a very long time. The reason is the very high costs of the taxes and fees involved, which even a healthy rise in property prices is highly unlikely to counterbalance. You'll have to pay property tax (about 1 per cent of the total value), administrative fees plus a massive 12.5 per cent registration fee (though this is reduced to 6 per cent for especially small or cheap places, and rates in Flanders dropped to 10 per cent/5 per cent respectively in 2002). Even then, the buying procedure takes about four months of bureaucracy before you can move in. This can rarely be speeded up. All in all, if you're only intending to stay a couple of years, renting is probably more sensible. On the other hand, the taxes keep property prices relatively low, and if you need to borrow money to purchase your house, interest rates are low and are usually fixed for a considerable part of the mortgage period.

Buying Technicalities

Many houses are advertised for sale in local newspapers: in Brussels, try *Le Soir* or *The Bulletin*, or magazines like *Vlan*, *Immo Transit*, etc. Only some 30 per cent of house sales are conducted through realtors/estate agents. Whether an agent is involved or not, all sales must go through a notary who plays a role somewhere between that of a lawyer and a tax collector. The notary arranges and witnesses the legalities, checks mortgage liabilities, verifies ownership details, etc. The paperwork for all existing homes should be lodged at the *cadastral/kadastraal* offices of the local commune.

Though illegal, it is not uncommon for buyer and seller to notarise an agreement in which the stated selling price is lower than the one actually agreed in private. The idea is to pay the rest in cash, thereby avoiding taxes on that portion of the transaction. This obviously appeals to the Belgian tax-dodging passion. But it is very dangerous for the buyer since there's no proof that the payment has been made, should the seller deny its receipt at some later date.

According to its age, location and size, a house is officially assessed for property tax (*revenue cadastral/kadastraal inkomen*) by region i.e. Brussels/Flanders/Wallonia. This represents approximately 1 per cent of the total value or the income that you would receive if you had rented it out (rent minus typical costs). Whether you actually rent your house out or not, you must add this sum to your annual declared income and pay tax on it.

Note that there are state subsidies for renovating houses of more than 15 years old, mainly in the form of tax payback on materials and labour.

Renting Technicalities

As with renting anywhere, you'll be expected to pay a deposit before moving in. This is usually equivalent to around three months' rent and is paid into a dual signature account so that neither you nor the landlord can remove it without negotiation. One key thing to note is that the tenant is liable for any damage to the interior of a rented property. This includes disasters like fires or gas explosions; so to avoid the possibility of being bankrupted by such a misfortune, you are strongly advised to take out a tenant's liability insurance policy. Occasionally tenants undertake major renovation work on their places to be counted against rent, but landlords can be pretty devious, so be sure to get a watertight contract if you attempt this.

The advantage of long leases are that once signed, the landlord cannot arbitrarily raise the rent in real terms. But he or she can 'adjust it for inflation' to maintain the same real-term value. If you want to leave the property before the end of the lease, you should find a replacement tenant yourself or risk incurring penalties (according to the rental contract). At the end of your lease, the law assumes that you'll extend the agreement if you don't say otherwise. So if you intend to leave at that point, you'll still need to inform your landlord—preferably by registered letter—three months before the termination of your contract.

A CITIZEN'S RESPONSIBILITIES

If you've got a house, you are responsible for keeping the walkway outside your residence clear. Theoretically if you don't, you could be held responsible for accidents which occur on the pavement. If you've got a garden, there are certain rules about tree height that neighbours can have enforced should your arboretum threaten to cast too much of a shadow. More importantly, you're not allowed to make noise on a Sunday (by cutting your hedge with electrical shears, felling trees, mowing the lawn, etc.). You may be surprised to see how seriously some suburban folk take this law.

DOMESTIC HELP

That Belgium is wealthy is apparent from the number of people who hire their own cleaning staff. Twenty years ago, many such workers were stereotypically Portuguese and referred to colloquially as *conchitas*. These days, the majority of domestic workers are more likely to be Eastern Europeans. Their services are generally procured through word of mouth or small advertisement boards in supermarkets. Note that few have legal work papers. Legally, you are supposed to have insured your domestic help against any harm that may come to your them while on your premises.

An alternative to expensive laundry services for busy people is to find an ironing lady who will smarten up your washing once you've pulled it out of your washing machine. These folks, too, are likely to be working illegally so won't necessarily advertise.

> The members of the manual professions — plumbers, electricians and handymen — are stars of the national sport of tax evasion. Everyone knows someone who can provide just what you need at a remarkable price, although you could always pay the full rate and call a bona fide company!

UTILITIES

There are many different companies supplying water, electricity and other utility services but there is usually only one option per sector in any particular area.

Where there are choices, readers wanting the latest reviews of the services should refer to the magazine *Test Achats/Test Aankoop* (http://www.test-achats.be, the equivalent of the *British Which?*). Water quality is excellent, usage is metered.

Rubbish Collection

Most communes organise their own systems of refuse disposal. In some you pay a fixed rate as part of local taxes, in others you have to pre-purchase special plastic sacks whose price (usually around € 0.60) includes the collection fee. Rubbish collectors in the latter areas will ignore non-regulation bags. Often, they will not even deign to collect regulation bags if you don't place them conveniently on the pavement outside your house. You would not be the first to think of simply dumping your rubbish along a quiet street, in a public bin or across the boundary line of a commune where collection is free. However, such behaviour is illegal and there are roving rubbish inspectors with the unpleasant chore of scrabbling through your waste. They look for telltale clues such credit card receipts or addressed envelopes that identify the offender's address. Fines start at a few hundred Euros.

There are days where 'special' trash is collected. The commune will post you a colour-coded schedule of which days you can leave what. Read the schedule carefully as there are often a number of rules for each collection. In my commune, collections include (on different days) paper for recycling, furniture, wood and garden waste, plastics, cans and drinks cartons, and, in early January, Christmas trees! The night before the rare furniture-trash days, there's a constant trickle of vans cruising the neighborhood looking for valuable or at least resaleable items.

Most communes also provide dumps for the use of their citizens but you may be required to give your address as proof of residency before unloading your waste.

As in most developed countries, there are bottle banks for recycling glass. But note that many types of bottles (some wine, most beer) can be taken back to the store for a refund. This is generally done in supermarkets by feeding the empties into a machine at the store's entrance which adds up the total value of the glass deposited, then issues a receipt ticket which can be reimbursed at the cash registers.

Belgians are particularly good about recycling batteries, and most homes keep a special little bag for the purpose. These are provided by Bebat (http://www.bebat.be) and are available free from many shops, supermarkets and even schools.

WHAT TO BRING FROM HOME?

There's little that you're likely to want that you can't buy in Belgium. Most apartments are rented unfurnished so some people prefer to ship their furniture, though this can often prove almost as expensive as buying replacements. Bringing books might be worthwhile because although there are English language bookshops in Belgium, prices are relatively high and incur VAT. If you order books by mail order or via the Internet, beware that the post office may charge you the due VAT. Although that's likely to be a relatively small sum, they'll also charge you a paperwork fee of nearly € 10 for the pleasure.

EDUCATION

In choosing a school for your children, you're spoilt for choice. Especially in and around Brussels, there is a wide variety of good free options within the state sector, offering education in either Flemish or French. Many have overt religious orientations. There is also a wide selection of (expensive) international schools aimed mainly at expatriates: education is possible in English, German, Japanese,and other languages around Brussels, and there are further English-language options in Antwerp and at Mons (for SHAPE employees). Brussels has an inordinate number of language schools, if you want to learn French, Flemish, or virtually any other language. And various universities offer courses in English. An invaluable reference for information about all available options is the quarterly *Newcomer* magazine or http://www.xpats.com.

Local Schools

The choice of school is up to the parents, assuming sufficient places are available. Particularly in bilingual Brussels, this is an important choice as different schools work in different languages and have specific religious affiliations. Catholic schools are often considered to offer a higher standard of education. As the system is linguistically divided, the divide between Flemish and Francophone children begins early on with little social mixing, although some enlightened parents specifically put their kids in schools of the 'other' linguistic group to advance their children's bilingual prospects.

Education is mandatory until the age of 18. Belgian school kids start *gardiennes/kleutertuin* (infant school) at three and proceed to *primaires/lagereschool* (juniors) at six. When they're 12 years old, there comes the traumatic move to *humanités/middelbarschool* (secondary school) which involves a great deal more research-based study and a difficult choice of subject options.

Unlike in the UK, students in Belgium must attain a minimum standard to progress at the end of each academic year. Those who fail by a small margin are allowed to try again toward the end of the summer, by which time family holiday plans have been shot to pieces. More significant failure means resitting the whole year. Those failing repeatedly at *humanités* level are encouraged to seek apprenticeships or entry to a vocational school (*école supérieure/hogeschool*). which develop practical skills more than academic ones. Normally, only those who complete the sixth grade of *humanités* are eligible for university, though it is technically possible to qualify by completing an extra (seventh) year of vocational school.

In principle, school education is free for all registered residents, regardless of whether you are a Belgian citizen or not. However, parents are asked to pay a series of small *frais scolaires/inschrijvingsgeld* charges (carefully itemised for photocopies, library fees, report books, school rules manual, etc.) which add up to around € 50, twice a year. Parents are also expected to buy all school books, a list of which is presented at the beginning of each academic year (September). Textbooks can be bought second-hand at the Bourse des Livres in Brussels, ordered through the school, or (most expensively) bought from bookshops.

Schools have no personal lockers, so students have to carry around all their books for the day in big cartable bags, the designs of which make something of a fashion statement.

Discipline

In the local secondary schools, rules seem lax by my parochial standards e.g. smoking is banned from the classroom but openly tolerated in the school grounds. This admirable attitude adopted by the education board is supposed to make discipline less of an issue and to encourage the student to study with his or her career interests in mind. In cases where the child needs discipline, parents are frequently asked to intervene: punishment is generally not administered by the teacher.

Parents beware. The Belgian Civil Code holds parents responsible for damage caused by the actions of their children. This was originally intended to help recoup the damages caused by teenage vandalism, but recently the law has been invoked against families of children who are disruptive at school. In one case, a family was fined nearly € 1000 for failing to instill proper values in their child who was accused of taunting a fellow classmate into truancy.

Some Belgians are quick to blame recently arrived asylum seekers for behavioural problems in schools, especially recently arrived teenagers who often lack basic Flemish or French language skills. In addition, there is doubtless racism in schools, as in the rest of Belgian society, particularly toward the Turkish, North African and Muslim minority.

Help for Parents

Belgian local schools are carefully geared to deal with working parents. Most schools have supervised drop-off facilities from 7:00 am even though classes don't start until after 8:00 am. Similarly, schools can take care of the children for a couple of hours after the end of classes (4:00 pm) to make it possible for parents to pick them up again around 6:00 pm. This pro-work attitude is also reflected in the common use of crèches, though places are increasingly hard to find. For babies (three months and older) there are two types: private crèches which are expensive but usually have high supervisor to child ratios, and the cheaper, communally subsidised crèches. Forward-thinking couples are advised to book a place at a communal crèche before their wedding and just hope they can produce a baby in time!

Universities

The best-known Belgian universities are the KUL at Leuven (Flemish language, founded in 1425) and the UCL at Louvain-la-Neuve (French language, broke away from Leuven after the 1968 riots). Brussels' top universities VUB (Flemish) and ULB (Francophone) are side by side, yet by a pedantic quirk of the communal bad-blood a lecturer qualified in one is not qualified to teach in the other.

The vast majority of university students study close to their parental homes and thus commute rather than live on campus. This gives many universities a rather 'dead' feel in comparison to British or American colleges. Those student pads that do exist are known colloquially as *kots*. On average only 38 per cent of those who sign up for the first year's course will make it through to the second.

Assistance

For guidance with university or higher education choices, there are several helplines (e.g. tel: (02) 640-8008) and career guidance booklets (like the annual *Francophone Etudes*, *toutes Directions*). Many Belgian universities have entire courses in English as do outposts of a variety of American and English universities including the Open University (tel: (02) 644-3368).

BANKING

Belgium's extraordinary plethora of banks has been considerably reduced over the last few years by a rash of mergers. Banking hours are not standardised, but those which open on Saturday mornings may take one afternoon off in the middle of the week. Many but not all banks close for lunch, typically from 1:00pm–2:30 pm.

Opening a bank account is extremely straightforward. You will need some sort of identification, preferably a residence card. Most banks offer no significant interest on accounts and there may be charges associated with the statements posted to you every time there's activity on your account. However, few banks, such as Argenta (http://www.argenta.be), do operate without bank charges, give a modest interest on current accounts and generous rates on savings accounts with annual bonuses. They also give charge-free Visa and Mister Cash cards but don't offer a full range of other banking services; Argenta, for example, cannot handle foreign cheques or change money.

If you need such service, you might try:

- KBC (http://www.kbc.be/expats)
- Fortis (http://www.fortis.be)
- Citibank (http://www.citibank.be) which also provides a banking guide for expatriates, free of charge (fax: (02) 626-5624).

Debit versus Credit Cards

Shops in Belgium accept the usual range of credit cards: Visa, MasterCard, AmEx and, less commonly, Diners Club. However, if you open an account, you should request a debit card (Mister Cash, Bancontact, Maestro or the equivalent). Some supermarkets only accept debit cards. Supermarkets are usually happy to give you 'cash back'—i.e. they can charge you more than your shopping bill and give you the change in cash.

Most shops have terminals like these which can directly debit a customer's account (right) or take small sums from a Proton electronic purse (left). Just enter the PIN code.

Proton Electronic Purse

The Proton electronic purse (e-purse) is a third type of card that is accepted in many corner shops as well as by some parking meters. Effectively this is a microchip wallet which you top up by going to an ATM or a pay phone and transferring (free of charge) a sum from your account to the card. To spend this money, a shop's card reader removes the required electronic money units from the card onto the account of the shop. This is convenient for small sums where using a credit or debit card is not economically viable. But don't load too much money at one time—if you lose the card, it's like losing cash. The only way to take the credit off a Proton card is to spend it; transfers are not possible. Most Belgian debit cards now have a additional Proton function built in. Once the debit card has expired, the Proton card remains valid but only so long as you don't activate the replacement debit card. Go to http://load.proton.be for a demonstration on how to load your card.

Cheques and Transfers

The use of personal cheques in Belgium is relatively rare. A much more common method of settling bills uses the ubiquitous red and white *virement/overschrijvingsbewijf* form. For example, the electricity bill might come with a pre-printed *virement*. You sign it, add your own account details, then drop it off at your bank. The bank will then send the requested funds to the account of the utility-provider. No need for a cheque, so no fear that the cheque will get stolen along the way. *Virement* forms work equally well for transferring money to friends and family if you know their account details.

TAXES

Taxes, social security and other assorted contributions typically eat up around half of an employee's salary (*see* Chapter 9: Business and Work, *page 235*). But nothing upsets a Belgian more than a tax bill. Watch the annoyance of Belgians when they're overtaken by someone driving a car with blue-on-white plates. It's envy— that's a Eurocrat who gets to live here tax free!

As in most countries each citizen is expected to file tax papers. The submission dates are usually 30 June, unless as in 2005, somebody messes up the mail-out of forms in the first place. These days, it's possible to file on-line using the Internet (http://minfin.fgov.be/taxonweb/). Being self-employed is something of a fiscal minefield given the need to pay your own social security charges in full and to register expensively for a commercial certificate.

Tax Policy

Full details of the tax policy are explained by the Finance Ministry (http://www.minfin.fgov.be) or accessed via http://www.belgium.be.

As well as direct taxation, there is a whopping 21 per cent VAT on most (but not all) purchases. As in most of Europe (but unlike the USA), this is always included in quoted prices and not tacked on at the time of payment.

Other smaller, unexpected taxes include those on owning a car radio (http://www.redevances.cfwb.be).

SHOPPING

Shops in the cities have plenty of character. There is a high concentration of delightful speciality outlets and many assistants speak surprisingly good English. Bargaining is not common but is possible to a certain degree when buying high price-tag items e.g. by offering to pay cash rather than by credit card, or (illegally) by suggesting that you don't need a receipt.

The bigger supermarkets stock products from virtually all corners of the globe, supplemented by Turkish and North African corner shops, a couple of East Asian food stores and even a few British and American speciality shops in case you're desperate for Marmite or Hersheys chocolate.

Don't expect to find 24-hour hypermarkets. Supermarkets are usually open Mondays to Saturdays until 8:00 pm or 9:00 pm, though the newer, upmarket 'Deli-Delhaize' chain opens till 10:00 pm and even works on Sundays—still quite a novelty in Belgium. Most smaller businesses operate from 10:00 am–6:30 pm, often closing for an hour at lunchtime though without the lengthy Italian-style siesta. At Christmas time, it is very common for shops to wrap purchases for their customers at no extra expense. Some supermarkets provide big rolls of free Christmas gift wrap beyond the checkouts so that you can do the job yourself . You'll often see sneaky customers surreptitiously pulling out a few extra metres for later use.

Markets and Sales

Markets and fairs are held regularly in town and commune squares. These usually offer high quality fruit and vegetables, selections of cheeses and olives, barbecued meats, bargain clothes and (probably fake) perfumes. While there are many antique shops, a good place to start your search for antiques and bric-a-brac is the *puces* (literally 'fleas')/*vlooienmarkt*, like the daily morning market on Brussels' Place du Jeu de Balle. The vast majority of stuff sold here is rubbish, especially after about 6:00 am when the dealers' buyers have passed through. But the place retains a brilliant atmosphere thanks to its Marollian characters who, by early afternoon, are selling off what's left for a few coins a piece. The stalls in Brussels' Sablon area are a big step up in quality. There are dozens of other markets, the biggest of which jams the roads around Brussels' south station on Sundays selling virtually anything moveable. The Anderlecht abattoir holds various livestock markets during the week, there's a horse market in Molenbeek-St-Jean on Friday mornings, and a daily plant and flower market in the Brussels Grand Place.

A *brocante*/*rommelmarkt* is equivalent to a British car boot sale—like a flea market but open to ordinary people to sell their motley selection of unwanted clothes, furniture, books and bric-a-brac. For the most popular ones (e.g. at the Carrefour/ex-Biggs car park in Waterloo every Sunday), vendors arrive before dawn to claim a valuable pitch. Often, a roadside *brocante* is one feature of a village *braderie*—a kind of fête at which the town centre is closed to traffic while various cafés and street sellers serve drinks and snacks on the pavements and shops offer limited discounts. This is not, as Belgians are swift to point out, the same as the sales (*soldes/ solden*), which are legally limited to two officially designated periods in January and July. Suburban homes also run garage sales, known in Belgium as, well, garage sales.

Special Regional Products	
Lace	Brussels, Bruges
Diamonds, gold, avant-garde fashion	Antwerp
Crystal glassware	Seraing
Hand-beaten copperware	Dinant

HEALTH AND HOSPITALS
Medicine

Belgium has one of the best health services anywhere. While health care is not entirely free in Belgium, one can choose one's doctor and seeking a second opinion is very easy and relatively inexpensive. Nor are there the infamous British delays for operations. Treatment tends to cost much less in Belgium than in the US as the insurance is funnelled through non-profit 'mutual societies' (*mutualités/mutualiteit*). Citizens must sign up with one such society to receive medical reimbursements from the social security system. Whatever the actual cost of treatment incurred, the state repays at the basic INAMI rate. (INAMI stands for National Institute of Medical and Disability Insurance.) This is almost, but not quite, enough to cover the cheapest option/consultation and means that those covered are not bankrupted. Note that doctors listed as *conventionné* usually charge fees nearest to the INAMI level and are likely to be every bit as good as private *non-conventionné* medics. Of course, the social security system only pays out for those patients who are paying contributions as an employee, officially self-employed, or the state-funded unemployed. To top up the state system, many companies provide their employees with extra health and life insurance, and a few even pay for prescription medicines which you must otherwise buy yourself. For minor afflictions, you can save a doctor's appointment and simply ask for a pharmacist's advice. The green cross symbols of pharmacies shine like beacons and attract a steady stream of customers, but beware—most close at lunchtime, and those which open in the evenings or on Sundays (by a rotating schedule) will charge a supplement for drugs dispensed at non-standard times. Assuming you're paying social security, be sure to take your 'SIS' card (a credit-card shaped health ID) to the pharmacy to get subsidised prices on your prescription drugs.

Hospitalisation

If you are warded in a state or university hospital (which are perfectly good), your social security repayments will cover all but about € 5 per day (about £ 3 or US$ 6) for your accommodation charges in the cheapest rooms. If you want to save money on your medical bills, try to get yourself to the hospital. This not only saves you paying for the ambulance, but allows you to choose the cheapest option. Ambulances, in contrast, will take you to the hospital that's nearest, regardless of how high that institution's charges may be.

All patients are expected to bring their own towels, toiletries, pyjamas, etc. Note that the same taboo against serving tap water that is so visible in Belgian restaurants (*see* Chapter 6: Food and Drink, *page 149*) also applies in hospital; if you ask for a glass of water to wash down your pills, you'll be given (and charged for) a bottle of mineral water. There are also separate charges for using the telephone beside your bed and the TV in your room.

Medical Paperwork for Foreigners

If you are paying Belgian social security payments through your business or via your employer, you should receive the normal social security reimbursements via a *mutualité/ mutualiteit*—so don't forget to join one! Non-resident visitors, especially from EU nations, often enjoy fairly comprehensive reciprocal health agreements. Until recently, British visitors could use a date-stamped E111 form for up to 12 months. However, since 2006, an EHIC (European Health Insurance

Card) is required. Apply online at http://www.ehic.org.uk. If you need to claim, you'll need to make arrangements with a mutual society like any normal Belgian citizen, which will receive INAMI rate reimbursements on your behalf.

WILLS AND DEATH DUTIES

Should disaster strike and you die while you are a resident in Belgium, your inheritance will be subject to Belgian rules and taxes. Since these may be very different to those in your country of origin, it's well worth taking the time and trouble to make a specific will for your time here. Obviously if you're dead, it won't be of great concern to you, but those left behind may be in for a surprise. For example, your spouse might be horrified to discover that unless you name him or her specifically as recipient, your possessions would bypass him or her and go directly to your children, parents or siblings. So write down what you intend. And not just any-old how. The will should be HANDWRITTEN, ideally in the language of the commune where you are resident. Even if the intention is clear, incorrectly formulated wills may later be challenged or nullified. And be aware that certain direct descendants (*héritiers réservataires*) have the right to claim a certain portion of your estate, regardless of what you have written in the will. That's why most wills have a clause minimising what an unnamed, unanticipated *héritier réservataire* (perhaps a hitherto unsuspected illegitimate child) can claim.

A notary will be able to help you with finding your way through all the minutae. Remarkably, there's no charge for this help, but you'd be wise to pay him or her € 100 to lodge the will as an official record in the notary database. Any time you want to change or update the will. you simply deliver the new version to the same notary—no further fees apply.

Death duties vary considerably according to three factors:
- who receives the money,
- how much each receives and
- whether you live in Brussels, Flanders or Wallonia, each of which have different tax scales.

Wherever you live, taxes are vastly lower when giving to parents, children, spouse or registered 'partner' than to siblings. Nephews, nieces, uncles and aunts pay even more while any other recipient is likely to pay a truly colossal tax bill. For example, in Wallonia, someone recently left € 3 million to their favourite charity. But with a tax rate approaching 80 per cent (for a large gift to a non-relative), the real charity-case was Wallonia's government. Had the same sum been split between 200 charities, the tax would have only been around 30 per cent.

TRANSPORTATION
Belgium is blessed with many good things. But great public transport is not really one of them. Buses and trains cover most of the country but suburban services don't quite run frequently enough to really generate mass usage. Even in the city of Brussels, you may often have to wait up to 20 minutes before a metro train arrives. This encourages commuters to drive, which further reduces passenger revenues and worsens the traffic load. It's a vicious circle. All the more vicious considering the discourteous and dangerous Belgian driving style. The car is king but, as you'll see from the second half of this section, there are plenty of challenges for drivers, foreign and local alike.

Public Transport
Train-SNCB/NMBS
Belgium is reputed to have the densest railway network in the world. The Brussels-Mechelen line was the first on the European continent to run a passenger service. These days, services are moderately priced and run at hourly intervals on most routes. At main stations, departure boards are usually clearly marked but remember that place names look different in French and Flemish. When reading timetables, note that yellow posters quote departures while white ones are for arrivals. There are quite different but similar looking timetables for weekdays, and for weekends or holidays.

There are weekend discounted return tickets and 'B-excursion' tickets which may include the entrance fee to an event or attraction. For major events such as the carnival at Binche, return tickets to the site are sold at a

Some stations are works of art. Binche's (pictured here) has great wrought ironwork, Gent's has a brilliant neo-medieval buffet-café and Antwerp's Centraal Station is one of the city's most splendid buildings.

major reduction (60 per cent) to encourage drivers to leave their cars behind. For very special events, Belgian railways sometimes get generous and give away tickets, as they did for the wedding of Prince Philip on 4 December 1999. Strangely on that day, you could get a pair of free tickets from anywhere to anywhere, not just to Brussels to see the spectacle. So rather than watch the wedding, Belgians left the capital en masse for a free weekend at the seaside! The B-Tourrail offers the best deal: free travel anywhere within the country for five stated days within a one-month period for only € 68 (€ 104 for first class). There are also special deals for people over 60 years of age and for big families (very Catholic!). You can find out more by visiting the website http://www.b-rail.be.

Belgium has at least two seasonal steam railways. Trois Vallées runs from Treignes to Mariembourg in Hainaut from April–October only. Vennbahn (tel: (087) 858-285, http://www.vennbahn.de) links Eupen and Robertville a few weekends per year.

Buses and Trams
Belgium has three main public bus companies. For Brussels, that's STIB/MIVB (http://www.stib.irisnet.be) in French which

Give way! You are always in the wrong in a tangle with a tram.

also operates the capital's tram and metro system. De Lijn (http://www.delijn.be), literally 'The Line', runs buses and trams in Flanders while Transport en Commun (TEC) is the equivalent in Wallonia, with different contact details in each province (e.g. http://www.tecbw.com in Brabant Wallon).

Bus frequency on many routes diminishes considerably at weekends. Brussels and certain other cities have fairly extensive tram networks but be careful when driving near or across the tracks: if a tram hits you, it is always considered 'your fault'.

Tram Party

The Brussels Tramway Museum shows off a great variety of trams which are mostly still in working order and, on special occasions, are still used as public transport. An intriguing way to celebrate is to rent out a party-tram and driver from STIB (evenings and weekends only, up to 40 revellers per tram).

Taxis

In taxis, as in restaurants, there is absolutely no compunction to tip. The gratuity is already included in the quoted fare, though this doesn't stop certain drivers trying to persuade you otherwise. Taxi fares can usually be paid by credit card in the car. In Brussels, the minimum charge is € 2.35 (€ 4.21 night) plus € 1.14 per km and € 0.364 per minute waiting time (which includes travel at under 20 kmph). You should note that the rate doubles if you want to travel beyond city limits (e.g. to 'Brussels' airport, which is actually in Zaventem). Brussels Taxis have their own website at http://www.taxi.irisnet.be/)

Owning and Renting A Car
Rush Hour Chaos

Rush hour traffic is bad anywhere. And bus drivers' frequent strikes don't help. The Gent, Antwerp and Brussels Ring roads often resemble car parks during rush hour. It's not unusual to see drivers reading a book at the wheel as they inch forward. The blockages are bad enough if everyone's driving sensibly. If there's a crash, the whole system comes to a standstill. And there's nowhere more likely to cause a crash than that most infamous of blackspots, the Carrefour Léonard. Here, the Brussels Ring intersects the Brussels-Namur motorway with an interchange so confusing it requires a PhD to negotiate. Turning certain directions involves several perilous stops and starts while attempting to cross the oncoming streams of international juggernauts. An amusing advertisement quipped ironically 'A user's manual for the Carrefour Léonard? If one exists, you'll find it in the Yellow Pages!' In 2004, some bright spark finally decided to restrict the most dangerous permutations, though the result has been an almost equally confusing set of detours and U-turns at neighbouring junctions.

Traffic is noticeably lighter (except on weekends) between 1 July and 31 August, i.e. during the school holiday season. However, on Sunday evenings in summer or at the end of long weekends, the motorways back to Brussels from Ostend and from the Ardennes can be chock-full of cars.

Driving in Belgium

Belgian driving standards are infamous. Glance at the walls of the tunnels that wind beneath each of the bigger cities and you will see that barely an inch has not been

scratched and scarred by a vehicle that has lost control. Curve-barriers are repeatedly buckled from crashes, motorway tarmac is artistically adorned with skid tracks and small suburban shrubberies are felled every weekend by sozzled chauffeurs.

There was once a good reason for all this mayhem. Driving tests were only introduced in 1967. Prior to that, to get a driver's licence, you simply had to go to the commune, pay a fee and swear that you knew how to drive. A suitable hole was punched in your identification card and that was it. Off you go. Notwithstanding the better training today's drivers undergo, many still seem addicted to speeding, drink-driving, bullying pedestrians and tailgating. When driving abroad, my wife occasionally mutters darkly at other road users, "Watch out! Don't you know there's a Belgian behind you!" And she's only half joking.

Despite all of the above, compared to most European capitals, Brussels is a relatively easy place to drive. A key is learning how to use the sometimes very lengthy under-city tunnels which can spit you out halfway across town—handy when you've learnt how to navigate them. Certainly the rush hour periods are appalling, but especially at night there remains a reasonable chance of finding street parking right outside the place you're going. Don't try this in Gent or Bruges, however. Those cities have a one-way system so complex that even residents get lost. And West Flanders police's zero-tolerance policy to any parking or motoring infraction horrifies show-off Ixelles drivers grown blasé at triple parking around Brussels' Place Chatelein.

Driving Tests

If you're learning to drive, GOCA (rue de la Technologie 21-25, B1080 Brussels, tel: (02) 469-0600) has lists of driving test centres. Sample questions from the theory test are available online at http://www.brocom.be or on the French Language CD-ROM *Feu Vert*.

Bob Tonight?

A high-profile publicity campaign has long tried to persuade Belgium's notoriously merry motorists that it's sexy to be 'Bob'. A 'Bob' (or 'Bobette') stays sober to drive the rest of his (or her) friends home after a party. For those found to be over the 0.5g/l blood alcohol limit, fines start at € 137.50 (vastly more if you can't pay up immediately). Blood alcohol over 0.8 g/l will get you anything from a € 400 fine to the immediate confiscation of your drivers' licence plus a year in jail for good measure. Nonetheless, for years, most Belgians have simply scorned the drink-driving laws. They simply didn't expect to be caught. This may finally be changing. Since 2003, a new campaign to randomly breathalyse drivers has sent shivers of fear (if not sobriety) through many a motorist. At crash sites, police frequently find cars abandoned and their injured drivers lurking in the undergrowth to avoid the breath test rather than seek medical help. There have even been bizarre cases where drunk drivers, spying a police car approaching, have nimbly jumped into the back seat with their passengers. Thus, when the police officer opens the door, he finds the driver's seat empty and the back seat crammed with 'hitchhikers'.

Drink-driving Limits

The Belgian Society for Road Safety (http://www.bivv.be) and the Francophone website http://www.jesuispour.be both offer extensive information on driver security. The latter offers a downloadable chart of traffic fines and drink driving limits.

Yet even when caught, there is still hope. I've seen cases myself where helpful traffic policemen simply ask about a crashed driver's welfare, apparently choosing not to notice his near paralytic condition. And if you are stopped by the police, you're allowed to request 30 minutes to breathe, drink water and crunch garlic to mask the smell of alcohol before you are eventually breathalysed. The very fair-minded principle is to prevent unfairly punishing those who may have happened to have just one single drink (swigged on departure to steady the nerves for the journey?!).

If you want to be law-abiding and find yourself without a 'Bob' at hand, on special occasions (like New Year's Eve) you can still reach home drunk and in one piece with the help of a volunteer group called Responsible Young Drivers. The volunteers work in pairs—one drives you home in your own car while the other follows in a second vehicle to pick up his partner after the ride. On millennium night, the group aided some 3,080 revellers in various states of intoxication. Of those who did choose to drive that night, only 10 per cent caught were legally 'intoxicated'—a score that my Belgian wife deemed 'suspiciously low'.

Speeding

Belgian motorists seem to perceive posted speed limits as minima rather than maxima and growl bitterly at those law-abiding slowcoaches who persist in sticking to the generally disdained limit. Things get especially dangerous in the rare but severe snows that occasionally catch the country unawares and put skates beneath those macho lorry drivers who frighteningly consider their trucks immune to skidding.

The chances of being caught for speeding may be higher than for boozing. But that is not saying much. The idea of fixed speed traps is a novelty. Many were put in position during 2004 but well into 2005, none were yet operational. Meanwhile, speed checks are done by police with radar guns—you may not even notice you've been caught until the fine notice turns up in the mail. Thus it's worth listening to daily radio announcements... Incredibly, the police tell radio stations where many of the speed traps are going to be placed each day. And radio stations make regular bulletins. The possible logic for divulging the speed guns' positions is delightfully Belgian. Radio stations can't be prevented from divulging such information—that's free press. And motorists who spot a radar trap might phone in reports to radio stations on mobile phones. But such phones are illegal and dangerous to use while driving. So why not be safe and simply have the gendarmerie announce the trap locations in the first place.

Pedestrian Crossings

There are two types of pedestrian crossings, and neither are entirely safe. Those at traffic lights are the better of the two. But many show the 'green-man' symbol while turning traffic is simultaneously allowed to filter around the corners, straight into the pedestrians' path. So watch very carefully. Then there are the 'normal' crossings: thick (if tellingly faded) black and white stripes painted across the street and marked on the roadside by a blue triangular sign. Legally, pedestrians have the right of way to cross here. But believe that at your mortal peril. It is a relatively new rule, and the stream of traffic is unlikely to even slow down for you. If you stride forth confidently asserting your rights (as one would on a British zebra crossing), most drivers will simply look at you with a mixture of bemusement and annoyance as they try to knock you down.

Driving instructors are in a quandary over these crossings. Since the correct (if rarely observed) rule says that drivers should stop for pedestrians, learner drivers ought, theoretically, to be so taught. The problem is that practising the manoeuvre is dangerous for student and instructor alike. Driving schools claim it's their major cause of crashes: the drivers behind simply don't expect anyone to stop for pedestrians, so slam straight into the back of the practice car.

Priorité à Droite

As if all the other dangers weren't enough, traffic on Belgian roads has the extra challenge of observing the suicidal French-style *priorité à droite* rule. This gives the right of way to a vehicle shooting out from the right rather than to the stream of traffic going straight ahead. The rule makes sense at the unmarked junction of two roads of similar sizes. But when a tiny country lane joins a big thoroughfare, the potential for disaster is obvious. It is compounded by the caveat that you lose the priority should you slow to a halt. Thus, to maintain the right to advance, it's important not to watch where you're going. Silly? So it would seem to most visitors. And in private, many Belgians quietly admit that *priorité à droite* is a well-intentioned but potentially lethal anachronism. But God help any foreigner who criticises it—you may be seen as making a cultural attack, rubbing salt into an open wound or, at best, being boringly predictable.

Note that not all roads are ruled by *priorité à droite*. You can relax somewhat when you see occasional yellow-on-white diamond roadside signs along your route. And if you see a row of triangular white 'teeth' painted across your path at a junction, you must give way—even if you are advancing from the right. Finally, at a roundabout (rotary), the vehicle going around the circle has priority over another vehicle approaching from a side road. That is normal the world over, isn't it? Well, yes. But beware. In Belgium, the very opposite was true until recently. And even sober drivers can be a little forgetful.

Buying Cars

Belgium was once one of the cheapest places in Europe to buy new cars, though the advantages have been whittled away recently. Belgians themselves show an extraordinary enthusiasm for the Salon de l'Auto car show held every two years at the Heysel exhibition grounds in Brussels. Some car brands take as much as 40 per cent of their annual order during the fair, which draws a phenomenal 10 per cent of the national population each time!

Besides the fair, there is the usual network of dealers (bargain hard!) and you can get a price guide from *Auto Gids* or *Moniteur de l'Automobile*. For second-hand cars, check the fortnightly *Auto-Occasion* or watch for bright orange signs displayed in the back windows of the target cars themselves. Note that unlike the UK, it's usually better to sell a car second-hand than to trade it in with a dealer, though either way, prices are pretty low. Generally, it's required that the seller proves the road-worthiness of the car in question through an MOT-style test when a sale is agreed, even when the car is relatively new and still under guarantee.

Even the most comprehensive Belgian automobile insurance scheme may not cover the loss of a car's contents. And it's very wise to get legal defence liability coverage too. Insurance normally covers the car rather than the driver.

Number Plates

In Belgium, licence plates are registered to a driver not a car (except for company or commercial vehicles). The front number plate is simply a copy that the owner has made at a key-cutting store but the back plate has security markings and a fluorescent backing. It's the back plate that carries all the legal importance, so stealing it from a car is an extremely cruel practical joke which can cause months of bureaucratic difficulties for the owner and is almost worse than having the whole car taken.

Private plates have red characters on a white background. 'CD' in green letters on an otherwise ordinary plate means the driver has diplomatic immunity, so keep out of his or her way! They won't be responsible if they crash into you.

If a lad turns up on a date in a flashy Ferrari, he is much less likely to impress the girl if the licence plates are in green letters. She'll assume that his dad is a car salesman; such plates are for cars held by the dealer awaiting a buyer.

White letters on a red plate indicate a car 'in transit', i.e. bought here but destined for export. The owners of these cars may avoid the 21 per cent VAT, but the car must be exported within a year.

Blue letters on white plates with the EU symbol denote the number plates of cars driven by those who work at the EU. The plates give certain preferential parking possibilities to Eurocrats who are mostly expatriates with large tax-free salaries. The result is a certain degree of resentment from ordinary Belgians, beaten at their own national sport of tax-avoidance. Thus, drivers of cars bearing blue plates suffer the same nagging insecurities as wearers of fur coats in London.

Paying Traffic Fines

Parking fines are generally paid by virement bank transfer. Speeding or other infractions might require a visit to the post office to buy fiscal stamps. Stick them on the fine-form, cut off the bottom strip as a receipt then deliver the rest to the police station. If you contest the decision but lose, you'll be charged five times the fine.

Renting or Leasing a Car

Renting a car is as straightforward as anywhere in the EU. More common for long-term residents is the long-term lease of a company car provided by your employer. The latter is a favourite amongst tax-dodging Belgians as the hidden benefits of free petrol, paid insurance and regular new models rapidly offset the relatively small tax increase that receiving a company car incurs.

Petrol

Service stations may not sell petrol above an officially announced maximum price per litre, though several (such as Octa +) regularly charge less. Changes in this official price are announced on the evening news almost daily.

On weekends or late evenings, many garages appear to be closed but, in fact, you can often still use the petrol pumps and make payment with a debit card or by putting a € 20 note into a self-service slot. If a Belgian finds himself anywhere near Luxembourg, he or she will naturally be tempted to detour through the Grand-Duchy to fill the tank virtually tax free. Unless, of course they're driving a company car, in which case they'll be cursing the fact that they can't fill up for free just before crossing the border. (Company car deals often include petrol but only when bought within Belgium on a special account-card... but no petrol station can survive too close to low-tax Luxembourg).

Cycling and Rambling

In the provinces, particularly Flanders, there are extensive cycle paths and signposted hiking trails. You can rent mountain bikes at certain railway stations, and many tourist offices provide fairly detailed walking and cycling maps to help you explore the area. Attractive VTT (mountain bike) trails are also found in the Ardennes. However, on the busy city streets of Brussels, cycling approximates to attempted suicide. This is ironic considering the popularity of the sport of cycle racing (*see* Chapter 7: Culture, Sport and Travel, *page 176*). Roadside cycle paths in the suburbs frequently end suddenly or slam into high kerbs. Drivers have no more respect for cyclists than they do for pedestrians, and are highly unlikely to grant priority to cycle lanes even where they are legally supposed to. If you have a bike (or indeed a horse) in Brussels, the best place to ride it is the glorious Forêt de Soignes/Zoniënwoud, through a cathedral of beech trees with miles of peaceful bridle paths and cycle tracks. And no cars.

If you want to buy a bike, there are plenty of specialist but pricy bicycle shops. The hypermarkets sometimes have great deals on bicycles but usually stock only a limited range of sizes which may come in a box, making it rather difficult to test ride before you buy. You can buy a second-hand bicycle at a special market on the Blvd du Midi/Zuidlaan near the Brussels Midi/Zuid station (Sundays, 7:00 am–2:00 pm) or through small ads like those posted on http://www.xpats.com.

Water Transport

While canals in Britain have been largely relegated to servicing pleasure cruise holiday-makers, in Belgium waterways still carry significant industrial cargoes and receive major investment. Huge vessels of up to 9,000 tonnes can reach Liège via the Albert canal. The curious inclined lock at Ronquières, like a massive bath on wheels, allows sizeable barges to reach Charleroi from Antwerp. And the brand new rotating hydraulic lift at Strépy-Thieu has been built to expedite heavy boat traffic between the Rhine, Scheldt/Escaut, and Maas/Meuse rivers.

Despite the major industrial traffic, several sections of Belgian waterways are accessible to pleasure boats. Tourists seem to love the Damme-Bruges paddleboat run. An appealing 21 km (13 miles) of the Lesse between Anseremme and Dinant have been set aside for kayaking, and there are summer rides between the rocks and trees down the Semois from Chiny (by reservation, call tel: (09) 554 9372).

LEAVING BELGIUM
By Air
By air, Brussels is connected to most other European countries, and directly to the US and many African destinations. Indirect flights via London, Frankfurt, Vienna, Paris or Amsterdam can get you virtually anywhere else. Note that Air France 'flights' from Brussels actually depart from Brussels Midi/Zuid train station. That's not an error—the connecting 'flight' to Paris is actually on the Thalys train! Also beware if you book a budget airline ticket to or from 'Brussels South'. That's not Brussels at all but a marketing name for Charleroi.

At Brussels Airport, Le Chat welcomes you and bids you farewell all in one breath. Note the use of English with French and Flemish translations relegated below!

Flying Away

Airports

Antwerp Airport	http://www.antwerpairport.be
Brussels Airport	http://www.biac.be
Charleroi Airport	http://www.charleroi-airport.com
Liège Airport	http://www.liegeairport.com (charters/cargo)

Airlines

British Airways	http://www.ba.com
British European	http://www.flybe.com (several British destinations)
BMI	http://www.flybmi.com (many British destinations)
Ryanair	http://www.ryanair.com (budget flights from Charleroi)
SN Brussels Airlines	http://www.flysn.be (major Belgian airline)
Virgin Express	http://www.virgin-express.com (mostly Meditterranean destinations ex Brussels)
VLM	http://www.flyvlm.be (to the UK from Antwerp and Brussels)
Wizz Air	www.wizzair.com (low-cost flights to Eastern Europe from Charleroi)

Travel Agents

USIT Connections	http://www.connections.be English language telesales tel: (02) 550-0100
Airstop	http://www.airstop.be Telesales tel: (070) 233-188 (high toll number)

By Land and Sea

Belgium is ideally placed as a starting point to head off to somewhere else. Amsterdam, Cologne, Paris, Lille and London are all short hops away from Brussels by high speed Thalys or Eurostar trains. Trains originating in Belgium cross into neighbouring countries and even go as far as Moscow. Eurolines buses (http://www.eurolines.be/

http://www.gobycoach.com) link most European cities and there are several small private operators offering coaches to North Africa and Eastern Europe. There are ferries from Zeebrugge to Hull, and from Ostend to Ramsgate. Alternatively, reaching England is easy by car via northern France with regular ferries from Calais or Dunkerque to Dover or using the Eurotunnel car-train (http://www.eurotunnel.com). However, reaching Calais by public transport from western Flanders is surprisingly awkward.

Train and Boat Contacts

Trains To and In Nearby Countries

Belgian railways	http://www.b-rail.be
Thalys	http://www.thalys.com
	(Amsterdam, Cologne, Paris)
Eurostar	http://www.eurostar.com (London and Lille)
French railways	http://www.sncf.com
British railways	http://www.nationalrail.co.uk
Italian railways	http://www.trenitalia.com
German railways	http://www.bahn.de
Dutch railways	http://ns.nl/domestic/index.cgi

Ferry Links to UK

TransEuropean	http://www.transeuropaferries.com
	(Ostend–Ramsgate)
Norfolk Line	http://www.norfolkline.com
	(Dunkerque–Dover)
P&O	http://www.poferries.com
	(Calais–Dover and Zeebrugge–Hull)
Seafrance	http://www.seafrance.net
	(ferries Calais - Dover)

TELECOMMUNICATIONS
Telephone and Internet

Unlike in the US, there is a per-minute charge for local phone calls (i.e. anywhere in Belgium), and a minimum per call charge of around 5cents. The per-minute rates are somewhat lower for calls to Internet providers. When you are making a telephone call, note that all numbers including the city code should be dialled, even when you're within that town. The main telephone company, Belgacom (toll free 0800-33-800), can generally install a phone line relatively rapidly but there's a standard charge for line rental. Discounted long distance calls are possible through a variety of smaller companies using access numbers (e.g. 070-777-777), using pre-paid code cards or by dial-via-Internet services like Skype (http://www.skype.com).

Pay Phones

Except at stations and airports, pay phones are few and far between and relatively rarely take coins. If you find a box that does take coins, there's a € 0.60 minimum call fee, rates are € 0.30 per minute or € 0.60 per minute, Mondays–Fridays 8:00 am–7:00 pm. Most public telephones take credit cards or prepaid phonecards which you can buy at kiosks, train stations and newsagents. If you have a bank card with an attached Proton electronic purse you can conveniently charge your card with credit in most Belgacom phone booths and then use the Proton credits to call (minimum only € 0.50 per call).

Telephone Companies

- Belgacom
  Tel: 0800-55-800 (in English)
  Website: http://www.belgacom.be
- Telenet
  Tel: 0800-66-000
  Website: http://www.telenet.be
  Offers a wide range of local and long distance calls in Flanders

---

Toll Numbers

There is a range of special toll rate telephone prefixes. Some important ones to be aware of include:

- 0800   toll free
- 078   € 0.025/min off peak, € 0.05/min peak
- 070   € 0.0875/min off peak, € 0.17min peak
- 077   € 0.45/min; adults only, mostly for pornographic and chat-line services

- 0900   € 0.45/min
- 0902   € 0.745/min
- 0903   € 1.12/min
- 0908/9   Variable but can be up to € 2.5/min and with a fixed dial up charge of as much as € 25!

Belgacom can block calls to toll numbers. Blocking 077 calls is free, but they will charge you around € 15 plus an annual € 2.5 for blocking the various options that start with the numbers 090. Calling a mobile telephone from a fixed line incurs a € 0.10–0.11 connection charge and costs between € 0.116–0.281/min depending on the time of day, day of the week and company called.

Mobile Phones

Belgian mobile phones follow the usual GSM standard as in the rest of Europe, but use a different waveband to North America. There are three main providers: Proximus, Mobistar and Base. Each has its pluses and minuses according to what exactly you need from your phone and at what price. In a totally unscientific poll of some personal friends who seemed sober enough at the time, Proximus came out as overall favourite. A pay-as-you-go SIM card for your phone will generally cost around € 20–30 including a phone number and € 10 of call credit. Such cards can be topped up from most ATM cash machines outside banks by tapping in your telephone number along with your bankcard PIN.

Mobile Phones Companies

- Proximus
  Tel: (02) 205-4000
  Website: http://www.proximus.be
- Mobistar
  Tel: 0800-95-951 or (0495) 959-501 from abroad
  Website: http://www.mobistar.be
- Base
  Tel: (0486) 191-999
  Website: http://www.base.be

Internet Service Providers

An explosion in the number of service providers in the late 1990s has been countered recently by a major consolidation. As of 2006, the main players are Scarlet (http://www.scarlet.be) and Skynet (http://www.skynet.be), the latter run by Belgacom, the major terrestrial telephone company. For a complete discussion of ISP issues in Belgium consult http://www.ispa.be

Post

Deliveries in Belgium are usually made only once daily during normal work hours and not at all during weekends, though collections are made on Saturday mornings.

If you are sending a letter, beware that the Belgian post office strictly enforces size and shape norms. Thus, a letter that is too big, too small or simply an unusual shape is likely to incur a hefty premium. When shopping for Christmas cards, take with you one of the letter size templates as many British and American designed cards are the wrong dimensions.

If you're sending parcels heavier than 10 kg (about 22 lbs) abroad, you may find it considerably cheaper to send the contents as two smaller parcels: 10 kg is the cut off between the small package rate and the more expensive 'kilopost'. Check rates on http://www.laposte.be.

For international letters, post clerks will assume you want to pay the faster *prioritaire* rate unless you state otherwise. It is important to attach the little blue prior airmail sticker on your letters to ensure that you actually get that faster service. There is, however, a second-class airmail (*non prioritaire*) rate. This saves just a couple of cents on EU mail but virtually halves the cost to Australia, Japan and North America. A small packet that I sent thus to Japan arrived in barely two weeks.

In October 2005, the Belgian and Danish post offices joined forces in an unusual alternative to full privatisation.

The major courier mail services operate in Belgium including DHL (tel: (02) 715-5050), FedEx (tel: 0800-13-555), TNT (tel: 070-233-633) and UPS (tel: 0800-12-828)

FOOD AND DRINK

CHAPTER 6

'As I walk along the streets with my mayonnaise and frites,
you can tell I'm happy as can be
With my Duvel in my hand, then you must understand,
I'm a Belgian—so nothing worries me'
—From the song 'Potverdekke, it's great to be a Belgian'
an amusingly tongue-in cheek little ditty that you can hear
on http://users.pandora.be/filip.geerts/potverdekke.mp3

BRITS WITH LONG MEMORIES may remember *Not the Nine O'Clock News*. It was a partly-topical comedy show in the early 1980s. In one sketch a pre-Mr Bean Rowan Atkinson played a Belgian cultural attaché who was asked to explain cultural nuances that Belgians use to express their appreciation of their food. The hilarious, if utterly untrue, answers included gratuitous farting and burping, and culminated in the question, "But what if you wanted to say, 'that's the best meal I've ever tasted'?" Answer? "Not a very likely contingency... in Belgium." Across the UK, people roared with laughter.

Clearly very few viewers had actually eaten in Belgium. The collective assumption back then was that 'Belgian = boring = bad food'. The reality couldn't be more different. Belgians love to eat out. And a relatively wealthy, demanding clientele supports a very high quality and competitive restauration trade.

These days, the world is better informed. One Internet site gushes accurately (if inelegantly) that gastronomically, Belgium is 'not the sleepy sister of France; it's a chowhound Mecca'. The establishment of the Belgo restaurant chain (since 1992) has helped to change images. So have all the the Euroland expatriates, many of whom become happily overweight and reluctant to go home. The taste for luxury is emphasised at Christmas: while the English-speaking world stuffs

'Everyone eats well in Belgium.'
—Ruth Van Waerebeek-
Gonzalez (recipe book
title and general truism)

its turkey and the Eastern Europeans choose their carp, wealthier Belgians are off to the supermarket to collect their box-full of pre-ordered lobsters.

French visitors are frequently surprised to find that French food in Brussels restaurants and bakeries is consistently better and of better value than in much of France. Day-to-day home-cooked meals may be less inspired 'meat-and-two-veg' variants, but are typically rich and hearty offering few compromises to the concerns of dieticians. Beyond the evils of the Brussels sprout, Belgium's most famous contributions to gastronomy—chocolate, chips and mussels—reflect its international flavour. After all, potatoes and cocoa are New World products while the best 'Belgian' mussels are usually imported from the town of Yerseke, just across the Dutch border.

AT THE BAKERY
Belgian bakers reckon they make French bread better than the French. Sounds like an oxymoron. Yet on the whole,

I agree. And it's not just the *pain Français* (baguette); Belgian bread comes in all shapes and sizes. *Prokorn* is light and soft-centred yet stuffed with seeds. Try the various nut breads with hazelnuts and raisins. Unlike France, sliced bread is popular in Belgium. In bakeries, the slicing is performed to order by the shop assistant and you'll usually be charged a couple of cents for the service. In supermarkets, you'll have to slice it yourself. This means confronting a machine which looks like it belongs in a medieval dungeon. Put the loaf in through the flap in the rear section and close the door. Press the green button. A whirring of electric saws begins and the loaf starts to emerge from the set of metal teeth. Once the bread has escaped, place it onto the angular metal tongue on the top of the contraption to make bagging it up more straightforward.

What's What in a Baker's Shop

What's What In a Bakery...

The following are some other morsels you can find at a bakery:

- *pains à la Grecque*   neither Greek nor bread, this Belgian biscuit is a trademark of the venerable 1829 Dandoy patisserie at 31 rue au Beurre, Brussels
- *pain au chocolat* (French)   croissant with chocolate filling (*chocolade broodje* in Flemish)
- *pistolets* (Belgian-French)   not small guns but small, round bread rolls
- *achtje* (Flemish)   literally means 'eight' in Flemish, but in patisserie terms, these are pastries moulded into the shape of the number eight with a custard paste in each lobe
- *kaasflap* (Flemish)   cheese turnover
- *kersengebak* (Flemish)   small cherry tarts
- *rozijnkoek* (Flemish)   fruit cake
- *suikerwafel* (Flemish)   sugar waffle
- worstenbrood (Flemish)   sausage roll

Fresh bread should be available most of the day but towards closing time, the choice is considerably diminished. *Couques* such as croissants and *pain au chocolat* are usually available only in the mornings. Most *boulangerie/ patisserie* shops have a wide range of cakes and other temptations on offer including a selection of chocolates and tarts. *Tarte au sucre/zuikertort* is caramelised sugar in an open pastry base. There is also a wide variety of fruit pies such as the classic Walloon *tarte aux groseilles vertes* (gooseberry tart). Arguably, some of the country's best tarts come from a small roadside *tarterie* in the tiny township of Chaumont-Gistoux, south-east of Wavre. People making the considerable drive from Brussels don't seem to mind the lengthy wait and curt service they get from the shop attendants. Many bakeries have an attached coffee shop where you can enjoy the pastries at slightly higher than takeaway prices. And the coffee is usually delicious.

Traiteurs and Sandwich Bars

Belgian delicatessens (*traiteurs*) offer a wide range of cooked meats and pre-prepared gourmet meals, as well as a selection of salads and sandwich fillers. A sandwich (*belegd broodje* in Flemish) makes a quick working lunch—the assistant will cut and fill half a baguette to order for around € 2–3.

What No Bakery?

Belgium has a fair range of vending machines. 'PAIN' daubed above such a machine does not imply masochistic potential for self-torture. And 'BROOD' is not a command for you to act miserable. In fact either term is likely to indicate a coin-operated bread dispenser. These are fairly common in villages where there are no shops.

Many tourists raise an enthusiastic eyebrow at discovering that most Belgian soft drinks machines also dispense beer. However, you'll only get 5 per cent-alcohol standard beers in this way, not the 'real' Belgian masterpieces.

CHEESE

Sandwiched between the great cheese producers, France and Holland, Belgium's brands are relatively unknown.

Yet some 300 cheeses are produced. The most celebrated is the infamously smelly Herve. Also much touted are the abbey cheeses, many of which are produced by the same religious institutions who turn out the famous beers (to which their cheeses make an ideal accompaniment). Obviously incorporating the beer into the recipe is a selling point. Gent's *pas de bleu*, the first Belgian blue cheese, is somewhat similar to a Stilton. *Aux orties* cheeses are flecked with what appear to be herbs but are, in fact, crushed and dried stinging nettles.

On the second last Sunday of August, don't be alarmed if you see men, who look curiously like gnomes in their traditional blue and red costumes, wheeling around huge slabs of creamy, white-skinned Passendale cheeses piled upon black, low-slung barrows on the streets. The spectacle before you is the Passendale's biennial cheese parade. In late October, Herve village also holds a cheese and wine fair; or you can sample a wider range of Belgian cheeses at the National Belgian Cheese Festival at Harzé Castle on the last weekend of August.

CHOCOLATE

Belgians eat almost 8 kg (18 lbs) of chocolate per person per year. Given the vast selection available, one might imagine that the figure was even higher. Wrapped confections provide temptation at supermarket checkouts, many Belgian homes stash a slab of Côte d'Or for a sly nibble and chocolate fingers or individually wrapped squares are de rigueur for coffee-dunking. But for gifts or treats, locals visit the specialist chocolate shops that line local high streets in economically improbable numbers. Belgians refer to their top quality, individually filled, bite-sized chocolates as *pralines*, though these need not strictly be praline (i.e. ground hazelnut) flavoured. The term was coined in 1912 in honour of the early chocoholic Comte de Praslin. The Swiss grandfather of their creator, Belgian chocolatier Jean Neuhaus, had set up shop in Brussels' glorious Galeries Royales St Hubert in 1857. The boutique is still there.

Specialist chocolate shops offer high
quality pralines which make ideal gifts.

Chocolate Controversies

The subject of chocolate is a matter of national pride and can raise a surprising degree of emotion amongst the masses as the two following examples reveal:

Côte d'Or

Established in 1883, Côte d'Or became Belgium's dominant mass market brand, equivalent to Cadbury in the UK or Hershey in the United States, though Belgians would baulk at the comparison. When the company was sold to the multinational conglomerate Kraft Jacobs Suchard, the sense of national loss was akin to that felt in Britain over the sale of the Rolls Royce car company.

What is Chocolate Anyway?

The political wrangling over this technical definition may sound silly, but in Belgium, the issue is major news. The problem is that the EU definition and the traditional Belgian definitions are different. Until recently, the Belgians could only call their product chocolate if it used 100 per cent cocoa butter. Now, the EU has decided in its fallible wisdom, that the exact meaning of the term chocolate should be standardised across the Union. After pressure from the UK industry where manufacturers customarily dilute their cocoa butter, this definition will henceforth allow chocolate-makers to use up to 5 per cent vegetable fats in their products. However, many Belgian producers claim they will retain the old standard.

Belgian Chocolates: Types and Tips

Beautifuly displayed in the nation's myriad chocolate shops, bite-sized *pralines* (as the chocolates are known) come in a bewildering array of types that's utterly confusing for a first-timer. Just as when visiting an American coffee shop, you can't just ask for a coffee, here it makes no sense to simply ask for chocolate. The easiest solution is to simply request a pre-boxed assortment. However, it's perfectly feasible to order which ever takes your fancy; even if you only want a single chocolate.

Types of Pralines

Pralines fall into the following main types:

- *Manon*   usually have a chocolate outer shell and a fresh cream centre. They are best eaten within a few days of purchase.

- *Gianduja*   my personal favourites. These are extremely smooth mixtures of chocolate, icing sugar and finely powdered nut. Commonly sold in little bars wrapped in gold paper.

- *Ganache*   the mainstay of the industry. *Ganache* is a smooth mix of chocolate and *crème fraîche*. Often used as a filling with various crunchy ingredients.

- *Truffles*   are ball-shaped *ganaches*, often with a hardened coat dusted in cocoa powder. Especially popular around Christmas time and often sold in small stalls at seasonal markets.

All types should be kept reasonably cool and dry, but not in a fridge.

Which Brand to Choose?

In choosing chocolates for gifts, there is a somewhat defined hierarchy of perceived qualities which is reflected in the price and the appropriateness of a specific brand. For myself or anyone abroad, I'd buy Leonidas-dream-like quality at great prices. But to impress a Belgian, I'd have to pay almost double and go for brands like Godiva, Corné or Neuhaus. There are also many smaller family chocolatier brands. Some, like Wittamer, will prove very successful presents, but the choice should be very carefully made, especially if you're buying a business gift.

MEAT AND MEAT ATTITUDES

Belgians like their meat and are not afraid of blood. 'Medium' steaks are served red. Rare ones walk away by themselves. Meat ordered 'blue' is simply warmed rather than cooked.

Filet Américain is frequently a disappointment to visitors from the United States who unwittingly assume it's a quaint term for hamburger or steak. In fact, it's raw minced beef, known in France as *steak tartare*. *Carpaccio*, Italian-style slices of raw beef make a popular and very acceptable starter when doused in parmesan cheese and olive oil.

Pork or beef are generally more common than lamb which is seen as a relative luxury. Even more prized are kidneys, sweetbreads and especially goose liver. Belgians are not sentimentally squeamish over Black Beauty, and horse meat is a traditional favourite; pony steak is said to be tender while steeplechase horses are reputed to have the best taste. Traditionally, horse butchers ran niche shops, but such specialist shops are increasingly rare. It's not that animal lovers are prevailing. These days, tastes are just getting more exotic. No major modern supermarket is complete without a fridge-full of springbok, crocodile or llama cuts. Ostrich steaks are slowly becoming accepted as rather superior to beefsteak for tender, velvety red meat. Winter is the season for game which features not just pheasant, duck and venison, but also wild boar. In French, there are two terms for wild-boar meat: *sanglier* is the strongly flavoured meat from the full-grown beast while *marcassin* is from the milder tasting young.

Boudins are various varieties of sausage, not unique to Belgium but much appreciated. A *boudin noir* is a blood and pork fat sausage, a little like black pudding. *Boudin blanc* is filled with stuffing and white poultry, and other varieties add to this herbs, spinach, vegetables and/or raisins. Small versions—some in spicy or curry flavours—are popular in summer barbecues. A plate of black and white *boudin* is known collectively as 'Sky and Earth' as the dish would originally have been served with mashed potatoes (the 'earth') and stewed apple (from 'heaven above'). *Boudin* in Francophone slang can also be equated to the English insult, 'fat slag', a less than flattering term for an overweight, meretricious female.

Vegetarians and Animal Rights
A Belgian Animal Liberation Front has very occasionally attacked fast food outlets and Gaia (http://www.animalrights.be) has recently campaigned to prosecute farmers who mistreat their cattle. However, 'animal rights' viewpoints are far from universally appreciated. Supermarkets stock 'bio' products for health-conscious customers but vegetarianism (http://www.vegetarisme.be) remains marginal. Meanwhile, the Ardennes is the homeland of the St Hubert Foundation which actively promotes game hunting and backs it up by providing New Year's dinners of fresh wild boar for the homeless in Luxembourg Province. Protesters against the consumption of veal calves are widely assumed to be weirdos who don't like drinking milk (of which veal is simply an economic side product). Most Belgians will happily nibble garlic-plastered frogs' legs unconcerned at how they were severed from the frogs. And they are unashamedly proud to serve the ultimate animal-lovers' taboo: *foie gras* (the smooth liver of force-fed geese), washing away any qualms with a sweet Sauternes or 20-year-old Tokaj *five-putunjos*.

VEGETABLES
In medieval times, most of the peasant population survived on a diet of cabbage and beet pottage. Thus, cabbage entered the European psyche where it has lodged for centuries: babies

were supposed to arrive in a cabbage leaf—stork assisted or otherwise—and cabbage soup was traditionally served to Belgian newly-weds the morning after their marriage.

In the 13th century, a group of Belgian farmers committed, what is for me, the culinary equivalent of a crime against humanity: they developed the Brussels sprout (*chou de Bruxelles/spruitje*). Even when braised by the best chefs or smothered Belgian-style with butter, nutmeg and onion, I have an irrational horror of these mini-cabbages. Fortunately, Brussels sprouts are not that popular. In fact, the most archetypal Belgian vegetable is something altogether different: the endive.

Endives

Known in Belgium as *chicons/witloof*, the nation has an inexplicable enthusiasm for these hand-sized yellow-white vegetables which look like gigantic rosebuds sucked pallid by a vegetarian vampire. Their discovery is ascribed to a careless 1830s Schaerbeek farmer by the name of Antonius Dekoster. He had been storing chicory roots intended for use as a coffee additive. He left them too long, however, and the roots started to germinate. Nibbling at the buds, he found them surprisingly tasty. Their deliberate production was undertaken by a botanist called Brézier who started marketing them in 1846.

There are three main Belgian preparations of endives: raw in salads, coarsely sliced and fried in butter then served as a vegetable side dish or, most notably, rolled in ham and baked whole in a calorie-packed cheese sauce.

White Asparagus

There's considerable demand for this home-grown delicacy, dubbed 'white gold' by those who promote it. Generally white asparagus is only in season from May to June.

SEAFOOD
A Craving for Crustacea

Belgians enjoy a great variety of prawn lookalikes, from the Christmas lobster to the decorative *écrevisse via gambas*,

No carvng is necessary for this Belgian Christmas dinner.

crevettes géantes, *langoustines* and *scampi*. The most popular of all are surely the home-produced North Sea *crevettes grises*, or in direct translation, 'grey shrimps'. Smaller and less visually attractive than their bigger pink cousins, they are nonetheless much tastier and more expensive. Fried in a parsley, cheese and cream croquette or stuffed into hollowed-out tomatoes, grey shrimps represent a little niche of Belgian culinary heaven. The minuscule creatures are traditionally collected by artisan *crevettiers* around Ostend. At Oostduinkerke, *crevettiers* still ride horseback through shallow waters, trawling for the little critters during the shrimp-catching festival which takes place in late June.

Moules/Mosselen/Mussels

Moules frites (mussels and chips) is about as Belgian as food gets. Belgians expect big, succulent, carefully de-bearded mussels which put to shame the piffling gritty minnows served in restaurants in some other countries. During mussel season, supermarkets sell hundreds of pounds of the live shellfish together with packets of the diced onions, celery and herbs you need to make the required broth cooking-

base. Then it's up to you to add your choice of beer, wine, garlic, etc. to the boiling pot. Then, the mussels are served, shells and all, in a steaming casserole dish. To eat, simply take the shell of the first mussel you attack to act as tweezers for eating the rest. Don't try to force a mussel that doesn't open easily; it was probably dead before cooking and won't do you any good.

The classic chain of restaurants for mussels is Chez Léon. But mussels are also ubiquitous on menus even in motorway service areas and supermarket cafeterias. Usually, the accompanying fries are *à volonté* (eat as many as you like).

For a whole series of mussels recipes, consult: http://www.naturalsciences.be/museum/exhibitions/mussels

Fish

If you're choosing a fish menu to impress the Belgian sense of snobbery, the best choice is monkfish (*lotte/zeeduivel*). In the Ardennes and notably at charming Crupet village, trout (*truite/forel*) is a speciality. *Truite au bleu* is trout served with carrots, leeks and potatoes and is not blue at all. However the traditional Flemish 'eel in green' (*Paling in 't groen/anguilles au vert*) is about as green as it can get, thanks to a rich sorrel sauce. The most appealing, typically Belgian, fish dish is probably *waterzooï*. Alternatively made using chicken, it's a classic meal in a bowl—somewhere between a creamy stew and a rich, thick soup with chunks of vegetable and potatoes. Fish dishes served *à l'Escavèche* come in a vinegar marinade. *Saurets/bokking* are salty, smoked herring, not as dry as kippers, and sold un-filleted in brown and white varieties.

Fishy French Slang

Maquereau (mackerel) and *morue* (cod) appear on menus but, in a different context, are terms in colloquial French used to denote pimps and prostitutes respectively. A *merlan* (whiting) is more innocuous: to 'make eyes like a fried whiting' means to roll your eyes. The slang usage of a single mussel (*moule*) is anatomically feminine and simply too rude to utter in public, so always play it safe and refer to mussels in the plural!

TRADITIONAL BELGIAN CUISINE

One of the delights of getting beneath the skin of a culture is learning about the ordinary day-to-day foods that most people traditionally ate—and often still do. Beneath the fine dining Belgian sophistication, lies the potato-mash of everyday reality. Some of the most archetypal Belgian meals simply don't feature on restaurant menus.

Boulettes/Ballekes

For Belgians, the gastronomic skeleton in the kitchen cupboard is undoubtedly *ballekes*. Traditionally, the quality of her *ballekes* was said to be the measure of a Belgian housewife, just as a good kimchi is proof of good Korean womanhood. It's an odd criterion. Basically, all you get is a plate of mini-meatballs in sauce, swimming around islands of boiled potato. It's not bad. Just plain dull.

Stoemp

Potato partially mashed together with whatever vegetable is at hand (carrots, leek, spinach, etc.). This then comes as an accompaniment to a basic protein dish (sausage, *boudin*, egg or bacon). Traditionally a yokel dish, it can now be found in a few restaurants as a 'rediscovered' traditional speciality.

Poulet Compote/Kip Met Appelmoes

Chicken with stewed apple. While quite acceptable eaten quietly at home, serving *poulet compote* to a middle-class Belgian guest, is about as appropriate as serving pie and mash at a wedding. Some Belgian friends decided against going to a colleague's dinner party on ascertaining that their poor children were to be humiliated with *poulet compote* rather than enjoying the full adult spread.

Hutsepot

Hutsepot is a Brussels hotpot of stewed turnips, potatoes, sausages, bacon and pigs trotters. It's supposedly traditional but I've yet to find anyone who will make it for me. Thankfully.

STREET FOOD

Offering the worst in nutrition per calorie, there are several typically local street snacks including the celebrated Belgian waffle and the mighty *frites* (chips), which really deserve a chapter of their own.

Beignet/Smoutebollen

Beignets/smoutebollen are greasy fried dough balls served by the dozen in a tray of icing sugar. Playing a social role similar to candy floss, you'll only see them at the fairground. The first couple taste great—messy little treats that add to the atmosphere of roundabouts, dodgems and teenage snogs. But by your 12th *beignet*, you'll promise yourself you'll never buy them again. Until the next time.

Caricoles

These are boiled water-snails, sold by street vendors at winter markets and fairs.

Chips

French fries? Belgian fries would be a much more appropriate name. The Belgians take their chips very seriously. Admitting that she often feels sick after a cone of *fritches*, my wife still declares Belgian chips the best in the world. She puts it down to technique. The chips are double fried. Once to create the soft centre, and again (to order) so the outer surface is always fresh and crispy.

How Do You Spell 'Chips'?

Fritches is the somewhat comic Bruxelloise term. In written Flemish, they would correctly be spelt *frieten* but are commonly rendered *fritten*. A *frituur* is the Flemish term for a chip stand, correctly written *friterie* in French but sometimes spelt as the hybrid *friture*.

Sauces for Your Chips

Any self-respecting *friture* will offer a bewildering variety of sauces to be squirted liberally on a cone of freshly fried chips. They'll charge you around € 0.40 a glob for the privilege. This introduces a whole list of necessary vocabulary to ensure that your snack is not rendered inedible. As well as ketchup, mayonnaise, curry and mustard, a typical list might include *andalouse* (like a slightly spicy Thousand Island dressing), *samurai* (similar but much spicier), *mammouth/mammoet* (smooth and creamy), *tomagrec* (half way between ketchup and tomato purée), and *brazil* (with an intriguing fruity tang).

Chip shacks also offer a selection of unhealthy deep-fried snacks. Common examples include the pallid, lightly battered *fricandel* sausage or the *brochette tzigane* (literally 'gypsy kebab') which is a stick of mincemeat balls coated in spicy breadcrumbs.

Gaufres/Wafels

Belgian waffles are sold hot from patisserie windows, ubiquitous griddles in shopping centres and trolleys at special events. There's even a booth in Brussels Airport. They are served with a sprinkling of icing sugar or, more creatively, with a range of fruit, syrup, ice cream or chocolate toppings.

REGIONAL SPECIALITIES

Areas or towns of Belgium associate themselves with gastronomic regional specialities, local produce or traditional local tastes. Some like *waterzooï* are now relatively widespread, but others like Poperinge's hop shoots, remain very localised and seasonal.

- Antwerp   mini-cakes in the shape of a hand; *elixir d'anvers* (the local fire water); eels 'in green' (i.e. cooked with sorrel)
- Ardennes   game (wild boar, pheasant, quail); trout; ham; a selection of cold cuts known in local dialect as *une dressée*
- Arlon   *bretzel*, *maitrank*
- Bruges   *noeuds de Bruges*
- Brussels   mussels; waffels; *stoemp*; *hutspoet*

Topped with fruit or smothered in chocolate, Belgian waffles taste best straight from the griddle.

- Chaumont-Gistoux   sugar-tart
- Crupet   trout
- Damme   river eels
- Dinant   *couques de Dinant*
- Gent   *waterzooï op gentse wijze* (*à la Gantoise*); *mokken* cakes in syrup
- Grammont   macaroons
- Hasselt   pea soup; *jenever*; *speculoos*
- Herve   smelly cheese; apple syrup
- Huy   *boulettes de Huy*
- Ieper   *babelutte*
- Kortrijk   *kalletaart* (a long bar of pastry)
- Jodoigne   cheese cake (*la blanke dorèye*)
- Liège   salad *liégeoise* containing bacon, potatoes, onions, parsley, and french beans with a lukewarm vinegar-based dressing
- Maaseik   *knapkoek* cake
- Namur   *la flamiche* (hot, salty cheese pie); *avisances* (a sort of sausage roll); *schubertine* (trout in cream)
- Nivelles   *tarte al djote* (hot flan with spicy cheese and spinach beet)
- Orp-le-Petit   *boudin vert*
- Poperinge   hop shoots in a cream sauce, served with a poached egg. 'Popering Pears' were occasionally referred to in medieval literature (e.g. by Mercutio in Shakespeare's *Romeo and Juliet*).
- Spa   mineral water; biscuits
- Tongeren   *Tongerse moppen*; *caesaarkes*
- Tubize   *mirandaise* tarts (sugar and almonds), adopted in 1966
- Veurne   *Vernse slaper* (pastry)
- Vielsalm   blueberries
- Villers-la-Ville   *bâton de St Bernard* (sausage)
- Virton/Arlon   *geheck*
- Wavre   *tarte au stofé*
- Wepion   strawberries

DINING IN BELGIUM
Entertaining

There are some basic rules to entertaining in Belgium. As anywhere, it's polite for a guest to bring a gift for the host. Flowers are generally more appropriate than wine, especially for a hostess. A € 20 bunch should do the job: don't expect to get away with a seasonal bundle of wild daffodils sold by one of the Romanian roadside gypsies. If you bring chocolates, remember that the brand is important.

If you are hosting a dinner party, you'll need a well-stocked drinks cabinet as the boozing typically continues a good while before and after the meal. The aperitif drink (e.g. port, whisky & Coke, sparkling wine) is typically served with *zakouski* snacks. The meal passes much as in any country, but remember to have chilled mineral water handy. Or, should you dare to serve tap water, hide your deceit in misleadingly labelled mineral water bottles. (See later in this chapter for reasons why.)

Restaurants and Chef-Artistes

Dining out in Belgium is a great pleasure. The standards are almost invariably high and while prices are not cheap, they usually reflect very good value for money. Set lunches and fixed menu *du jour/dagmenu* may be even better value. The biggest problem can be too much choice. An invaluable aid for anyone eating out in Brussels and the suburbs is the annual *Delta*, a guide with an exhaustive list of eateries reviewed under various criteria such as price and cuisine style. On the web, check http://www.resto.be which allows diners to comment upon their culinary experience, and to read the comments of others. While there is a certain suspicion of some restaurateurs adding their own eulogies at times, the site remains a generally good source of unbiased feedback.

The best restaurant in the country, is widely accepted to be Comme Chez Soi. Such a unanimous acceptance of superiority seems odd, but the fact remains that you'll need to book weeks (or even months) ahead for dinner in this family-run place on Brussels' otherwise unfashionable Place Rouppe. Its chef, Pierre Wynants has been described as a

Surveying the beach from the new Ostend Queen restaurant, co-owned by celebrity chef Pierre Wynants. There was an international furore when this restaurant received a coveted Michelin star rating—not because it didn't deserve it but because the place hadn't even been open when the book was 'exhaustively researched'!

'National Treasure'. Other great celebrity chefs include Geert Van Hecke at De Karmeliet, Jean-Pierre Bruneau at Bruneau, Alain Deluc at the Barbizon (also Brussels), Christian Ulweling at the Moulin Hideux (Bouillon), and Christian Denis at the Clos St Denis (Tongeren).

International Cuisine

Only the bigger cities are likely to have sushi bars or Mexican fare. Indian food is a relatively exotic experience in Belgium and commensurately expensive, on par with eating Thai. Chinese food is available in almost every town, with a wide range of prices and standards. Serving the sizeable North African community are plenty of couscous places and quaint cross-cultural hybrids like the Egyptian Pizzeria in Aalter, which serves pizzas baked on tandoori nan bread. Greek and Turkish restaurants are also ubiquitous.

Dining Caveats in Central Brussels

In central Brussels, the Rue des Bouchers and Petite Rue des Bouchers are narrow streets crammed with terrace restaurants. Even in winter, the open-air terraces are heaving with tourist diners and kept warm with powerful space heaters. Some of the restaurants along the streets (such as Aux Armes de Bruxelles which does an excellent *waterzooi*) are very well renowned, if pricy. But in many of the others, you should be wary before you make your order. You'll often see unbelievably reasonable prices on advertised set meals (maybe € 12 for a three-course fish meal). These are genuine bargains, but don't be fooled. Pretty much anything else on the menu is likely to be much more expensive. When you get inside, you may find that the menu list you're handed omits that '€ 12 Special'. Ask for it specifically if that's what you want, but remain cautious of the waiters' suggestions. Don't assume that dishes he proceeds to recommend are part of the menu deal, even if that sounds implied. Check! Usually they're not, and the tempting seafood platter which you merrily agree to is likely to cost more like € 60.

Also, be sure to look at the wine or drinks list and check carefully before casually ordering a bottle of *vin du patron*.

Brussels' restaurant-packed Pètit Rue des Bouchers is a visual feast, densely filled with tempting seafood eateries. However, it's also a tourist trap and in certain establishments, you'll need to be on your guard when ordering an apparently 'cheap' menu.

Menu 14,
CROQUETTES de CR
GRISES
ou HUÎTRES

In restaurants almost anywhere else in Belgium, you'd expect such house wine to be between € 10–20 per bottle (according to the class of the establishment). However, on these two streets, some restaurants use that Parisian trick of calling a vastly expensive fine wine 'the house special'. Whoops, another € 70! Don't let these slick tricks deter you from dining out elsewhere; you will be pleased to know that such practices are pretty much unheard of anywhere beyond the tiny tourist enclave mentioned.

Bistros, Cafés, and Fast Food

It's generally cheaper to eat in a bistro or café than in a full blown restaurant, though choice may be limited. Indeed, cafés (discussed later in this chapter) concentrate predominantly on drinks and many don't serve food at all. In fast food terms, McDonald's' main rival is the Quick burger chain which perplexed the nation by advertising its 'long burger for the long generation' in heavily-accented English. As in Britain, *döner kebabs* (or pita sandwiches) constitute typical post-pub snacks. The finest *döner* I've tasted anywhere, ever, came from Ilhan, an unassuming Kurdish takeaway at the top end of Wolstraat in Tienen.

THE LAND OF BEER

Alcoholic drinks are every bit as important as food to the Belgian palate. Beer is the undoubted king of local beverages, but there are plenty of other distinctive drinks. For those who want to stay sober, there's always mineral water from the town which gave us the English term 'spa'.

Belgium produces what many connoisseurs consider to be the world's finest beers. Beer became especially popular once the preservative effects of hops were discovered in the early Middle Ages. By the 16th century, visitors to the Low Countries were reportedly appalled by the huge national beer consumption. Although the 20th century has seen the number of breweries plummet from 3,000 in 1900 to barely 100 at the start of the new millennium, Belgium still produces nearly 1,000 different brews.

Types of Beer

The sheer variety is overwhelming. Beers can be variously classified according to different criteria e.g. by to brewing method (*geuze*, *lambic*, etc.), colour (*blond(e)* is straw colour, *bruin/brune* is dark), filtration (white beers are unfiltered), reputation (Trappist beers, abbey brews), etc. In addition there are a variety of systems for hinting at a beer's alcoholic strength:

- By an archaic specific-density number. For example, with Rochefort 6, 8 and 10,the numbers do not equate with the amount of alcohol by volume (abv). Indeed a Rochefort 10 is nearer 11.5 per cent abv.
- By label colour. For example Chimay's distinctive 7 per cent abv red-label brew is much more quaffable than the meaty 9 per cent blue-label or darker, more bitter white-label.
- By appellation. A *dubbel/double* is generally around 6–7 per cent while a *trippel/triple* typically kicks you with a fearsome 8–10 per cent punch.

Alternatively, there's a cover-all hierarchy of four broad legal categories:

- 1–2 per cent abv (Category III) for table beers
- 3–4 per cent abv (Category II) the rarely-made stronger table beers

- 5 per cent abv (Category I) includes most standard beers and ordinary draft lagers
- 6 per cent + (Category S) covering virtually the whole range of specialist ales which Belgium is so justifiably famous for

Lager/Pilsener

The day-to-day beer for the majority of Belgians is a basic 'blonde' lager—you can drink plenty without getting unduly plastered. Stella Artois was marketed to the top end UK lager market under the slogan 'Reassuringly Expensive'. Yet in Belgium, it is quite unexotically standard; one of the 'generic three' beers together with Jupiler and Maes. It's a 25-centiliter glass of such lagers that you'll be served if you just wander into a café and ask for a beer (*une bière/ pintje*). Lesser known brands include Cristal and Diekirch (from Luxembourg) plus there are the international standards like Kronenbourg, Heineken, Carlsberg, etc.

Speciality Beers

There is a hierarchy to Belgium's stronger speciality brews. Only six (Orval, Chimay, Westmalle, Rochefort, Achel and Westveleteren) fall into the premier league, known as Trappist beers. All are associated with the Cistercian monastery or

abbey which brews them. There is also a single non-Belgian Trappist beer (La Trappe, from the brewery of Koningshoeven in the Netherlands) but there's no need to upset fellow Belgian boozers with that upsetting little revelation. Many bars and shops do stock the first three or four. But finding the others is like seeking the holy grail. The only place in the world you can ever have much hope of finding magnificently complex Westvleteren 12 is the De Vrede café, opposite the abbey itself (about a mile from Westvleteren village, between Ieper and De Dolle). Even then beer supplies are sporadic so the abbey has a 'beer phone' (tel: (057) 401-057) so you can call ahead to check availability.

A second division of brews are known as Abbey beers, but these are not necessarily linked by more than a franchising agreement with the religious establishment whose name they bear. Grimbergen and the wonderfully complex Leffe, are both increasingly widely available on draft. Many locals argue that in reality these brews are every bit as good as their Trappist brethren. As bars may stay open most of the night, there's no reason to resolve such discussions quickly. Look out also for Corsendonk, Witkap-Pater, Tongerlo, Affligem and several others named after assorted saints (e.g. St Feuillien which can occasionally be found in jeroboam-sized bottles).

Beer Names

Other strong, archetypal Belgian beers which failed to become saints, have cut their losses and gone the other way entirely marketing themselves under names linked to occultism, sin and peril. Duvel, which is worthy of Abbey status, actually translates as 'devil'. You'll also find Satan, Lucifer, Diablos, Guillotine, Brigand, Mort Subite (Sudden Death) and Delirium. Reportedly the label of Verboten Vruct (Forbidden Fruit) featuring fig-leaved classical nudes enjoying a Garden-of-Eden brewski, was once considered too raunchy for import into the USA.

Many more Belgian beers bear names that are unintentionally amusing in English: try Silly beers from Silly, Prik Pils (from Oudenaarde), Slag lager (from Ninove),

La Plope (from Wareme), Pee Klak (from Zottegem) and Witte Dikke (from Neerpelt).

Lambic and Gueuze

The uniquely Brabantine *lambic* is special because it has no added yeast. It simply sets to work fermenting itself. Miraculous enough to keep the nation Catholic, you might think. In fact, the divine fermentation is aided by airborne *Brettanomyces bruxellensis* microbes, which are apparently unique to Brussels and the Senne valley. A straight *lambic* is rarely served—it's simply too unpleasant. However, by blending *lambics* of different ages together you can get the arguably more palatable beer known as *gueuze* (pronounced something like 'girls' without the letter l).

Flavoured Beers and Fruity Lambics

There are other ways in which breweries improve upon a *lambic*. Faro is simply *lambic* sweetened with dark brown caramelised sugar. This is perceived as an old man's drink, although it's undergoing something of a revival of late. Then there are the fruity *lambic* beers. The most popular varieties are *framboise*/*frambozen* (made with crushed raspberries) and *kriek* (with cherries) although peach and other novelty varieties are sometimes available. The most commonly found brands are Belle-Vue and Mort Subite, but to my taste, the Timmermans and Boon brews are tarter and fresher. A flute of *framboise* may be delicious, but note that fruit beers are thought of as women's drinks. A *kriek* would not be the ideal thing to order after a rugby match when you're out with the lads.

White Beers (Witbier/Bière Blanche)

These unfiltered wheat beers are delicately flavoured with orange peel and spices such as coriander. Unfiltered and thus cloudy, the tart, slightly cloying flavour is something of an acquired taste, improved with a squeeze of lemon, according to connoisseurs. Perhaps the most respected *witbier* is Hoegaarden, found on tap in bars across the country and beyond.

During festivals, the cafés can get so full that it can be hard to reach the bar. Fortunately, entrepreneurial individuals solve the problem by setting up street stands or (as here) by taking beer to potential customers along the procession route.

Other Beer Types

Several beers don't fall conveniently into any of the above style categories. Wood-aged Rodenbach is labelled red beer by some writers. Brews like De Koninck, Palm and Horse Ale fall somewhere between lager and the speciality beers. There are a number of supposedly Anglo-Irish style ales brewed for Belgian tastes, notably John Martin's Pale Ale, Gordon's Highland Scotch and the world's strongest bottled Guinness produced at a special 8 per cent abv.

Table Beer

Belgian beer's ugly sister is 'table beer'. But you'll never find it in a bar. Inoffensive with barely 1.5 per cent abv, locals don't really consider it beer at all. Traditionally it was served as a 'soft drink' at family meals, especially for younger children. These days, consumption is dwindling, but supermarkets still sell it in 75 cl screw top bottles for under a Euro. There are several varieties: *blond* (pale), *brune* (dark) and *multicéréal* (malty, brewed from a selection of grains). The best known brand is Piedboeuf.

Buying Beer

Any supermarket worth its car park offers the regular spectacle of housewives lugging home a returnable *bac*

(24-bottle crate) of Stella, Jupiler or Maes. The deposit on the crate is almost as much as the beer so remember to bring back the full set of empties. Supermarkets also stock a limited range of speciality beers. From Bruges to Bouillon, you'll also find an increasing choice of specialist beer shops pandering to the tourist market. You can taste as well as buy at the Brasserie Delépine in whose cellars many companies leave their beers to age. Or buy beer online—http://www.beermania.be will deliver the brew of your choice.

Beer Etiquette

In a Belgian bar, there are none of the juvenile jokes linking half pints and limp wrists. That's because in all but the odd Irish pub, beers are inevitably served in sculpted 25 or 33cl glasses which simply aren't full pints. Tap beers are given a sizeable head which is combed lovingly by the bartender. The inch of froth is considered integral to the presentation and is not a bar's ploy to save a few millilitres of brew, as some tight-fisted Brits are tempted to suspect. It is also good Belgian practice to dunk a lager glass in a sink of water before serving a *pintje*—a wet beer mug does not imply the sloppy lack of a tea towel. Where you can get shirty with your barman, however, is if your beer should come (heaven forbid) in the wrong glass. Mistakes are very unusual (except for basic lagers). Incorrect glasses would be all too easily spotted as the name of the brew is prominently engraved or printed on each glass and the design for each brand has a distinctive shape, culminating in the silly 'thistle' shape of 'Gordons Scotch'. Then there's Kwak...

Kwak

Kwak is a rich, rounded red-amber beer whose notoriety stems from its peculiar glass shaped like a gape-mouthed test-tube. Its bottom is so rounded that it simply can't stand up so it's held up by a specially designed wooden stand. The drinker is expected to balance the assemblage and get the glass to his or her lips by holding the wooden rod and not the glass itself. Any jerky movement could dislodge the

Kwak is a fine, rich beer but its farcically shapped glass presents the drinker with a few social dilemmas.

glass and the manoeuvre becomes increasingly precarious the more one drinks. Understandably, this results in some bars demanding a deposit for their Kwak glass to ensure that breakages are paid for. In some cases, bars will take anything as a deposit—even your right shoe! Sadly, recently redesigned anti-slip holders rather spoil the fun; and you should be aware that locals assume most Kwak drinkers to be tourists.

Some Belgian Beer Trivia

- There are beer museums in Brussels' Grand Place, at 20 Brouwerstraat Antwerp, and in the Leuven Stadhuis plus several others.
- Several working breweries are open by appointment. Straffe Hendrick in Bruges with its canal-side provides tours for 'drop-in' tourists.
- Certain Belgian recipes include beer as an ingredient, most famously *carbonnades flamandes*—a beef-and-beer casserole.
- The Den Dijver in Bruges is a high-class restaurant with a gourmet menu which consists entirely of delicacies cooked with beer, each course accompanied by the appropriate brew.
- Belgians drink an annual average of 101 litres of beer per capita, making them the world's sixth largest consumers after the Germans (131 l), Irish, Danish, Austrians and Brits (who drink a mere 2 l more).
- Around 3,500 of Belgium's 27,500 bars have plaques to show that the staff have passed beer pouring exams.
- The patron saint of Belgian brewers is St Arnou, an 11th century Flemish monk who saved believers from the plague by persuading them to drink beer instead of water.
- The Bruxellois term *flotchesbeer* is a slang term for a disappointingly weak beer. A very rare problem.

WINE

Despite all the beer drinking, Belgians also consume vast quantities of wine. There are Belgian wineries but production is limited and fairly expensive so the majority of wine is imported, predominantly from France.

Belgian Wine

In the 13th century, almost every village in the Hageland region of Belgium had a vineyard on its south-facing slopes. However, in the 1430s, the Burgundian dynasty took over the region. Their taste leant toward the finer wines of France and the Rheinland, and the lower-quality Belgian industry couldn't compete. Meanwhile, the introduction of hops meant that beers could be kept longer and were thus ever more popular amongst the poorer folk. The Hageland wine industry simply fizzled out. It was tentatively revived between 1815–1865 in the village of Wezemaal, protected from the vicious north winds by a unique man-made wine-wall which still stands today. The revival didn't last and the region ripped up its vines and turned to other fruits, notably Jonagold apples. A second small, wine renaissance began in 1970s, and the region's vineyards have now been partially replanted.

Belgium has other wine areas in the provinces of Hainaut and Luxembourg. The Riesling-style Clos de la Zolette from the Gaume district is highly appreciated but hard to find beyond that region. Overijse on the Brussels outskirts is famous for its greenhouse-grown grapes and holds an annual Grapes in History pageant.

Imported Wine

Choosing wine poses a classic conundrum for the contradictions in the Belgian soul. On the one hand, there is the ever-present urge to seek out a bargain. On the other lurks a strong streak of French-style château-snobbery in choosing which wines are 'acceptable'. Some Belgians consider serving a *vin de pays* (rather than a true AOC wine) akin to offering baked beans at a dinner party (*see* Chapter 10: Fast Facts, *page 259*). A similar snobbism frowns on wines from 'lesser regions'. Even though regions like Minervois and Corbières may now be much better than their traditional reputations, God forbid that anyone should catch you uncorking a bottle in company. Of course, foreigners are suspected of wholesale ignorance. Making a bad wine choice allows everyone else to snigger behind their hands and later exclaim how uncultured the rest of the world is. The attitude is at its most unbearable when you take a Belgian to a restaurant in Britain or the States to hear that feigned amazement, "Why is it that people here actually seem to like *vin de table*?"

Getting it Cheaper

The trouble for wine drinkers is that the stuff costs up to twice as much in Belgium as in France. Problem? Of course not. You'll find the Belgians arriving en masse at Lille or Valenciennes (just off the Brussels-Paris road). Signs within the gigantic car parks of the Auchan hypermarkets point satisfied customers helpfully back to Belgium. Hurrah for company cars!

On one of my first visits to Belgium I was served a very good, if young, wine from an unlabelled bottle. I complemented my hosts on making such an amazing home brew—my Boots DIY wine kits had never turned out anything like that. Suitably insulted, they explained that the wine was actually a very fine Bordeaux. They'd simply bottled it themselves. Whoops. Bottling your own wine is another distinctly Belgian way to get cheaper wine. One family orders a big bulk shipment from a French winery. They take orders from friends and relations who come round on a prescribed day for a bottling party. Everyone brings their own bottles (so save and wash your empties) and a jolly party ensues as everyone takes turns filling bottles and corking them with a special (and rather expensive) machine. A lot of wine fails to reach the bottles at all!

Port/Porto

While they don't make the stuff, Belgians are amongst the world's largest per capita consumers of port (which they quite correctly call *Porto*). *Porto* is drunk as an aperitif rather than an after-dinner snifter. And, contrary to their normal passion for quality comestibles, for some reason Belgians seem satisfied with some of the shoddiest Portos around. The drink is seen as cheap, and is thus destined to remain so.

OTHER BELGIAN TIPPLES
Apéritif Maison

An *apéritif maison* is not an appetiser, but a restaurant's home-blended pre-prandial cocktail. This frequently combines a little white wine with a bizarre and colourful range of fruity flavours.

Jenever/Genièvre/Witteke

The town of Hasselt is famed for two liquid delicacies: pea soup and gin. Dutch-style gin, that is known in Flemish as *jenever* and once a mainstay of local hangovers. The drink is now much less popular in Belgium than it is in Holland (where it's spelt *genever*), thanks to a century of prohibition which forbade Belgian cafés from serving the stuff. Only four Belgian distilleries survived the prohibition. The fact that any did at all is thanks to Flemish *jenever*'s reputation as the best available. These days attitudes have changed. Some 70 distilleries now produce over 200 varieties and there's even a National Gin Museum (19 Witte Nonnenstraat, Hasselt, closed Mondays) where you can taste dozens of *jenevers*. Just as with Belgian beers, the producers offer a great range of fruit-flavoured versions. But unlike London gin, *jenever* should be drunk straight, not used in cocktails.

> Hasselt's version of the Manneken-Pis is the Borrelmanneke fountain. The little chap holds a *jenever* barrel with a small hole in the bottom from which the water flows. During the annual Jenever Festival, it flows with gin instead.

Péket/Péquet

This is a uniquely Belgian variant of *jenever* flavoured with juniper but slightly weaker than gin. It features heavily in the September Fêtes de Wallonie in Namur with revellers pouring sake-style cupfuls for each other like raucous Japanese at *hanami* (viewing of cherry blossoms). Cups are chained to wrists for safekeeping lest they get mislaid in the drinkers' drunken stupor.

Elixir d'Anvers

Antwerp's bitter-sweet firewater made using 32 herbal spices. Considered a favourite of the elderly or a remedy for stomach ache.

Maitrank

This typical May Drink of the Arlon region (Luxembourg Province) is made from very dry white wine in which woodruff (*Asperula odorantis*) has been left to soak. Maitrank should be served very cold with a slice of orange and can be used in certain recipes for cooking mussels.

Mandarine Napoléon

A sweet, commercially trademarked blend of tangerine-peel liqueur and cognac (http://www.mandarinenapoleon.com).

SOFT DRINKS

Belgians aren't entirely alcoholic. They consume essentially the same familiar range of non-alcoholic beverages as other Europeans. Coffee is a typical beverage at the breakfast table and after meals. Fizzy soft drinks have largely replaced table beers as the standard drink that goes with family meals.

WATER

A Belgian restaurant will happily bring you free bread with a meal. But ask for water and you'll get an expensive bottle of *eau minérale*. Beer would usually be cheaper. Although it is theoretically your right to demand tap water, no self-respecting Belgian seems capable of overcoming the stigma that ordering *eau du robinet/kraantjeswater confers*.

There are dozens of brands of mineral water named for their spring sources. High-profile Belgian examples are Chaudfontaine and Spa. The latter has been associated with curative water treatments for so long that its name and associated function have been adopted into the English language.

COFFEE AND TEA

In people's homes, instant coffee is fairly common. But in Belgian cafés, bars or bakery-coffee shops, one expects to receive a large but espresso-style brew at almost espresso strength. Unlike in France, this should always come with a little pot or jug of creamer so no need to specify 'white' or 'au lait'. And almost always, a coffee will also be accompanied by a little wrapped biscuit, a square of chocolate or a *speculoos*. The last is sculpted gingerbread, semi-sweet and hard enough that it doesn't sag if dunked. Special Santa-shaped *speculoos* are presented to children on St Nicolas Day (6 December).

Café coffee is usually of a remarkably high standard. And it's great value too. For between € 1.50–2, ordering a single cup might allow you to sit and read the paper for much of the morning. Cafés are rarely busy or impolite enough to push out 'slow' drinkers. But there's no such thing as an American-style bottomless cup.

Generally, it doesn't pay to order one of the more 'specialist' coffees. Notably, beware that many cafés consider a 'cappuccino' to be coffee smothered with whipped cream rather than with added steamed milk as you might be expecting.

Tea in Belgium can be a slight disappointment. Tea shops can be very atmospheric, but the tea itself is generally served as a bag in a sachet which one dunks into a cup of hot water. While this works well enough, for some tea purists, the off-the-boil water is tantamount to tea-blasphemy.

BARS AND CAFÉS

In Belgium, the term café can denote a vast range of possible establishments but all are more likely to be what

English speakers would define as a pub or bar. Unlike French bars and cafés, relatively few Belgian cafés serve food. You might get cubes of cheese, slices of salami or nuts from a dispenser or maybe, if you are lucky, a sandwich or *croque monsieur*. Spaghetti or light meals are offered by certain cafés with a sign in the window saying 'Petite Restauration'/'Klein Honger'.

Some cafés are fabulous architectural gems but many more are dismal, barely-decorated brick boxes where sorry-looking regulars say their hellos and then settle to a smoky night (or day) of solitary swigging. Belgium has an astonishing number of cafés: one for every 407 people. The rather dismal town of Mouscron, otherwise famed only for the occasional success of its football team, has a café for every 218 inhabitants.

A bar, to the Belgians, is a more upmarket place. A cocktail den like Ricks on Brussels' Avenue Louise, perhaps. Or the bar of a hotel—anywhere that the drinkers wear bow ties. Somewhere in between bars and cafés are the city pubs, often aimed at the expatriate crowd.

Café Types

Broadly speaking, there are three main types of cafés. I've dubbed these 'charmers', 'squealers' and 'locals'. Like the three primary colours, one can observe every shade of overlap between them.

Venerable Charmers

The most obviously attractive bars are the wonderful art nouveau, turn-of-the-century places—all polished brass, old mirrors and carved wood. Greatest amongst these are the Falstaff, the Cirio and the Mort Subite, all in Brussels, but most of the bigger towns have an equivalent. Other hidden gems are tucked away in historic houses as with Diest's 'Gasthof 1618', delightfully located within a medieval Begijnhof. In the countryside, several beer brewing abbeys have a pub nearby or en site so that you can sample the brew. Not all charmers are old. Some are simply well situated with a nice summer terrace. The only possible downside of these places

Terrace-cafés on the Markt, Bruges' main square.
The step-gable building façades behind are
typical of classical Flemish architecture.

is that for all their atmosphere, you'll rarely find yourself thrust into bizarre conversations with the locals. Reckon on € 1.80–2.20 for a *pintje*.

Young Squealers

The teenager crowd tends to migrate toward the modern décor and loud music of cafés that look like bars almost anywhere in the Western Hemisphere. They have relatively dim lighting and a remarkable preponderance of people who seem blissfully oblivious to all the Smoking Causes Cancer campaigns. Prices similar: € 1.60–2 for a pintje as long as you stick to non-imported beer.

Unpretentious Locals

These most archetypal Belgian bars are outwardly depressing dives. Typically, they're shoebox-shaped shop units marked with plain Maes, Stella or Jupiler name signs. The most intriguingly old-fashioned ones have bench seats fitted to wooden half-panelled walls that are set with mirrors around head height. Others are entirely unadorned. On a row of stools at the bar you'll usually find a motley selection of predominantly male social misfits making strained banter with the bored barman. These places are an anthropologist's dream. The price for a *pintje* is low—around € 1–1.60. A photographer specialising in strawberry noses and bizarre facial hair could find the opportunities overwhelming. Even a fellow Belgian may occasionally require an interpreter.

Don't venture in if you want a quiet drink—once you've overcome the 'all eyes on the stranger' entry, half the locals may decide to nestle in for a chat. It's a real opportunity for cultural immersion.

Country Pubs

The quaint country pubs familiar across the UK are relatively rare in Belgium. There are certainly café-pubs in villages, but they are typically very much of the brick-box local variety: often sadly unappealing. However, there are some notable exceptions. Examples around Brussels include two renovated watermills near Grimbergen, of which the Tommonmolen is the more atmospheric. There is a peaceful lakeside terrace at Sept Fontaines' La Piñeta, (off the Chaussée d'Alsemberg, south of St-Genesius-Rode) though this is frequently reserved for diners. You'll have to pay the € 3 entry fee to the stately Great Park to reach Enghien/Endigen's delightful little Halte du Miroir. A personal favourite is the sunset terrace beside the moat of Horst Castle, 7 km (4.2 miles) south of Aarschot down a quiet country lane from St Pieters-Rode. Or the timeless stone caverns of the Taverne du Moulin at Villers-la-Ville (http://www.moulindevillers.be). There are also some homely stalwart village inns where you can expect to be served by waddling old dears in black dresses with white aprons, and incomprehensible jokes—try the Huis Istas in Jezus-Eik, just beyond the Brussels Ring.

General Etiquette for Belgian Cafés & Bars

- Except, perhaps, in a few expatriate bars, tipping the bar staff is unnecessary and not expected.
- Drinks will be brought to your table unless noted otherwise. *Bestellen aan de bar a.u.b./ commander au bar s.v.p.* means 'please order at the bar'.
- Rather than charge for each successive round of drinks, most cafés run a tab that you pay just before leaving.
- Better bars often provide a little thimble full of peanuts or mini-crackers to accompany your drink. This doesn't cost extra and, in some places, there's a large bowl from which you can freely replenish your supply. In cheaper places, you may have to put a 50 cent coin into a snack dispenser. Some cafés also have a basic snack, sandwich and meal menu and virtually all serve decent coffee.
- Unlike in neighbouring Holland, it is not normal behaviour to hang up your coat at the entry to a café or bar. Less trusting Belgian drinkers usually feel safer draping their coats over their chairs where they can keep an eye on them.

Bars 'Without a Key'

The notorious 24-hour bars are not as common as some would have you believe. Still, wandering around Brussels cafés between 5:00 am and 8:00 am one Saturday (for research purposes only, you understand), I found an ample selection of watering holes still more than happy to pour me a *pintje*. And without cover charges or excessively inflated prices either. And just as these are closing, so others are opening for breakfast tipplers.

Beer Cafés

This sounds like a tautology as all bars and cafés have beers by the dozen. A beer café, however, is one where the choice of brews is so long you need a multi-paged menu to list them all. Such places are more common than you might imagine. Classics include Brussels' Moeder Lambic, Antwerp's Kulminator and almost a dozen in Gent, notably He Waterhuis aan de Bierkant (http://www.waterhuisaandebierkant.be) and Dulle Griet (http://www.dullegriet.be)

Bar Games

Cafés aimed at the younger market often have video games, table football, pinball machines, or perhaps a pool table. Others encourage old men to play dominoes or cards. And the Greenwich, a delightfully unpretentious Art Nouveau café in central Brussels, is the place to play chess. Once you get there, you'll notice that pretty much every table is likely to be deep in concentration over a game. There is no charge for the use of the sets and it's often possible to find other people to play against should you happen to walk in alone.

Traditional cafés also have a couple of distinctly Belgian games including a very un-American version of pool, called 'American' billiards. The table has two holes positioned well away from the cushions and guarded by rubber mushrooms.

More common is Den Tosh, a wonderfully archaic looking machine halfway between pinball and a fairground game. The aim is to get a series of balls to lodge in a specified set of numbered holes. Like in Japanese pachinko, there are

Why fly to Vegas (or drive to Ostend) if your local café has Den Tosh?

no flippers, so there is little you can do to affect where the ball ends up. However, by feeding in more money you can rearrange 'win grids' and buy extra balls to improve your chances. On the face of it, all this is purely for fun. Gambling is not allowed in cafés (one-arm bandit slot machines are relegated to gaming rooms and casinos) so in Den Tosh you simply win 'credits' to play again. Cafés often tacitly agree to 'buy back' any credits won, however, thereby encouraging gamblers to play for stakes vastly higher than the paltry 20 cent minimum.

CULTURE, SPORT AND TRAVEL

CHAPTER 7

'You're a tourist? In Belgium? Why?
Amsterdam is so much more beautiful.'
—Self-depracating Antwerp resident having
politely answered my request for directions.

Outwardly Belgians like to keep up the pretence that Belgium is boring. Perhaps they want to keep it for themselves?! But there is a truly astonishing variety of places to discover, events to witness and things to learn. One great way to get more immersed in any country is to delve deeper into its arts and to familiarise yourself with its famous contemporary and historical stars. Like so much in Belgium, what you investigate will depend considerably whether you're staying in Flanders or the French-speaking areas—each has a very separate pantheon of cultural icons. Sport, however, tends to cut across linguistic lines and there's plenty to discover in Belgium's passions from soccer to cycling to, yes, pigeon-racing. Although little known to the world at large, Belgium also has a quite extraordinary range of processions and carnivals, some of which rate amongst Europe's most spectacular. And how can you beat a perfect coffee or master-brewed beer on one of the fabulous medieval city squares around which most old Belgian towns are ranged?

BELGIAN ART AND ARTISTS

"Belgian art?—Do you mean lace-making or the Manneken-Pis?" Foreigners have a grossly unfair disdain for Belgium's contributions in the field of the arts. Not all the decorative arts are sold from kitschily twee souvenir boutiques in Bruges. Indeed, some of the greatest artists in history came from Belgian soil. Before heading off to the magnificent galleries of

Brussels, Gent, Antwerp and Bruges, it's worth familiarising yourself with a few of these historical greats.

Early Artists

Before the 15th century, European painters had a pretty wobbly feel for perspective and concentrated mostly on religious subjects or portraits of noble patrons. Flemish artists were the first to really change this. Jan van Eyck (1390–1441), one of the artists known collectively as the Flemish Primitives, certainly started out painting royal mugshots—indeed his portrait of Isabella of Portugal was so good that his master, Philip the Good, decided to marry her. But along with his brother Hubert, Jan perfected oil painting, allowing previously unprecedented levels of realism.

Flemish artists started backing portraits with landscapes instead of solid colours or gold leaf. These glimpses of everyday life would eventually become subjects in themselves. This was encouraged by the new wealth of the Flemish merchants who were happy to pay enticing fees for painted 'snapshots' of their families, homes and possessions.

Other great Flemish Primitives of the same era include the artists Rogier van der Weyden (1399–1464), Hugo van der Goes (1440–1482) and Hans Memling (1435–1494, a naturalised Bruges citizen though born in Frankfurt). Great places to see their works include the Groeninge Museum in Bruges and the Galerie des Beaux Arts in Brussels. The collected works of the van Eycks are exhibited in their entirety (albeit in photographic reproduction) at the Couvent des Frères Mineurs on Boomgaardstraat in Maaseik.

In this period, tapestry making was every bit as important as painting. Especially for the then Flemish town of Arras, it was a major craft-industry, and one which moved en masse to Brussels when artists fled in 1477 following Arras' annexation and destruction by French king Louis IX. Fine examples of medieval Belgian tapestries are displayed in the Maison du Roi on Brussels' Grand Place.

Renaissance And Baroque

Sixteenth century Flemish painting styles varied considerably. Contrast the Leonardo da Vinci-inspired realism of artists like Quentin Metsys/Matsijs (1465–1530), with the surreal imagery of the Breughels, which belongs in the darkly bizarre pictorial world of Hieronymous Bosch. Some of the most remarkable canvases in Brussels' Heulens Van der Mieren collection are landscapes peopled with contorted anthropomorphic figures. The names of their artists are unknown (the paintings are not signed), but were they not 450 years old, it would be tempting to suspect Salvador Dali imitators.

The aftermath of the Dutch revolts meant that art as well as the economy and culture of 17th century Belgium were force-fed heavy doses of Catholicism. The great paintings of the new era tried to ram home the message with vast, overpowering images of sumptuous heavens and brooding hells.

Despite the drastic decline in trade, Antwerp developed as a formidable artistic centre thanks in part to a trio of great painters: Peter Paul Rubens (1577–1640), Anthony (Antoon) Van Dyck (1599–1641, who was later appointed court painter

The Manneken Pis (1619)—a humorously ironic choice of icon for a country of such artistic pedigree.

to Charles I of England) and Jacob Jordaens (1593–1678). The works of these and other great baroque artists are to be found in many Belgian museums and churches. On 15 August, Antwerp celebrates with a Rubens Market—stallholders dress up in period costumes, adding to the charm of the antique market on Handschoenmarkt.

19th And 20th Century Art

Independent Belgium developed a range of artistic talents including the Romantic/neoclassical Antoine Wiertz (1806–1865), great naturalist Constantin Meunier (1831–1905), and the symbolist Ferdinand Knopff (1853–1921) whose delightful work echoes the pre-Raphaelites and deserves a much wider appreciation. Belgium was one of the first places to embrace the naturalistic curves and serifs of art nouveau, notably in decorative arts, furniture and architecture. Belgians are almost universally proud of the elegant buildings by architects Henri van der Velde (1863–1957), Paul Hankar (1859–1901) and, especially, Victor Horta (1861–1947). Yet oddly, little was done to protect that heritage until relatively recently.

Remarkably ahead of his time, James Ensor (1860–1949), was an Ostend-born pre-expressionist painter whose works ranged from attractive Manet-like scenes to macabre masks and human faces with a dash of Van Gogh. He has been particularly *en vogue* since a major 1999 retrospective in Brussels on the 50th anniversary of his death. Probably the greatest 20th century Belgian artist was René Magritte (1898–1967). His surrealist figures are notable for their lack of faces as in *Les Amants* where a pair of lovers kiss, apparently oblivious to the bags across their heads. His most famous painting strikes a particularly resonant chord with the Belgian sense of the absurd. It is a simple depiction of a pipe. Underneath, the prominently inscribed title proclaims (in French) 'This is not a pipe'.

The Belgian surrealist Paul Delvaux has gained a certain notoriety for his obsessively repetitive theme of semi-surrealist nudes, almost universally based on his wife. With a delightful tea shop and garden, the Delvaux museum offers a charming oasis of calm in the seaside town of St-Idesbald.

Modern And Contemporary Art

Without much fanfare, Belgium continues to drape itself in art, albeit to mixed reviews. Large, lumpy metal-&-stone hunks sometimes prove remarkably appealing, as along the Franklin Rooseveltlaan in Brussels. Other examples are downright peculiar, as in Turnhout where a modernist metal nude bathes in the castle moat and a strange rusty structure outside the station looks like a gigantic, bent 'tuning fork' with a rock precariously balanced on its tip. Like it or loathe it, new art is everywhere, from *trompe l'oeil* murals to the intimidatingly colourful graffitti of suburban railway halts. The effect is to insert unexpected visual stimuli amid the mediocrity of even the drabbest suburbs. You may have to wait a while for the Brussels metro, but at least there's something to look at—each station has been decorated by different contemporary artists. And around the capital, the walls of 25 unsightly end-of-terrace houses have been adorned with what is arguably that most popular of all Belgian art forms: the cartoon strip.

CARTOON STRIPS (BANDE DESSINÉE/STRIPVERHAAL)

Belgians (adults just as much as children) have a passion for comic books that is second only to that of the Japanese. Cartoons are taken seriously as an art form and most Belgian homes quietly shelter a shelf or two of hardback albums.

Internationally, Hergé's Tintin and Peyo's Schtroumpf (Smurfs) are probably Belgium's best known *bande dessinée* characters. But dozens of others are household names locally. Many Belgians are astounded to discover that characters like the lonesome cowboy Lucky Luke are not world-famous. Other classics to read if you want to sound knowledgeable include Vandersteen's *Suske & Wiske/Bob & Bobette*, Franquin's *Gaston Lagaffe* and *Spirou*, and Hergé's *Quick & Flupke*. A visit to the Centre Belge de la Bande Dessinée (comic museum) will introduce you to many more.

Hergé's *Quick and Flupke* get down to some comic peeping tommery on a Brussels end-of-terrace house wall.

Belgium's political cartoonists can be merciless on the country's leaders. Astute observers include Vadot in *Le Vif L'Express* and Kroll in the *Télé Moustique* magazine. *Le Chat* is a ubiquitous single frame cartoon character who is fond of making obvious yet sagacious statements (*see photo on page 105*). Philippe Geluck, its creator, is now a popular TV personality in both Belgium and France.

OPERA, THEATRE AND DANCE

Belgium owes its very independence to a gang of rowdy Brussels opera-goers who got over-excited by Auber's *Muette de Portici* in 1830. Forgoing a beer and a pita after the performance, they settled on a revolution instead and the rest is history.

For a country so small, there remains a remarkable wealth and variety in the performing arts. This is not limited to Brussels. Antwerp (all summer) and Gent (June/July) are particularly active during their festival seasons and both, like Liège, have their own opera houses.

Dance is extremely well patronised. Performances are common in a variety of styles and both Flanders and Wallonia have their own Royal Ballet companies—the latter based in the unlikely setting of post-industrial Charleroi. Although it moved to Lausanne in 1988, Belgian dance fans remain proud that Maurice Béjart's groundbreaking 'Ballet of the 20th Century' company and Mudra dance school were based in Brussels from 1960. There are a number of dance festivals; one for international folk groups is held at the dramatic venue of the Schoten castle during the second weekend of July.

Unlike London or New York, the Brussels theatre scene is not dominated by long-running slick musicals, although when these arrive for brief spells, they tend to sell out very fast.

Puppet theatres were once very popular and were regarded as the poor man's TV. There are still half a dozen in Gent. In Brussels, there are only two: most famously at Toone (http://www.toone.be) but also in the basement of Poechenellekelder (opposite the Mannekin Pis). Both double as atmospheric pub-cafés.

CINEMA
The good news for Anglophone movie goers is that you can find most English-language films screened in VO, i.e. subtitled rather than dubbed. For a superb listing of what's showing where, surf to http://www.cinebel.be (in French or Flemish) which allows you to search a film by name, actor, director

The Nova (http://www.nova-cinema.com) is Brussel's art house cinema. Despite a great 'student-style' bar and an imaginatively esoteric playlist, it continues to teeter on the edge of bankruptcy.

or per town or province where you live. You can even win free tickets in frequent online competitions.

Traditionally, the scourge of smaller cinemas was the dreaded usherette. In return for tearing your ticket and handing you a free magazine, she'd expect a tip—not much, say 50 cents—but refusing to pay up could cause a scene. However, these uniquely Belgian dragons are a dying breed, killed off since the 1990s by the opening of big US-style multi-screen cinemas (notably Kinepolis and Imagibraine).

The major cities each have their own film festivals, and Brussels and Antwerp film museums screen art movies and popular classics plus dust off old, rare spools for the connoisseurs. On summer weekends from July to August, the park around Brussels' Cinquantenaire transforms into one of the world's more idiosyncratic drive-in movie theatres. You get the sound on the car radio.

Belgian Films and Film Stars

'Muscles from Brussels' Jean Claude Van Damme was born Jean Claude van Varenburg. In 1999, he deigned to come home to Belgium for his wedding—his fifth marriage. To action film aficionados, he's the greatest star on the planet. But for some Belgians, the upstart 5'8" fist-fighter is only marginally more appealing as a national symbol than chips and child molesters. It's easier to be proud of the timeless screen idol Audrey Hepburn who was also born in Brussels (as Edda Kathleen van Heemstra Hepburn-Ruston). Star of *My Fair Lady* and *Breakfast at Tiffany's*, her first known screen role was a non-credited bit part in a 1948 teach-yourself Dutch/Flemish instruction film! Understandably, *Nederlands in Zeven Lesen* was not a great box office storm. Indeed, until recently, the world seemed blissfully unaware of the Belgian movie industry. OK, so even today it's not Hollywood, or even Shepperton. But Belgian films have been claiming great critical success in the last few years, thanks to Chantal Akerman's *La Captive* (inspired by Proust's *La Prisonnière*) and Luc and Jean-Pierre Dardenne's *Rosetta*.

The Dardenne Brothers

Belgium's most successful film-makers are brothers Luc and Jean-Pierre Dardenne who have won the prestigious Cannes Palme d'Or twice (1999 and 2005). Presenting the harrowing, harsh life of a no-hope, fired factory hand, their first success was *Rosetta*, a brilliant close-up view of life in a dismal Liège backwater which also won best actress award for teenage discovery, Emilie Dequenne. Their 2005 *L'Enfant* offers an equally miserable-yet-fascinating glimpse of petty criminals in Seraing.

Other Belgian successes included Mike van Diem's *Karakter* which won the 1998 Foreign Film Oscar. It featured Jan Decleir who also played in the 1992 Oscar-nominated *Daens*, directed by fellow Belgian Stijn Coninx. The most popular Belgian movies amongst local cinema-goers were probably *Ma Vie en Rose*, about a boy growing up wanting to be a girl, and *Le Huitième Jour*, Jaco van Dormael's moving tale of a Down's syndrome sufferer. Van Dormael's *Toto le Héros* and *Between Heaven and Earth* also received critical acclaim.

Other Belgian directors to watch out for include Jan Bucquoy (*The Sexual Life of the Belgians*, 1994; *Camping Cosmos*, 1996), André Delvaux (*L'homme au Crâne Rasé*, 1965; *Un Soir, Un Train*, 1968) and Jean-Paul Picha (*The Big Bang*, 1987).

Foremost Belgian actor of recent years is Benoît Poelvoorde whose *Man Bites Dog* (1992 with Rémy Belvaux and André Bonzel) was a disturbing classic-like *Natural Born Killers* set in Namur. His acclaimed role in *Podium* (2004) as an obsessed Claude François tribute-artist was his greatest box office success to date. Dark-eyed Belgian beauty Marie Gillain was the star of *Le Dernier Harem* and a model for Lancôme. She raised great local press interest by her improbable 1999 confession, "C'est très à la mode d'être Belge" ('It's very trendy to be Belgian'). Naturally that didn't last long. Nonetheless, a record number of Belgians were cited for their work during the 2005 César awards (France's Oscars), notably Yolande Moreau who won best actress.

MUSIC
Classical

By the age of 11, Liège-born César Franck (1822–1890) was already touring the then brand new country as a piano prodigy. Even if you don't recognise the name, you'll probably recognise his *Symphony in D Minor*. Other Belgian composers include André Grétry (1731–1813), Henri Vieuxtemps (1820–1881), and Paul Gilson (1865–1942). My wife claims she only knows these names because they are streets in Brussels.

These days, Philippe Boesmans is Belgium's foremost composer of contemporary opera, having created *Reigen* in 1993 and *Wintermärchen* in 1999. The latter is based loosely on Shakespeare's *A Winter's Tale*.

Arguably Belgium's most prestigious musical event is the Concours Reine Elisabeth/Koningin Elisabethwedstrijd—a contest to find the world's best young classical singers, composers and musicians. Started in 1937 by violin impresario Eugene Ysaye (1858–1931), it soon received the patronage of Queen Elisabeth, the wife of King Albert I and Ysaye's most famous violin student. It's held in May. See http://www.concours-reine-elisabeth.be for more details.

Jazz and Blues

Not surprisingly, the country which gave the world the saxophone is passionate about jazz. In Belgium, the term is interpreted in its widest possible sense to encompass everything from avant-garde to zydeco. There is also a vein of great *soukous/zingé* music to be mined, thanks to the Congolese community based around the Matongé area of Brussels. There are numerous blues festivals and the Brussels Jazz Marathon (in late May) is one of the city's most festive weekends. Mainstream pop-radio carries regular world music and several blues shows (see Classic 21 under the section 'Radio', later in this chapter).

Internationally, perhaps the best known Belgium-born jazz star was Django Reinhardt (1910–1953), the great gypsy virtuoso who joined violin maestro Stefan Grappelli in the quintet Hot Club de France. A living legend is the recently knighted Toots Thielemans, one of the world's only musicians who've managed to make a career out of playing the harmonica. Other locally renowned jazz greats include Philippe Catherine, Charles Loos, Steve Houben and the experimental cello and bassist José Bedeur.

Popular Music

Belgian popular music is heavily divided along linguistic lines, although both communities eagerly lap up American and British rock, dance and pop music too. French French music is also a mainstay of Francophone radio play. Contemporary bands have often taken to singing in English to gain more international exposure. Throughout the summer, rock festivals are held almost weekly and many (notably Wechter and Pukkelpop) attract big names from all over the world.

French-language Belgian stars

Jacques Brel (1928–1978) is one of the classic '3B's' that rule the pantheon of popular French music (along with Georges Brassens and Gilbert Bécaud). Yet he was Brussels-born, and evoked Belgium in some of his classic songs ('Le Plat Pays', 'Les Flamandes') which ranged from heart-rending ballads to bittersweet cabaret numbers. Brussels made a big show of the 25th anniversary of his death during 2003 (http://www.brel-2003.be). Adamo (Salvador Adamo)—now a UNICEF envoy as well as top-selling singer and songwriter—has proved one of the most successful figures in French-language pop. His 1963 classic 'Tombe la Neige' has been covered by an astounding 500 other performers. Adamo was born to one of those Italian mining families who had settled in Belgium in return for a ton of coal. His career started as a child when he secretly participated in a singing contest to win himself 2 kg (4.4 lb) of chocolate. Flame-haired Axelle Red is a more recent star in Francophone countries. But despite her wistful French lyrics (including 'Manhattan-Kabul', a powerfully humanist 2002 duet with Renaud), she's in fact Flemish. Despite being long defunct, Dani Klein's group Vaya con Dios remains popular, having adopted Latin rhythms long before the present fad made them trendy. Other major Belgian stars include Maurane, Annie Cordy (also a comedienne and actress), and the Canada-based songstress Lara Fabian who has been labelled the 'new Céline Dion' (a compliment?).

French French Pop

To socialise with Francophones, it may be tactful to develop a liking (or at least tolerance) for French *chanson*—a catch-all term for everything from melodic ballads to insipid soft-rock. It's also wise to familiarise yourself with at least some of the classic stars of French French pop. Eternal rocker Johnny Hallyday (part Belgian, born Jean Philippe Smets) is the French Elvis. Charles 'For Me... Dable' Aznavour remains one of the great crooners along with the 3B's (see above). Cringe at Claude 'Clo-Clo' François' videos. Mourn for Michel Berger. Wonder how alcoholic Serge Gainsbourg managed to bed Brigitte Bardot or ask anyone what he said to Whitney Houston on live TV. Gainsbourg becomes more fashionable every year, even though he's been dead for a decade. Other long-standing stars include goat-voiced Julien Clerc, heartthrob Patrick Bruel, and veteran rapper MC Solar. Classic female artists include Sylvie Vartan, France Gall and the ever-warbling Véronique Sanson.

The Lotti Paradox

Where middle-of-the-road *chanson* crosses into pop, you'll find a Belgian reigning as the unlikely king of the European ratings. Helmut Lotti, a Flemish Mr Clean singer from Gent, is the Belgian Barry Manilow. He's frequently the top-selling artist in the Benelux. Lotti started his career as an Elvis impersonator and since his second album, has given up singing in Nederlands (the language, not the country). The antithesis of a rock archetype, he usually appears neatly groomed in a smart suit and tie. He continues to be successful by singing a vast range of styles from pop to opera to African to Russian, each accompanied by soaring symphonic background and rock beat. Seen as every mother's ideal son-in-law, he is an embarrassing joke to many: interviewed on radio, even his biographer was swift to deny being a fan. Nonetheless, there remain vast hordes of loyal Lotti followers, 90 per cent female (see http://www.helmutlotti.be).

If you thought Helmut Lotti was unfashionable, then listen to Frank Michaël. His blend of soft-rock/oompah/waltz music is so un-trendy that he's studiously ignored by TV and Radio, even though his records almost inevitably reach the top ten, snapped up by his loyal over-50-year-old fan base. Frank's concerts fill small stadia with screaming female-pensioners competing to give him cuddly toys and other mementos which are almost more tacky than his songs. He claims to keep them all. Right. Flanders' answer to Frank Michaël is Will Tura whose sugary tones manage to remain mysteriously popular after more than 40 years of touring.

Flemish Folk Music

Many contemporary Flemish bands sing in English (see below). For the best selection of Flemish folk CDs, visit Den Appel in Asse. Styles range from ponderous polkas to haunting pseudo-Irish melodies, or folk music heavy on the fiddle.

Lais is the Flemish folk movement's equivalent of the Corrs: three young women producing music of striking variety from highly traditional semi-Gaelic sounds to rock-beat hoedown. They even sing occasionally in French or Swedish! Arno (Arno Hintjens) also sings in three languages. Don't confuse Lais with Lucy Loes, a rotund septuagenarian 'oompah' singer, dubbed the queen of Ostend fisherfolk ballads.

Belgian Rock

In the late 1960s, Belgium produced a surprising number of inspirational rock bands, but most were predominantly live acts which recorded relatively few discs. Thus classic formations Hiroshima, influentially flamboyant Kleptomania and blues-purists Burning Plague are not widely known by younger generations of Belgians. The best selling Belgian bands of that era were Jess & James, the Pebbles and most notably, Wallace Collection with a sound reminiscent of early Jefferson Airplane. In the 1970s, Machiavel emerged as Belgium's best-known progressive rock outfit while

The Kits were likened to the Stranglers and Chainsaw barked out a local version of punk rock.

Rockers SweateR and club stars dEUS are amongst the latest proponents of the misspell-your-way-to-fame approach pioneered in the 1980s by fellow Belgian group Sttellla. Along with K's Choice ('I'm not an addict', 'Everything for free'), dEUS are probably the best known band to emerge from the very active 1990s Antwerp music scene. Conservatory-trained DAAU combines clarinets and strings, with samples and synths for a unique musical blend with varied influences including hip-hop and reggae. Hooverphonic, once pigeonholed as a trip-hop act, is in fact a boundary-breaking band from St Niklaas who are edging towards international recognition. Zornik is Belgium's answer to Coldplay and has toured with Muse. For more up-to-date information on the Belgian music scene, see http://houbi.com/belpop/links.htm.

Memorable Musical One-offs

Middle-aged Brits probably remember the very brief appearance of Le Punk when Belgian misfit Plastic Bertrand's catchy if monotonous ditty 'Ça Plane Pour Moi' became an unlikely UK hit. About as punk as Abba, he swiftly disappeared and his appalling attempt at a revival with a Belgian entry for the Eurovision Song Contest was an unmitigated failure. Indeed, Belgium's only success in that competition was in 1986, the night before the Chernobyl disaster. The winner was a 14-year-old schoolgirl by the name of Sandra Kim (real name Sandra Caldarone) who declared herself 'Italian by extraction, Walloon at heart'. The greatest Eurovision failure was Fud Leclerc who represented Belgium in 1958, 1960 and 1962, and on the last occasion managed astoundingly to score no points whatever, a feat nearly repeated in 2000 by Nathalie Sorce who finally scooped a pitiful three votes. This resulted in Belgium being booted out of the May 2001 competition, a fact heralded with typical self-effacing humour in *Télé Moustique* with the quip: 'Belgium—no point'. The most bizarre of all Belgian one-off's was the annoyingly catchy little song that starts, 'Domini-ka-nik-a-ni-que' and went on to global chart success. It was sung by Soeur Sourire (aka Janine Deckers), a gay Belgian nun who ended up committing suicide in Wavre.

TELEVISION

For obvious practical reasons, the press and entertainment industries are divided along linguistic lines. What is surprising is how rabidly independent the apparently equivalent institutions are in relation to one another. British or American programmes may be dubbed or subtitled in French or Flemish but Belgian programmes almost never cross the linguistic divide. Each community admits knowing more about the rest of Europe than about the other Belgium.

The main terrestrial TV networks are state-run VRT (in Flemish, http://www.vrt.be) and RTBF (in French, http://www.rtbf.be) plus VTM (Flemish, http://www.vtm.be) and RTL (nominally from Luxembourg but focused on Francophone Belgium).

Belgian news programmes (in French at 7:00 pm on RTL and 7:30 pm on RTBF1; in Flemish at 7:00 pm and 11:00 pm on TV1, 7:00 pm on VTM) are reassuringly down-to-earth without the infuriating breaks, pointless conjectural pontificating or constant headline recaps of BBC, CNN, etc. Reports are laced with ironic humour rather than confrontational interviews. This means that politicians are generally prepared to speak candidly off the cuff. Although RTBF and VRT are government-run and subject to political influence, they are generally seen to be fair and neutral, although TV news does tend to plug Belgian folkloric events and business deals.

Television Fees

You'll have to pay a TV licence fee (around € 200 for a colour set) to the Service Redevances /Dienst Kijk en Luistergeld offices in Wallonia/Flanders respectively. On top of this, you'll have to pay an extra fee if you want cable connection (€ 50–80 connection plus around € 100 per year subscription).

Some 90 per cent of households have cable TV, making Belgium the most cabled country anywhere. With access to more than 30 channels, virtually anyone can flick between programmes in German, Spanish and English (typically CNN, BBC1 and 2, CNBC and MTV). Many households receive Portuguese and Turkish programming too. Ironically, the cable companies often fail to provide the full range of Flemish channels in Wallonia or Francophone Belgian channels in Flanders. For the linguistically challenged TV addict wanting a wider range of English-language programmes, there is a slight advantage to living in Brussels or Flanders as many subtitled foreign programmes appear only on Flemish channels (such as *Frasier* on VTM, *Jonathon Creek* on Canvas, *Friends* and *Cheers* on VT4, etc.).

If the standard cable selection doesn't offer enough choice, you can add further pay channels (like Be TV) or get a satellite dish. Beware of possible installation restrictions on your house/apartment lease if you opt for the latter.

RADIO

As in Britain, the main radio stations are state-run. RTBF1 ('La Première', 96.1 FM) and VRT Radio1 (91.7 FM) offer mixed programming. Classic 21 (99.1 FM) plays pop and rock oldies climaxing on Sunday evenings (6:00 pm– 8:00 pm) with the stupendous Dr Boogie showcasing upbeat blues, rockabilly and zydeco—good enough to salvage the wreckage of even the rainiest weekend. Nostalgie (100.0 FM) also has 'classic hits' but with a more French tilt. StuBru (Studio Brussel, 100.6 FM) is Flanders' equivalent of the UK's Radio 1, offering a trendsetting blend of rock, house, and techno sounds. Pure FM (http://www.purefm.be, 101.1 FM) is Francophone Belgium's nearest equivalent, proffering current chart music, recent releases, dance, and indie music. Insipid VivaCité (97.3 FM in Wallonia) features music that is more mainstream with a fair sprinkling of French *chanson* and plenty of meaningless chat. The Flemish version is Radio Donna (88.3 FM). Air Libre (87.7 FM), run by the North African community, plays plenty of rai. Reception of the BBC World Service is reasonably clear on 648kHz MW with programming in both English and German. For classical music, try Musiq 3 (91.2 FM, with some Jazz), Klara (89.5 FM, including Flemish cultural features), France Musique (99.4 or 88.7 FM), Holland 4 (98.7 FM) and the German station WDR3 (95.1 FM). Note that frequencies given here are for Brussels but vary considerably in different regions (details via the relevant websites). RVI (Radio Flanders International, http://www.rvi.be) is the Flemish equivalent of the BBC World Service. Charleroi/La Louvière has an Italian language radio station.

Radio Fees

In Belgium, car radios incur an annual licence fee of around € 25. There is no such fee for a radio kept at home.

LITERATURE

For Belgian writers, the nature of the linguistic divide tends to ensure that their popularity is limited to one or the other language community. Flemish writers might seek fame and fortune in the Netherlands and Francophone Belgians, in France. A notable example is Georges Simenon (1903–1989) whose *Maigret* is considered the classic detective character in French popular literature, though Simenon himself was Belgian. Despite his demure, pipe-in-hand appearance, Simenon is said to have bedded more women than Bill Clinton and David Mellor put together—10,000, by his own modest estimate. If you're interested in doing a Simenon tour of Liège, start at his birthplace, 24 Rue Léopold.

Other Francophone literary greats include playwright Michel de Ghelderôde (1898–1962), Antwerp-born poet Emile Verhaeren (1855–1916) and Camille Lemonnier (1844–1913), the Zola-influenced founder of the so-called Belgian Literary Renaissance. More recently acclaimed authors include Françoise Mallet-Joris and Jacqueline Harmpan (Prix Medicis award for *Orlanda* in 1996).

Hendrik Conscience (1812–1883) is an interesting Belgian literary figure of the 19th century. A prolific sentimental historical novelist and short story writer, he is credited with the development of the Flemish novel, even though his father was French-speaking and he himself started out writing Francophone poetry. His most famous works are *In't Wonderjaar* (a series of 16th-century historical life sketches) and *De Leeuw van Vlaanderen* ('The Lion of Flanders'). The latter tells the story of the Battle of the Golden Spurs in 1302. Its publication in 1838 was an important rallying point for Flemish nationalism, while the much later film version directed by Hugo Claus is strikingly Monty Pythonesque.

At the turn of the century, the Flemish literature movement was an important source of renewed community pride. Leading figures were Guido Gezelle (1830–1899), Herman Teirlinck (1879–1967) and Frank Lateur (1871–1961), who wrote under the appropriately Flemish-sounding pen name Stijn Streuvels and is best known for *De Vlaschaard*, which was written in 1907. Priest and poet, Gezelle wrote direct simple evocations of religious and rural life and was posthumously adopted as a literary icon by Flemish nationalists. His centenary in 1999 was very widely celebrated in Flanders. Sculptures of Gezelle are considered 'accurate' if the skin is suitably lumpy and the head oversized—he was hydrocephalic 'with such a surfeit of brains that he had constant headaches'.

Twentieth-century Flemish writer Hugo Claus was shortlisted for the Nobel Literature Prize for *Het Verdriet van België*—which translates as 'The Sorrow of Belgium'. The title refers not to the depressing weather but to a phrase the hero's mother uses to describe her son. The book is a masterpiece exploring the stoical Belgian character through a portrayal of life under Nazi occupation (1939–1945). Its use of archaic, yokel and French terms (retained when possible in the English translation) is an integral element of the book's satire on Flemish nationalism.

The Flemish equivalent of the Booker Prize is the Libris while Francophone writers aspire to the Prix Rossel, Prix Medicis or even toward the Grand Prix of France's National Academy. *Stupeur et Tremblements* won the latter in 1999 for Amélie Nothomb, a prolific young Francophone Belgian authoress born in Kobé, Japan to a diplomatic family.

SPORTS

Anywhere in the world, a sure way to bluster into conversations is through a shared appreciation of sports. In Pakistan, it's cricket and hockey; in Japan, it's sumo and volleyball; in Papua New Guinea, it's mini wars. The events that come closest to pushing football from the Belgian sports headlines are Formula One motor racing, tennis and cycling.

Cycling

In the first 60 years of the cycling World Championships, Belgians won a phenomenal 22 times. Recent Belgian stars are Johan Museeuw (champion in 1995 and 1996), Frank Vandenbroucke (1999) and Russian-born Belgian Andreï Tchmil, 'the lion of Siberia' who won the 1999 World Cup. Arguably the world's most famous cyclist ever was Belgian Eddy Merckx, five times winner of the Tour de France in 1969, 1970, 1971, 1972 and 1974.

But it's not just great sportsmen who share the passion. On Sunday mornings, most towns have a veterans cycling club that consists mostly of pensioners who cycle a substantial circuit, although not, of course, before tucking into a fortifying beer or three.

Key Belgian Cycling Events

▪ Le Tour des Flandres	one of the 12 stages in the cycling World Cup, held in early April. Its most gruelling stretch is the infamously steep, cobbled slopes of the Muur van Geraardsbergen/ Mur de Grammont.
▪ La Flèche Wallonne	Charleroi to Huy, in mid-April
▪ La Flèche Brabançonne	late March
▪ Liège-Bastogne-Liège	mid-April
▪ The Gent 'six days'	November
▪ The Ciney '24-hours'	August

Motor Racing

Even though local Formula One heroes Jacky Ickx and Thierry Boutsen are no longer racing, Formula One remains extremely popular amongst ordinary Belgians who stay glued to their TV sets until 3:00 am to see the latest rally live from one of the world's least convenient time zones. The Belgian Grand Prix at Francorchamps near Spa was frequently cited as the 'drivers' favourite'. However, it was cancelled in 2006 following a financial scandal. Its future had been in doubt since 2003 when new laws outlawed tobacco advertising thus removing the race's major source of sponsorship. To most Belgians, banning cigarette commercials seemed rather silly in the first place—surely tobacco-advertising tells smokers what brand to buy rather than inspiring anyone to put cancerous sticks of burnable leaves in their mouths.

The Francorchamps course also hosts a classic 24-hour motor rally: a punishing endurance contest like the better-known equivalent at Le Mans (France), which, incidentally, Jacky Ickx won six times.

Football

It's often said that along with the monarchy, Belgium's national team, the Red Devils, are one of the main things that keep the nation together. If so the team's failure to qualify for the 2006 World Cup seems to poigniantly reflect the increasing lack of national unity.

Belgium's top domestic teams are FC Brugge (of Bruges) and Anderlecht, from an inner city commune of Brussels otherwise associated with Erasmus and ethnic unrest. The two teams are well known for the traditional enmity of their fans. This erupted in what was dubbed 'British-style hooliganism' when the teams met in January 1999. Some 400 seats were ripped up and thrown onto the pitch and Anderlecht fans were subsequently banned from Bruges altogether. Nonetheless, during Euro 2000, co-hosted by Belgium and the Netherlands, it was still the British fans who were considered the most dangerous. The authorities' fear dates back to the traumatic Juventus versus Liverpool European Cup final in 1985 when 39 supporters died in what is now the rebuilt King Baudouin stadium at Heysel (Brussels).

Belgian football has seen plenty of recent controversy. In 2003, Beveren (near Antwerp) surprised everyone by signing up a virtually complete team from the west African nation of Ivory Coast. Much more seriously, it was revealed in February 2006 that players in some Belgian league teams had apparently lost matches to order for the Chinese betting mafia.

For expatriates itching for a game, British United FC (http://www.bufc.org) has several teams playing at different levels.

Tennis

Tennis hadn't featured enormously on the Belgian sporting radar until 1997 when Sabine Appelmans reached the giddy heights of world number 16 then promptly retired. Few would have guessed that just five years later, two more Belgian women players would be at the very summit of world rankings... but so it proved with Kim Clijsters and Justine Henin-Hardenne. When the two met at Roland Garros for the 2003 French Open finals, much of Belgium closed down to watch. The King, Queen and Prime Minister all went to Paris to see the game in person.

The Belgian men's game is less developed but Kortijk-born Xavier Malisse along with the Rochus brothers are constantly improving.

Basketball

Basketball is another less traditionally Belgian sport to be gaining popularity. Almost undefeated in 2002–2003, Charleroi plays at the impressive 7,000-seater Spirou Stadium, though in February 2003, the game that gained it most press attention did so because thieves managed to escape with all the bar takings! For match schedules, results and standings in Belgian Basketball surf to http://www.b-all.be/basketball.

CURIOUS ALTERNATIVE SPORTS IN RURAL BELGIUM

Balle Pelotte

With a certain similarity to the jai alai (pelota) of the Basque country, *balle pelotte* is a game in which two teams slap a bouncy powerball toward each other using bare or gloved hands on an open court. Televised on little-watched Belgian provincial channels, the event of a big match is like a rural fête with impromptu bands of three or four gently inebriated musicians serenading the crowd. The irregularly shaped Ballodrome (court) is usually little more than lines marked on a village square with painted oil cans for distance markers.

Animal and Bird Competitions

Recently, the curious sport of pigeon racing hit the headlines when a Belgian fancier's birds were stolen from their dovecotes. The audacity of the theft was shocking, but so too was the discovery that these birds were valued at some € 250,000! April 2001 brought the offbeat sports story of the year: some 80 pigeon-fanciers were under investigation for suspected doping of their birds with performance enhancing drugs!

And this is not the only popular bird sport. Some eccentric folks in West Flanders spend their Sunday mornings taking their caged finches to the park. In a bizarre competition, the birds are judged for their ability to sing a very specific song. Birds that get it wrong are corrected, although the most stubborn and slow learners are usually released, eventually.

There are more than 40,000 competition finches registered in Belgium. There are similar competitions for singing dogs, although these are less uniquely Belgian.

FESTIVALS AND EVENTS

The sheer endless variety of folkloric parades as well as exhibitions, shows, festivals and other events in Belgium means that there need never be a weekend without a dozen choices of something new to see. The biggest problem is sifting through the myriad possibilities.

Public Holidays in Belgium

- New Year   1 January
- Easter Monday   dates vary
- Labour Day   1 May
- Flemish Community Day   11 July,
                                        not in Wallonia
- National Day   21 July
- Assumption   15 August
- Francophone Community Day   27 September,
                                        not in Flanders
- All Saints' Day   1 November
- Armistice Day   11 November
- German-speaking Community Day   15 November,
                                        only in the East Cantons
- Christmas Day   25 December

Winter

During the cold months of January and February, indoor activities predominate: there are plenty of trade fairs (homes, cars, travel, antiques, etc.) plus the Brussels International Film Festival. The Fête des Rois Mages (Feast of the Magi) falls on 6 January. All over Belgium, households celebrate the late arrival of Jesus' Biblical birthday presents (of gold, frankincense and myrrh) by eating a special cake into which is baked a 'lucky' coin. Increasingly, other novelties are substituted for the coin. In 2000, popular versions of this cake contained a ceramic Tarzan figure for kids to joyfully break their teeth on.

The honour of being a Gilles de Binche is usually passed from father to son. Seen here BEFORE donning masks or tarantula headgear.

Lenten Festivals

Mardi Gras (the 'fat' Tuesday before Lent) is six weeks before Easter. It's the culmination of many days of preliminary festivities in Binche, Belgium's greatest carnival town. The famous Gilles de Binche briefly don their spooky masks at around 11:00 am, then reassemble at 3:30 pm for the orange-throwing procession, wearing their exotically quivering ostrich headgear. Being hit by an Gilles-thrown orange is considered a blessing. Throwing one back would be considered extremely offensive.

Dozens of other towns have carnivals of their own. Aalst's raucous, onion-throwing bonanza is also held during Mardi Gras together with the Voil Jeanetten (Dirty Prostitute) procession of garishly cross-dressed men in giant bras and old corsets carrying broken umbrellas. Eupen's more picturesque Rosenmontag (Rose Monday) is the day before, and other carnivals occur each weekend between Dimanche Gras (e.g. at Malmédy and at Tongeren) and Palm Sunday (e.g. at Genappe, a quaintly banal affair of purely local interest).

Binche may have the finest Gilles, but several other towns have their own versions. Stavelot's carnival (fourth Saturday of Lent) is famous for its Blancs Moussis. These are white-capped figures with long-nosed masks, originally donned to protect the participants from the plague. Or, according to another story, so that monks could join in the fun without being noticed. The next day in Tilff, carnival participants wear extraordinary tall green headgear which turns them into giant pineapples, while in Hélécine they're dressed as witches. Somewhat more refined is Ostend's Dead Rat Ball, held on the first Saturday of March at the Kursaal Casino. Celebrated since 1898, it is touted as the biggest fancy dress ball in Europe. Book well ahead.

On Ash Wednesday, traditional Walloon villages spend the afternoon in the ancient ritual of *crossage de rue*, which is a sort of primitive mini-golf where a (traditionally wooden) *chôlette* ball is struck with a *rabot* stick. The target, in lieu of a hole, is usually a beer barrel placed in front of a café or bar where brewed refreshment can be found at gratifyingly short notice. You can join the fun in the Hainaut village of Chièvres.

The first Sunday of Lent goes by several names, including the Sunday of Brandons, Escouvillons or Feûreû. Its climax is the burning of Mr Winter (*le Bonhomme Hiver*) at Bouge on the biggest of seven great simultaneous bonfires on hillsides ringing Namur. The folks in the red robes are the 'brotherhood of the great fire'. If you see people with big batons, these are not for causing crowd trouble but to beat the trees in local orchards—a practice which traditionally was said to bring a good fruit crop.

The spirit of winter is ceremonially torched many more times throughout March, but mostly in rural villages, such as Orp-le-Grand and Walhain in Walloon Brabant. These events are totally un-commercialised and barely known beyond the village limits—a really great way to delve into rural culture.

Spring

By Easter, things have calmed down a little. Children burrow around the garden looking for Easter eggs which are delivered, so they're told, courtesy of the 'Bells of Rome'. If you're looking for a spectacle, there's the curious egg-throwing festival at Kruishoutem and an eerie penitents procession at Lessines (Good Friday). Torch-bearing figures at the latter wear costumes resembling monks' habits. A similar procession in late July at Veurne involves the penitents carrying huge crosses around the old town centre.

As is common across all of Europe, 1 April is the day of practical jokes. In Belgium, the classic gag is to stick a paper cut-out of the *poisson d'avril* fish on someone's back. 1 May is Labour Day, on which it is an almost expected custom for men to present a small posy of *muguet/meiklokje* (lily of the valley) to female friends, family and colleagues.

Ascension Day is celebrated with the Holy Blood Procession—a grand cortège of horsemen, archers and musicians riding through Bruges escorting a 12th-century reliquary which supposedly contains a few drops of Christ's blood. The Sunday before is the similarly dramatic Hanswijk procession in Mechelen in which citizens traditionally thank the Virgin Mary for her supposed role in the town's 'miraculous' deliverance from the plague in 1272.

Several towns (e.g. Soignies, Wasmes, Gerpines) have religious festivals on Whit Monday. Then six days later on Trinity Sunday, Mons erupts with the brilliant Ducasse de St Waudru featuring the procession of the Car d'Or— a golden carriage which holds the saint's relics. The morning's mayhem culminates at Mons' Grande Place around 1:00 pm with the Lumeçon battle. This sees 'St George', dressed as an 18th-century cavalryman, defeat a dragon with the unfortunate name of Doudou. Bands play, musketeers fire and a melee of heaving humanity fights to retrieve hairs from the doomed dragon's long stick-like tail.

There are many other late spring festivities, notably the blessing of the sea at Knokke, *maitrank* drinking in Arlon, the Ros Beiaardommegang medieval pageant in Dendermonde and the fabulous Brussels Jazz Marathon. For something more sedate, you can join the queues to visit the Royal greenhouses at Laken (Brussels) around the end of April.

Summer

Summer sees a deluge of music festivals and commercial events at the seaside: in the most impressive, part of the beach at Zeebrugge is turned into a gigantic art gallery of enormous sand sculptures. Meanwhile virtually every commune in Belgium has its own summer *braderie* fête, or fair, though this might be little more than a big car boot sale, perhaps with a couple of minor roundabouts, beignet fryers, shooting stands and lucky dip stalls around the village square. The biggest is Brussels' Foire du Midi which commandeers half of the Boulevard de Midi for over a month to host an extensive fairground with a reputation for thrills, candy floss and pickpockets.

National Day (21 July) sees a military parade in Brussels but it's more fun to head to Vielsalm the night before where the local Blueberry festival is preceded by the town's 'capture' by Macralle witches who then put on a late night open-air show parodying themselves and local celebrity guests in hilarious Walloon dialects.

On 9 August, a somewhat chaotic cortège of giants and revellers block Brussels city traffic for the planting of

While Binche hosts Belgium's most famous and distinctive carnival, there are dozens of others. One of the most joyous is the lively Rosenmontag, held the day before Mardi Gras, in the German-speaking town of Eupen.

Sand sculptures on the beach at
Zeebrugge. Impressive... until it rains.

the Meiboom (http://www.meyboom.be) which strangely, considering the date, translates as 'May Tree'. The festival is loosely based on a historic conflict involving a wedding party, a saint and a gang of disruptive youths arguing over beer taxes. Assumption (15 August) is Catholic-Europe's busiest holiday of all with something happening in almost every town: fireworks, fairs, bathtub races, etc. Giants roll through Liège, which re-declares itself the 'Free Republic of Outre-Meuse' (http://www.tchantches.be). Bruges has its lace days (http://www.kantcentrum.com). Aarschot turns off all its electric lights and illuminates itself with thousands of candles. Malmédy scrambles 10,000 eggs for a giant omelette.

On the fourth week of August with the school holidays petering out, David takes on Goliath in the culmination of the Ducasse giants' parade at Ath, a procession dating back to the 15th century.

The Ommegang

The first Thursday in July, the Ommegang (http://www. ommegang.be) is Brussels' most dramatic pageant. Soon after the 1348 construction of a chapel at the Sablon, an impoverished cloth worker, Beatrice Soetkens, saw a vision of the Virgin. The apparition, while grateful for the new chapel in her honour, urged Soetkens to furnish it with a much venerated 13th century Madonna statuette known as O.L.V. op 't Stokske ('Our Lady of the Branch'). Convinced, she somehow persuaded her pious husband to row her all the way to Antwerp so that she could steal the figure. Her adventure proved remarkably successful and the sheer bizarre audacity of the mission made it seem almost a miracle. God's will, it seemed, had paralysed all those who tried to stop her and once, when the poor husband collapsed with exhaustion at the oars, the Lord even deigned to blow the couple's boat back to Brussels. Given such obvious divine intervention, even the Antwerp authorities decided to accept the fait accompli. In Brussels, the mysterious myth became the focus for a great procession in which the statuette was displayed by walking it around the city: hence Ommegang, (*omme* means 'around', *gang* means 'walk').

Over the years, the Ommegang has evolved beyond recognition. In its 21st century form, the main focus is no longer the Virgin statuette, but an impressive evocation of Charles V and Philip II's Joyeuse Entrée of 1549 (*see also* Chapter 2: Land and History, *page 14*). In full medieval garb, the pair is flanked by standard-bearers on horseback, heralds, pages and nobles mixed in with a hotchpotch of Gilles, Giants and Merchtem waterbirds. Real historical characters from the original Entrée are represented, right down to the royal pets. 'Charles' carries the emblem of the Golden Fleece. Some of the characters are played by the direct descendants of Charles' original noble entourage. Watching the afternoon procession is free but you need a ticket to attend the finale in the Grand Place. The day culminates in fireworks and a great costume ball.

Autumn

In autumn, things turn alcoholic. In mid-September the boisterous Fêtes de Wallonie give the French-speaking community the excuse to tuck into the *peket* firewater. In Poperinge, there's a hop parade every three years (next in 2008). And in mid-October is Hasselt's *jenever* festival. Perhaps as a counterbalance, the beginning of September also heralds the Heritage Days.

Amongst the odder local festivities are Jodoigne's pig festival (second week in October), the intriguing 'Day of the Edible Landscape' at Bokrijk's open-air museum (end of September) and the festival in Mol Ginderbuiten where 100,000 light bulbs illuminate a jolly parade of giants and bands on the evening of the last Saturday of September (but never on the 30th!).

Halloween is a recently imported idea celebrated by trick-or-treating kids but without any real cultural pedigree in Belgium (though the country has plenty of homegrown witch festivals e.g. at Beselare in July). All Saints' Day, on the first of November, is a national holiday which was traditionally

Even straw gets merry
in September!

the time for visiting family graves. These days most Belgians treat it with their usual irreverence by beetling off somewhere for the long weekend. The most pious head for Scherpenheuvel on the first Sunday of November. Armistice Day on the 11th is the time to remember the war dead.

Avoid central Brussels on St Verhaegen's Day (third Friday in November) unless you're happy to be plastered with flour and eggs. Actually Verhaegen wasn't a saint at all, but the founder of the Brussels Free University and the celebration is anarchic, booze-fueled mayhem. For a week before, you'll see students in laboratory coats walking the city streets, waving collection buckets at motorists, begging for beer money.

The first of December is St Eloi's Day, the workers' equivalent of St Verhaegen's Day, where public drunkenness is not only acceptable, it's expected.

Christmas

In some European countries, it's St Nicholas' Day (on 6 December) rather than Christmas on which children receive their presents from a white-bearded old housebreaker who sneaks down the chimney and violates their shoes, stockings or socks (with presents, that is). Belgian kids are lucky—they receive presents on both days. The term 'Santa Claus' probably originates from the shortened Dutch/Flemish name for St Nicholas, 'Sintiklaas'. To encourage Santa to be generous, it's fair tactics for children to leave a little present for him (typically a beer) and a carrot for his donkey (Rudolf the Reindeer hasn't caught on here). Next day, along with the shoes or socks full of presents, the children expect to see a bite taken out of the carrot. But no explanation is offered as to how the donkey got in to do that nibbling. Santa is traditionally accompanied by the curiously boot-blackened figure of Black Peter (Zwarte Piet/Pére Fouettard). It's Black Peter's job to check that children have been good. Good children get their gifts. But bad Belgian children supposedly receive coal instead and also risk the wrath of Black Peter's big stick, designed for whacking sinners. Hopefully symbolically.

As in many countries, Santa moonlights between night-time deliveries, sitting around in shopping malls and Christmas markets handing out gifts (once parents have paid). These commercial Santas sport red uniforms and white beards similar to the American and British versions, though generally they wear a hat that is like a stylised Archbishop's mitre. Black Peter sometimes lurks menacingly beside him.

For much of December, town centres hold festive Christmas markets. A common feature, besides the hot *glühwein* and chocolate truffles, are full-sized Nativity scenes. In some such scenes, the stables are populated with real animals and occasionally, there's even a live 'Virgin' in attendance with a real baby bawling in the manger. The job can be rather cold, if, like in Anderlecht, it's performed outdoors.

Christmas day itself is typically a relatively quiet family afair, though many minimally-religious Belgians still attend midnight mass on the night of Christmas Eve (24 December).

NON-ANNUAL PAGEANTS

Some of the most dramatic pageants do not occur every year including those below:

- The Golden Tree Pageant
  Roughly every five years in Bruges, this majestic event evokes the 1468 wedding of Charles the Bold (of Burgundy and Flanders) to theEnglish princess Margaret of York.

- Halle's Pilgrims' Procession
  Commemorates a legend in which the Virgin Mary appeared in Halle, her face blackened with smoke, when the city was under siege in 1498. Celebrated on Whit Sunday in odd years.

- Brussels Flower Carpet (Tapis Fleuri)
  The whole Grand Place is carpeted with designs made of flower petals in even numbered years around 15 August.

- The Kattestoet Festival
  Since as early as AD 932, there's been an odd tradition of hurling cats off the balcony of the Cloth Hall in Ieper. Some claim that the cats were kept in winter to guard the

The Tapis Fleuri. Every two years, the Grand Place in Brussels is covered in an incredible patterned carpet of flower petals.

wool, but weren't needed in summer so were disposed of. Another explanation links the cat-killing to a symbolic anti-sorcery display. Either way, these days cloth replicas are used instead of live felines and gigantic cats are wheeled around in a procession. Celebrated on the second Sunday in May every three years (2006, 2009, 2112).

- St Dympna Ommegang
  Some 2,000 players act out a historical pageant related to the 7th-century Christian Irish princess Dympna who fled from her incestuous, heathen father, only to end up beheaded in Belgium. Celebrated in Geel in late April or May every five years (next in 2010)

GOING ABROAD
Airlines

The November 2001 bankruptcy of SABENA (the national airline) was Belgium's worst ever corporate collapse. Labelled a 'social and economic' disaster by then employment minister Laurette Onkelinx, the result was a great public outrage against Switzerland as Swissair, the parent airline, was widely suspected of cynically defaulting on its SABENA bail-out plan by declaring its own technical demise. However, despite a particularly fine route network in Europe and to Africa, the airline had only ever been profitable for two of its 78 years of existence and for years had been nicknamed 'Such A Bad Experience, Never Again'. Much of the former fleet has since been recycled into the slightly more modest SN Brussels Airlines (http://www.flysn.be) which maintains the old Sabena logo. Along with British Airways (http://www.ba.com) and British Midland (http://www.flybmi.com) they now offer very competitive fares to the UK. VLM (http://www.flyvlm.com) serves several UK airports from Brussels and Antwerp. SN Brussels has recently announced a merger with Virgin Express (http://www.virginexpress.com), the only other major scheduled airline to have a hub at Brussels (Zaventem) Airport, whose website (http://www.biac.be) lists all current airlines and timetables. Beware that budget airlines including Ryanair (http://www.ryanair.com), and Poland's WizzAir (http://www.wizzair.com) use the term

Brussels South when in fact referring to Charleroi Airport. For cheap, last minute charter flights from Brussels, Liège and Ostend, keep watching the website of TUI Belgium (http://www.jetonly.com/en/) which has been known to offer deals to Cuba for as little as € 200 return.

Note that it's worth considering long haul flights from Schiphol (Amsterdam) and Charles de Gaulle (Paris) airports, both of which have direct, super-fast Thalys train connections from Brussels and Antwerp.

Travel Agencies

USIT Connections (http://www.connections.be/en/) and Airstop/Taxistop (http://www.airstop.be) are the most prominent travel agencies, each with an email service which can alert you to cheap deals and student and discount tickets. (*See* Chapter 5: Settling In *for details, page 104*)

The Last Call shop within Brussels Airport provides absolute last-minute tickets. They take no telephone calls. You just turn up between 6:00 am–7:00 am with your bags packed and hope for tickets to your desired destination. Or go wherever's cheapest! Prices quoted are for return trips with minimum one weekend stay, maximum one month.

Getting to the Airports

- You can reach Brussels Airport by 'express' trains that leave four times an hour from Brussels Midi/Zuid via Brussels Central and North stations. You've rarely seen a slower express. If travelling by road, you'll have to use the dauntingly large but feebly signposted intersection 4 off the Brussels Ring, following the minuscule signs for 'Zaventem' with the airplane symbol (but NOT 'cargo'). If you're planning to do this any time near rush hour, add an hour or more in anticipation of the traffic chaos.

- Antwerp Airport is located in Deurne, 5 km by bus number 16 from the Antwerpen Centraal station.

- Charleroi Airport is served by bus number 68 from Charleroi Sud station (one to two buses per hour) and by Ryanair buses direct from Brussels.

To or From Belgium by Land

From Brussels Midi station, high speed Eurostar (http://www.eurostar.com) trains reach London in under three hours while sleek super-fast Thalys (www.thalys.com/be/en) run direct to services to Amsterdam, Cologne, Paris and even Marseille (in little more than five hours). Tickets for those services must be booked ahead. You can also buy tickets from railway stations or the Belgian national railway website (http://www.b-rail.be) which also offers cheaper inter-city tickets to the same and many other destinations. Eurolines buses (https://webapp.eurolines.be/Eurolines/ssl_index.asp) offer a range of international services from outside Brussels North railway station and also from Liège, Gent, Antwerp and Kortrijk. There are several smaller international bus companies: look around Brussels Midi/Zuid Station for operations to Spain and Morocco, and behind the Central Station where the buses bound for Eastern Europe park. Another cheap way to travel to European destinations is with a car-share which pairs long-distance drivers with passengers who pay per kilometre. With Taxistop's 'Eurostop' scheme, you give € 0.025 per km to the driver plus pay an additional € 0.008 per km fee for the arrangement (minimum € 6.20, tel: (070) 222-292, http://www.taxistop.be/4index.html).

If you're driving out of Belgium on holiday, bear in mind the appalling traffic jams that can afflict the E411 Ardennes highway. In winter, it's ice that causes crashes. On summer weekends, it's the great southbound exodus. And added to all of that are the miscalculations of drivers desperately hoping that their petrol will last them till Luxembourg (where a fill up is so much cheaper). Police claim that up to 20 traffic jams a month are caused by such calculations going wrong, cars running out of petrol and blocking a busy carriageway! How Belgian.

WHERE TO GO?

One of the joys of living in Belgium is the sheer ease of going somewhere else. Hop on the Eurostar to London, the Thalys to Amsterdam, or drive to France for a boot-load of cheap wine (*see* Chapter 6: Food and Drink, *page 146*). But why rush away? There's loads to see in Belgium: medieval town squares, soaring belfries, moated castles, battlegrounds and the most idiosyncratic collection of museums imaginable. Bruges is arguably the best-preserved medieval city in Europe, and there are plenty of other gems to explore.

Historic Town Centres

Belgium's towns grew wealthy much earlier than those of many other European nations. Although the country subsequently suffered considerably from wars, invasions and town planners, a surprising wealth of medieval architecture has survived and/or has been restored. Even Ieper, almost entirely flattened during World War I, has had its historic centre attractively rebuilt. The main cities have beautiful centres, especially Antwerp, Mons and Mechelen. Brussels' Grand Place is arguably the most beautiful medieval square in Europe and it's worth seeking out the city's brilliant art nouveau treasures—a special pleasure since many of the best host atmospheric café and bars. St-Truiden, Tienen, Tournai, Grimbergen and Enghien are other particular delights but a personal top five would be:

- Gent
  Fabulous bars, beautiful architecture, a cute city-centre castle and a riotous arts festival summer, yet all in a city that's very real and down-to-earth. Wonderful.
- Bruges
  Brilliantly preserved with myriad attractive canal views. Probably Europe's most picturesque small town though over-touristy for much of the year.
- Lier
  Less extensive than Bruges but with less bustle
- Leuven
  Magnificent city hall, great student atmosphere
- Tongeren
  Belgium's oldest town. Charming begijnhof area.

Belfries and Curious Clocks

In the Middle Ages, the height and grandeur of a town's belfry tower was a symbol of a town's prosperity and independence.

Many still stand, especially in Flanders. In 1999, UNESCO recognised Belgium's 30 great belfries as a world heritage collection. Eye-catching examples include those at Aalst, Bruges, Mons, Lier and St-Truiden.

The latter two towns also display unique timepieces. The extraordinarily intricate Zimmer tower clock in Lier was built in the early 1930s but looks medieval. In the building next to the St-Truiden's *begijnhof*, you can see 'performances' of the Festraets Astronomical Clock, complete with a Foucault Pendulum. If you visit Nivelles, Kortrijk or Virton, keep an eye on the church towers as the hour approaches. Chimes are rung by intriguing mechanical bell-ringer figurines.

Fountains

The typically understated Belgian sense of humour is evident in the joy the population takes in dressing up the Manneken-Pis. The minuscule statue of a little boy taking a leak actually owns more than 600 fanciful costumes. His wardrobe is kept in the Maison du Roi city-museum on the Brussels Grand Place. The original 1619 statuette was stolen and destroyed in 1817 but the smashed pieces were eventually recovered and a new cast made. A spare was constructed in case anyone tries to steal the original again! If you visit the town of Geraardsbergen, which has its own version, locals will tell you that theirs was the original all along. Even lesser known is Brussels' Jeanneke-Pis, a female equivalent who does her thing at the far end of a little alley off the Petit Rue des Bouchers. Other intriguing fountains include the Hasselt gin barrel (*see* Chapter Six: Food and Drink, *page 147*) and the 1887 Brabo fountain in Antwerp's Grote Markt. The latter is a gory depiction of the first count of Flanders flinging the severed hand of the giant Antigonus into the river Scheldt—a deed which is the apocryphal derivation for the town's name (*werp* is 'throw', *ant* is a mispronunciation of 'hand').

Castles

There are so many fantastic castles in Belgium that tourist offices sell packs of cards, each one featuring a different château. A large number are well-preserved and dramatically set in well-maintained moats, all spiky with towers. A very condensed list is given below, chosen more for overall visual appearance and atmosphere than for historical merit.

- Antwerp   Antwerp's Sterckshof Provincial Museum is housed in a very dramatic moated castle
- Beersel   conveniently near Brussels, dramatic but unfurnished
- Bouillon   massive ridge-top fortress of Godfrey, the leader-bankroller of the first Crusade
- Gent   a picturesque addition to the city centre
- Gaasbeek   set in splendid grounds and with luxurious interiors
- Harvé   partially restored ruin on a big island
- Horst   moated beauty near St-Peters-Rode
- Modave   perched on a cliff, although you wouldn't notice this from the palatial main entry
- Namur   extensive hilltop citadel and fortress that dominates the town

Great Religious Buildings

The Belgian abbeys took a hammering after the French Revolution and relatively few retain much of their former grandeur. Those that have been rebuilt are generally rather austere and more interesting for their breweries than for their architecture. However, some outstanding religious structures remain.

To get a sense of its grandeur, Tournai's classic five-spired 12th-century cathedral is best viewed from the west end of the Grand Place. Nivelles' St Gertrude's and Soignies' Collégiale St Vincent are similarly massive, austere Romanesque structures. Villers-la-Ville's once great abbey was sacked in 1794 but the atmospheric ruins are protected and used occasionally as the venue for musical or theatrical performances.

The St Leonarduskerk in Zoutleeuw is unique in retaining its incredible pre-Reformation interior and artworks, but is only open from Easter till the end of September between 2:00 pm and 5:00 pm. Closed on Mondays too! Antwerp's Onze Lieve Vrouw cathedral has a splendid Gothic nave

The fairy tale castle of Beersel—peace and tranquility just three minutes off the Brussels Ring.

Aarschot is never likely to rate as much of a tourist attraction. But like several of Belgium's less exciting towns, it still manages the remnants of a *begijnhof* and an impressive if austere Demergothic church.

with baroque embellishments and paintings by Rubens. Aarschot and Halle have fine examples of Demergothic churches with bulbous spires, Walcourt has the onion-domed St Materne basilica while Jodoigne's dilapidated Notre Dame du Marché has a curiously twisted steeple.

Schepenheuvel, Belgium's mini Lourdes, has a heptagonal 1627 basilica on whose dome exterior are dozens of sparkling gilded stars. Brussels has several attractive churches and the splendid Gothic cathedral of Sts Michel & Gudule is reminiscent of Notre Dame in Paris. There's also the simply huge Koekelberg Basilica. It's the world's fifth biggest church and is really rather ugly. Attempts to make it a national monument have less to do with artistic merit than with persuading the federal government to pay for its maintenance and diabolical heating bills.

Begijnhofs/Beguinages

In the 13th and 14th centuries, many women in Flanders were accommodated in protective cloisters called *begijnhofs* (*beguinages* in French). Initially, these welcomed women of all classes and most notably the lonely wives of crusaders who needed protection while their warrior husbands were killing infidels abroad. Unlike nuns, these women didn't have to take permanent chastity or poverty vows, but could retreat from the harsh predatory world to a life of relative contemplative calm. They passed their days developing the art of lace-making. Later, the institutions became more like religious poorhouses. Gent still has an active *begijnhof*. Many other Flemish towns—such as Antwerp, Bruges, Diest, Kortrijk, Lier, St Truiden, and Tongeren—have retained at least part of these complexes which make delightful spots for a stroll. The Leuven *begijnhof* is now used as student accommodation.

Spa and Francorchamps

Not quite city or countryside, what sleepy Spa lacks in visual appeal it makes up for with curious historical connections and events. Spa is the original spa town. It was here that Kaiser Wilhelm signed the armistice ending World War I.

And it was in Spa's Hotel du Midi, that King Leopold II's estranged wife Maria-Henrietta took refuge for seven years. Despite its casino, Spa is a fairly sleepy place most of the year, coming alive for the 'Francofolies' festival, and for car rallies at nearby Francorchamps including the former Belgian Formula One Grand Prix.

Battlegrounds

Caught between powerful neighbours, Belgium has long been the unlucky venue for foreigners' wars. Most famously, Napoleon met his Waterloo at, well, Waterloo. Neutrality in World War I didn't stop Belgium being pounded into the mud so severely that for many, the fields of Flanders are still associated primarily with trench warfare and not feeding milk cows. World War II was every bit as traumatic—Belgium had to deal with German occupation and aerial bombardment from both sides. Today, the sad legacies of these and other battles hold a curious attraction for visitors. But to make a visit to a battlefield interesting, one really needs a good guide to make sense of what are, after all, simply fields.

Waterloo

The battlefield is about 5 km (3 miles) south of Waterloo town (take bus W from Brussels). The battlefield topography is interesting once one realises the significance of what at first appears to be a very understated, gentle slope. It was this feature that fooled the advancing French infantry, who hadn't expected to find Wellington's redcoats hiding behind a now disappeared hedgerow on the little ridge. In the lee of a huge artificial memorial hill topped with a bronze lion is a museum whose displays glorify Napoleon to the extent that you begin to wonder who actually won! The balance is redressed at the Wellington museum in central Waterloo.

Ramillies

In 1706, the British commander Duke of Marlborough, with the help of Dutch and Danish troops, decimated a French force and prevented its attack on Namur. Howard Green's

The Waterloo Battle Memorial. Technically, the battlefield now falls just outside the Waterloo commune boundary. But nobody really considers renaming it the Battle of Braine l'Alleud.

1976 book, *Cockpit of Europe*, helps visitors make sense of the rather widely spread battlefield sights near Taviers, some 25 km (15 miles) north of Namur.

Fontenoy

Three kilometres (1.8 miles) from Ramecroix, off the Tournai–Mons Road, is the site where a British force impeded a French attack on the Spanish Netherlands (Belgium). French commander Marshal Saxe was hardly helped by the arrival of his king, Louis XV, who turned up to watch with a vast foppish entourage of wig makers, clock winders, shoeshiners and a myriad other useless hangers-on. There's a curious monument to Irish soldiers who were, at the time, fighting with the French against the Brits.

Kortrijk/Courtrai

The 1302 Battle of the Golden Spurs (*see* Chapter 2: Land and History, *page 14*) was fought less than a kilometre from Kortrijk's Grote Markt. The exact site is now lost within the town sprawl and was around a stream which has since disappeared beneath the Groeningelaan road. Nonetheless, Kortrijk organises a Golden Spurs festival in early July.

World War I

Between 1914–1918, a horrifying 250,000 men lost their lives in one small area of Flanders, with 65,000 more missing in action. Their names are recorded on Ieper's Menin Gate (Menentoren), dozens of smaller memorials and 155 war graveyards in the region. Passchendaele (now spelt Passendale), one of the most emotive of the battlefields, is marked by the Crest Farm Memorial commemorating Canadians who bloodily regained the ridge in 1917. In Mesen (Messines), ANZAC day is still commemorated, remembering the heavy Kiwi troop casualties there. Overgrown, shell-pocked World War I fortresses remain in Liège Province including Fort le Loncin whose ammo store was exploded on 15 August 1914 taking with it most of the occupants.

World War II

Fought in 1944, the 'Battle of the Bulge' was not so named for a fat commander on a mission to slim. With World War II coming to a climax, Hitler had made a last-ditch counter attack and divided the advancing Allied lines with a 'bulge' of German forces pushing into the Ardennes. These troops encircled the US 101st Airborne Division at Bastogne. When asked to surrender, commander McAuliffe (now commemorated by a statue and a tank) retorted with the abrupt and much quoted response, "Nuts!". To celebrate this outburst, the Bastogne has adopted a walnut-throwing ceremony in early December. The area where the fighting raged is very extensive, but the Historical Centre in Bastogne can help define the boundaries. There are more ideas on http://www.visitbelgium.com/worldwar.htm.

Royal Exhibits

If you're really interested in the Belgian royal family, there's a dynastic museum in Brussels and visits to the Royal Palace in Brussels are possible in the summer. On Sunday afternoons, All Saints' Day and special occasions (like the death anniversaries of the kings), the public is allowed to visit the crypt at Laeken Royal Castle, the last resting place of deceased Belgian monarchs. It's free. Crowds flock to view the botanical collection in the great art nouveau royal conservatory which is open briefly to the public in the last week of April or the first week of May. Check at the tourist offices for details.

Museums: Belgium's Weird Collections

Belgium is graced with some truly splendid museums. The fine arts collections in each of the main cities are remarkable: Tervuren's African museum offers a fascinating colonial cameo, and the Brussels war museum has an unrivalled collection of military memorabilia if you're into that sort of thing. There are many open-air museums and wildlife parks. Antwerp's zoo is internationally famous. Almost every town, down to the smallest commune, has a local museum explaining some facet of local culture, demonstrating local crafts or displaying historical mementoes. Many are endearingly quaint as much for the dedication and love of their curators as for the museums themselves, although come closing time, you're likely to hear a very unambiguous rustling of keys.

Specialist Mini Museums

Belgium's sheer overload of specialist mini museums is quite exceptional. The strangest museum has to be Brussels' Museum of Veterinary Medicine (45 rue des Vétérinaires) with its stomach-churning collection of skulls and pickled organs, from dogs' prostates to a tuberculosis-afflicted parrot's head. There is even a horse torso—stuffed with a new born foal—designed for midwifery practice. All this, set in the neo-renaissance former Cureghem Veterinary School, makes for a very surreal experience. (It's currently closed for long-term reconstruction.)

In a quiet Brussels street, you can visit a Schindler Museum that has nothing to do with lists or the Holocaust. It houses a display of passenger lift apparatuses, and is hidden away in the premises of the eponymous Schindler company which

The Schindler elevator museum. Like several of Belgium's more idiosyncratic museums, just managing to get in is a large part of the fun.

built them. If that's whetted your appetite, here's a further selection from Belgium's encyclopedic catalogue of oddities. Note that some have extremely limited opening times. For example the harness-making museum in Ellezelles only opens 2:00 pm–6:00 pm on the first Sunday in the months from April to October. That's just 28 hours per year!

Bakery	Masseik, Aywaille
Barbers	St-Niklaas
Bee-keeping	Kalmthout, Tilff
Beer	*See* Chapter 6: Food and Drink, *page 136*
Biscuit boxes	Opheylissem
Blacksmithery	Ittre
Brushes	Izegem
Glass	Seraing, Charleroi, Liège
Ham	La Roche-en-Ardenne
Harnesses	Ellezelles
Heraldry	Temse
Hops	Poperinge

Hosiery	Quevaucamps
Iguanodon	Bernissart
Lace	Kortrijk, Brussels
Leather	Peruwelz
Masks	Binche
Nativity cribs	Manderfeld
Playing cards	Turnhout
Processions	Mons
Ribbons	Comines
Roots	Amel
Strawberries	Wépion
Taxidermy	Turnhout
Textiles	Oelegem
Tobacco	Wervik, Harelbeke, Vressesur-Semois
Traditional Flemish buildings	Bokrijk
Weapons	Liège, Brussels

Theme Parks

Belgium boasts several theme and adventure parks of which the best known is probably Walibi (http://www.walibi.be) near Wavre. In 1997, a car running along Walibi's 360-degree loop-the-loop ride suffered a mechanical failure and left its passengers dangling upside down for over half an hour. Fortunately, everyone was strapped in securely. But it was a major blow to its public relations: the park's advertising jingle was rapidly reworded as the popular joke version: '*Walibi-bi-bi, tête en bas bas bas*' ('Walibi-bi-bi, head hangs down-down-down').

Ports and Waterways

The port of Antwerp is Europe's second largest port (after Rotterdam). Bristling with petrochemical refinery towers, one couldn't call it beautiful, but the sheer scale of it is impressive.

The amazing lock gate systems serving the waterways of Belgium would be of interest to the engineer-tourist. The four hydraulic boat-lifts on the Canal du Centre between Houdeng and Bracquegnies are considered by some industrial architects to be the horizontal waterway equivalent of the Eiffel Tower. More modern, but as remarkable, is the 1967 plan incliné at Ronquières (tours are conducted from May to August only). Here, barges get into a huge, moveable bathtub in which they're wheeled up or down a long 5-degree slope, achieving a height difference of 67 m (220 feet) and saving dozens of lock gates. The Strépy Thieu boat-elevator achieves an essentially similar aim using a 110-m (361-ft) high rotating carrousel, capable of transporting four ships at a time (two up, two down) through a vertical height of 73 m (240 feet). The project was only officially inaugurated in 2002 and cost over € 500 million. Flemish spoilsports protested about this 'waste' of money (the project being in Wallonia) by ceremonially driving truckloads of cash and dumping it in the nearby canal. Don't worry, the money was fake.

Beauty Spots

It's intriguing to see what Belgians place in this category: a typical selection might include the Zwin's extensive sand-dune nature reserve east of Knokke-Heist, the Signal de Botrange, which is Belgium's highest point, or the Tombeau du Géant, a curl of forested valley in the Ardennes.

None of these do much for me. The popular areas of the Ardennes are either thickly forested with coniferous monoculture or littered with unexciting holiday homes and caravan parks full of curiously satisfied Dutch tourists. And while the Zwin is a refreshing break from the otherwise concrete blighted strip of coastal towns, it hardly warrants a special journey unless you're a birdwatcher. Personally, I prefer the vistas along tree-lined canals (e.g. north of Damme), the majestic beech forest of the Forêt de Soignes/ Zoniënwoud (south-east of Brussels) and the rolling hillside patchworks of woods and farmland that you find in small enclaves throughout the central areas of Wallonia (e.g. near Spontin and Crupet).

Caves

In the Ardennes region, there are some curious geological features and several cave systems you can explore. Look for the French term *grottes*, (though this can also apply to religious grottoes graced with a Virgin Mary statue à la Lourdes). You can visit caves at Sougné-Remouchamps and at Rochefort. But the Grottes de Han at Han-sur-Lesse, between Namur and Luxembourg, are probably the most impressive for a casual visit as the tour is by tram.

Superstitious Spots

Although Belgians are a generally level-headed people, they have numerous pilgrimage spots (Banneux, Scherpenheuvel, St Hubert, etc.) and a couple of very celebrated ways to score a free wish. One is to rub the head of the Grand Garde monkey on the wall of Mons town hall. Another is to touch the brass arm of Everard 't Serclaes just across the arched passage from the city hall on Brussels' Grand Place. 'T Serclaes was the celebrated deputy mayor of Brussels who had fought as a military leader against the count of Flanders. Whether or not his 1388 murder was really the work of the lord of Gaasbeek, the people of Brussels burnt down the Gaasbeek castle in revenge.

The deathbed statue of Everard 't Sercleas needs periodic repairs as superstitious Brussels citizens rub holes into the brass of his right arm.

Country Villages and Small Towns

Belgium is much less noted for its quaint villages than for its historic towns. All too often the soaring church spire and graciously walled, fortified farms are overwhelmed by a preponderance of sturdy, practical but characterless modern brick homes as one village sprawls formlessly into the next. Nonetheless, some cosy and attractive country villages and small towns include the following.

- Bouillon
  Castle-town that was sold by Duke Godfrey to pay for the first crusade
- Chimay
  Beer and castle town
- Crupet
  Sweet village overlooking a picturesque moated manor house. Famous for trout.
- Damme
  Historic and quaint canal-side village popularly visited on a boat trip from nearby Bruges
- Dinant
  Squeezed between cliffs and the river Meuse and overlooked by an extensive fortress. Traffic jams can be off-putting on summer weekends.
- Durbuy
  Based on dubious Francophone definitions, Durbuy is touted as the 'world's smallest town', and is still not much bigger than it was in 1331. When the population reached 10,000. the event merited a TV report.
- La Roche-en-Ardennes
  Castle ruins above a small town on a hilly bend on the river Ourthe
- Melin and Lô
  Two examples of unremarkable if pretty villages with archetypal fortified farms

OVERNIGHT ACCOMMODATION

As well as hotels, most towns have campsites, B&Bs (known as *chambres d'hôtes/gastenkamers*) and *gîtes/ langdelijke verblijven* (self-catering rural accommodation typically rented by the week). There are over 30 youth hostels (http://www.vjh.be), though several operate only in summer. Technically ,Wallonia has a separate federation (Wallonia Youth Hostel Federation, http://www.laj.be) from that of Flanders (Flemish Youth Hostel Federation, http://www.vjh.be).

Sometimes with *chambres d'hôtes* and *gîtes*, room prices for one person are listed, assuming a twin-sharing arrangement. Also, you should look very carefully at the supplements list before deciding that the place is a good deal; it is not an uncommon practice to add a considerable fee for stays of only one or two nights.

Hikers' cabins are sometimes available especially in Flanders. They hold up to five people in each cabin and you'll need your own sleeping bag. Get a copy of the useful pamphlet 'Trekkershutten in Zuid Nederland en Vlaanderen' from tourist offices.

INFORMATION ON EVENTS
Tourist Offices
Contact tourist authorities for regularly updated schedules of events. The central Belgian Tourist Office is helpful (call tel: (02) 504-0390 then press '4' for information in English) and can answer many questions on the more major events.

For less widely publicised events (of which there are thousands), call the local or provincial tourist offices or refer to the Wednesday edition of *Le Soir* newspaper whose 'MAD' section has a 'what's on' listing that covers events nationwide (in French).

Tourism Websites
- General
  http://www.visitbelgium.com
- Flanders/Brussels
  http://www.visitflanders.com
- Wallonia/Brussels
  http://www.belgium-tourism.net/
- Brussels
  http://www.brussels.irisnet.be

Provincial Tourist Offices

- Antwerp
  Tel: (03) 240-6373
  Website: http://www.tourprovantwerp.be
- East Flanders
  Tel: (09) 267-7020
  Website: http://www.tov.be/ (in Flemish)
- Flemish Brabant
  Tel: (016) 267-620
  Website: http://www.vlaamsbrabant.be/
- Hainaut
  Tel: (065) 360-464/(069) 354-285
  Website: http://www.hainaut.be/tourisme/ (in French)
- Liège
  Tel: (04) 232-6510
  Website: http://www.ftpl.be
- Limburg
  Tel: (011) 237-450
  Website: http://www.toerismelimburg.be (in Flemish)
- Luxembourg
  Tel: (084) 411-011
  Website: http://www.ftlb.be
- Namur
  Tel: (081) 749-900
  Website: http://www.ftpn.be
- Walloon Brabant
  Tel: (02) 351-1200
  Website: http://www.brabantwallon.be
- West Flanders
  Tel: (050) 380-296
  Website: http://www.westtoerisme.be

Town Tourist Offices

Most towns also have their own tourist office. Websites are usually in the form 'http://www.townname.be'. Site standards vary considerably. Otherwise try telephoning.

- Aalst   tel: (053) 732-270
- Aarschot   tel: (016) 569-705
- Antwerp   tel: (03) 232-0103

- Arlon   tel: (063) 220-256/216-360
- Bastogne   tel: (061) 215-790 /212-711
- Binche   tel: (064) 336 727
- Bouillon   tel: (061) 466-257
- Bruges   tel: (050) 448-624
- Brussels   tel: (02) 513-8940
- Charleroi   tel: (071) 866-152
- Chaudfontaine   tel: (04) 361-5630
- Dendermonde   tel: (052) 213-956
- Diksmuide   tel: (051) 519-146
- Dinant   tel: (082) 222-870
- Durbuy   tel: (086) 212-428
- Eupen   tel: (087) 553-450
- Geel   tel: (014) 570-950
- Genk   tel: (089) 309-561
- Gent   tel: (09) 225-3641
- Hasselt   tel: (011) 239-540
- Opheylissem/Hélécine   tel: (019) 655-100
- Herenthals   tel: (014) 219-088
- Huy   tel: (085) 212-915
- Ieper (Ypres)   tel: (057) 228-584
- Jodoigne   tel: (010) 819-951
- Kortrijk   tel: (056) 239-371
- Leuven   tel: (016) 211-539
- Liège   tel: (04) 221-9221
- Lier   tel: (03) 488-3888
- Maaseik   tel: (089) 566-372
- Malmédy   tel: (080) 330-250
- Mesen   tel: (057) 445-040
- Mons   tel: (065) 335-580
- Oostduin-kerke   tel: (058) 532-121
- Ostend   tel: (059) 701-199
- Oudenaarde   tel: (055) 317-251
- Passendale   tel: (051) 770-441
- Poperinge   tel: (057) 334-081
- Roeselare   tel: (051) 262-450
- St-Niklaas   tel: (03) 777-2704
- St-Truiden   tel: (011) 701-818
- St-Vith   tel: (080) 221-137

- Seraing   tel: (04) 336-6616
- Soignies   tel: (067) 347-376
- Spa   tel: (087) 795-353
- Stavelot   tel: (080) 862-706
- Tongeren   tel: (012) 390-255
- Tournai   tel: (069) 222-045
- Turnhout   tel: (014) 443-355
- Verne   tel: (058) 330-531
- Verviers   tel: (087) 307-926
- Visé   tel: (04) 379-6263
- Waterloo   tel: (02) 354-9910
- Westerlo   tel: (014) 545-428

CHAPTER 8

LANGUAGE

'Trop is te veel'
('Enough is enough')
—Classic Belgian aphorism combining French and Flemish
words and summing up many people's frustration with
everything from VAT on restaurants to the endless challenge
of the language divide.

FLEMISH AND FRENCH ARE THE MAIN LANGUAGES. However, Belgium is officially trilingual: German, the third language is spoken as a mother tongue by a mere 68,000 nationals in the far east

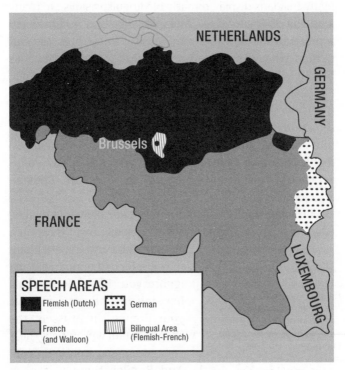

There are three Linguistic Communities in Belgium, one for each of the three main languages spoken.

of the country around Eupen. Even this three-way split is an over-simplification. There are several sub-dialects of Flemish and a variety of almost mutually unintelligible Walloon languages, only loosely based on French. And in the capital, there's the unique 'cockneyesque' Bruxellois dialect, spoken in the small Marolles area.

Help Available

Luckily for resident foreigners, there is a plethora of language courses available through local community colleges, at a relatively modest fee (around € 80 per year). Typically, these run weekly from October to May but you'll often need to sign up at a special college open day as early as June.

MULTILINGUAL BELGIANS

Many Belgians display remarkable linguistic skills.. In many jobs, the ability to speak multiple languages is considered a prerequisite. In an extreme case, I know of a 16-year-old lad who was refused a part-time job at McDonald's because he was 'only' bilingual—they wanted French, Flemish AND English from their burger salesmen. Some Brussels communes are short of policemen because the candidates flunk their language examinations. Even minor job postings might ask for two 'extra' languages: that's on top of French/Flemish AND English. My wife's secretary speaks French, English, German, Russian and Turkish.

The relative abundance of English speakers is a double-edged sword for long-term visitors. Speak bad French in a shop in Paris and the attendant may just tut bad-temperedly and ignore you. But at least you'll have an incentive to improve your French. In Brussels, the shop assistant will probably hear your accent and reply in English. And English fluency is even higher amongst the Flemish.

You'll almost always find someone who'll understand your English in Belgium, so it is not entirely necessary to learn the language(s) in order to survive. However, without at least one local language, escaping the expatriate circus and delving into the real culture will prove pretty much impossible.

Many locals speak excellent English but are not always aware of the funnier nuances, as you can see from name of this fishmonger's shop!

WHY DO THEY SPEAK ENGLISH SO WELL?

There are several theories. Generally, the Flemish seem more fluent than the Francophones, a fact put down to the more limiting nature of a 'small' language and, more likely, to the constant exposure to English on TV. The Flemish/Dutch market is apparently too small to justify dubbing TV shows. So when they sit glued to *The Simpsons*, Flemish kids are actually learning English. Francophones have the mixed blessing of pre-dubbed films aimed at the bigger French market, though in many cases, movies are offered in a choice of versions: dubbed or in Version Originale (VO) i.e. subtitled.

In the linguistic war, rather than speaking each other's language, English can at times be a diplomatic compromise for communication between French- and Flemish-speaking Belgians. Using English in advertising in bilingual areas or for pan-Belgian advertising slogans also saves the awkward decision of which language to place above the other.

FLEMISH AND NEDERLANDS

Flemish (Vlaams) is essentially a localised form of Dutch. At school, Flemish kids learn to read and write in Nederlands (the official name for the Dutch language). But between

Vlaams and Nederlands, there are many differences in vocabulary and some in structure and expression. Differences are distinctive enough that Nederlands-speakers are unlikely to confuse a Dutchman and a Belgian.

Flemish Dialects

Linguists once analysed the Dutch language into five main dialect groups, each subdivided into half a dozen sub-languages. Fortunately, many of these are only spoken within the Netherlands, and a mere dozen or so in Belgium. From 1893 to the 1960s, efforts were made to overcome this regionalism and create a standardised, officially 'correct' Flemish language. The result was not to everyone's taste: some considered it a sort of Flemish Esperanto. Verkaveling-svlaams, it was wittily dubbed by journalist Geert Van Istendael (a *verkaveling* being a characterless suburban housing development).

In reality, the old dialects continue to heavily affect the sound of Flemish spoken in the regions—from the languorous sloth of the Limburg accent to the 'sh-sh-shluring' sounds that give Aalst a reputation for producing the ugliest accent in Flanders. In Aalst dialect, 'Aalst' is pronounced 'Olsht'.

The most notable differences between Nederlands and standard Flemish show up in cases when a word of French extraction is used. Typically, Flemish tries to be more Dutch than the Dutch, and will often create a Flemish-sounding word where a Dutch-Nederlands-speakers would adopt the French word into their language. Thus, the Dutch call a spin dryer a *centrifuge* while the Flemish use the term *droogzwierder*. A sidewalk or pavement in Dutch is the same as the French word *trottoir*, but the Flemish use the word *voetpad*.

Flemish and Dutch Pronunciation

Flemish-Dutch transliteration is pretty systematic, but the following letters are pronounced rather differently from the way English speakers anticipate. Watch especially for double-letter vowels which suggest a lengthening rather than an alteration of the single-letter sound. Logically, this is eminently more systematic than in English and offers the bonus effect of keeping most Anglophones hopelessly confused.

Flemish Pronunciation Guide

Vowels

- **e**   like the *e* in *met*
- **ee**   like the *a* in *mate*
- **i**   like *ee* in *meet*
- **ij**   is effectively a single-letter vowel pronounced somewhere between *y* in *my* and the *ay* in *may*
- **o**   like the *o* in *mop*
- **oe**   like the *oo* in *moon* but a little less rounded
- **oo**   like the *o* in *mope*
- **u**   like a German *ü*
- **uu**   similar to German *ü* but longer
- **ui**   like *oh* said by a sneering upper-class toff attempting a Peter Sellers' mock French accent

Consonants

- **ch**   is a raspy *kh* sound
- **gh**   is similar to *kh* but slightly softer
- **g**   is a throaty *h!*. Many soccer fans know this thanks to the fame of Ruud Gullit (Rude H!oollit). Van Gogh was in fact Van H!okh.
- **j**   is a soft *y* sound as in *yes*

Eye-catching Flemish Details
Putting 't in Front of a Noun

This is not a crude attempt of Flemings to pretend that they're from Yorkshire. However, the **'t** does serve a similar grammatical purpose; it denotes 'the' (short for *het*, the neuter definite article).

Some nationalists have suggested that referring to the Flemish Lion (the national symbol) as Het Leeuw (neuter) would set it immediately apart from any less patriotic De Leeuw (masculine) that one might see in Antwerp's zoo.

The tje Suffix

This suffix implies 'smallness'. Thus a *potje* would be a 'little pot', while a *pintje* is a small beer ('little pint'). Applied to a close friend's name, the *-tje* ending can create a cute-sounding term of affection. But it might be fighting talk between two burly lumberjacks.

FRENCH-FRENCH VERSUS BELGIAN-FRENCH

Standard Belgian-French is not the same as French spoken in France, although the differences are no greater than that between American and British English.

On my first visit to the United States, I was bemused by waggish Americans using the peculiar greetings 'Hello bloke' and 'pip pip' with a Dick van Dyke fake-cockney accent. They apparently believed these strange phrases to be examples of archetypal English. The French-French seem to have a similar misconception that Belgians plonk the phrase *une fois* at the end of every other sentence. In the Belgium I know, the only time you're likely to hear this is in a signalled self-mimicking comedy sketch. However, there are some very real ways in which Belgian French does vary from that of France itself.

Numbers

The French-French count some of their numbers in base 20. Thus 96 is *quatre-vingt seize* (4x20 + 16). As far as I know it's the only European language to do so with the exception of Kartuli (the language of ex-Soviet Georgia). The practical Belgians have no truck with such oddities. Francophone Belgians call 70 *septante* rather than *soixante-dix*, and 90 *nonante* rather than *quatre vingt dix*. This is a common-sense solution that French-French snobbishly derides, much in the way that priggishly self-righteous Brits can't abide spelling 'colour' as 'color' in the common-sense American fashion. Strangely, Belgian-French does, however, keep the term *quatre-vingt* (4x20) for 80. Perhaps this is to prove that they too are capable of a little Latin idiosyncrasy. Or that they're not Swiss.

Le Lunch

Francophone Belgians suffer less from the terrors of Anglicised terminology (commonly nicknamed Franglais) than their Gallic cousins and there's no Belgian language police to prevent the spread of *le job*, *le weekend*, or *le board-meeting*. Belgians are not self-conscious in avoiding *le stress* by sitting down to *un bon lunch*, which is likely to be very *bon* indeed.

Too Cold or Too Familiar?

If you speak French, you'll realise that *tu* and *vous* both mean 'you'. But deciding which of the two terms to use in conversation is a diplomatic minefield. The standard rule is to use *tu* when speaking to children, family and close friends, and *vous* to pretty much anyone else you meet, unless the older of you gallantly suggests a switch to a friendlier *tu*. Using *vous* with a lover suggests you're angry with him or her. Using *tu* with your boss is downright insolent. At least that is the rule of thumb in France.

However, Francophone Belgians are noticeably quicker than the French in switching to *tu* and thus tend to think of the French as cold or arrogant. Meanwhile, the French see the Belgians as over-familiar. Watch the discomfort that results. Incidentally, inappropriate *tu* familiarity is accepted from foreigners—Moroccan and Turkish shopkeepers, particularly—whose total disdain of the *vous* is usually taken to be quaint and endearing rather than insulting. Note that in contrast, *vous* is used in some Walloon dialects in virtually any case without any implied formality. Indeed, my wife's aged Walloon aunt used to address her own mother as *vous* and still uses the term to address her sister.

Belgian-French Pronunciation

Exactly where thickly-accented Belgian-French blends into Walloon dialect remains a blurred line. The nasal *nin* ('not') used by some Walloons instead of the correct French *pas* is more than a pronunciational difference. But it is likely to be understood locally and is handy if you want to imitate the dull, flat Namur twang for deadpan comic effect.

French Belgian Pronunciation

Learning French pronunciation takes lots of time (or plenty of wine). Here, however, we will simply consider the differences between standard French pronunciation and that of Belgian-French. Most importantly, the Belgian **w** is correctly pronounced *w*, just as in English. That means that 'Waterloo' is indeed 'Waterloo', not 'Vaterloo' as the French-French insist on mispronouncing it. Otherwise, Belgian-French accents tend to extend vowels and often gargle exaggeratedly throaty sounds where textbook French has none—e.g. 'graaf' for *grave* ('bad'). Similarly a hard *kh* sound is thrown gratuitously into innocent words like *mon cher* ('my dear') which becomes more like 'mo' shairkh'. While such examples are commonly considered somewhat lower class, they can also be used deliberately to great comic effect.

USING FRANCOPHONE COMPUTERS

Francophone Belgian computer users often prefer to use the English operating system than the French one. Not surprising when a simple term like 'font' is rendered as the awkward mouthful: *police de caractères*.

Anglophone touch-typists are in for a shock if the keyboard has been designed for French-speaking users. While most of the keys seem to be in place, the Q and A keys have been swapped, as have Z and W. This so-called 'AZERTY' format also forces you to use the shift/upper case keys for numbers and full stops. This is to provide keys for accented letters, so typing what you'd expect to be '27.90' comes out as 'éè;çà'.

TRANSLATED SAYINGS

Enough is enough. *Trop is te veel*. There are hundreds of proverbs and sayings in any language. But the latter is most archetypally Belgian. Combining French and Flemish, it neatly displays a shared (if often exaggerated) exasperation that perversely unifies the antagonistic linguistic communities... especially when used to grumble against taxes. The phrase is commonly seen on bumper stickers and restaurant flyers calling for less VAT on feasting.

Idioms

Some English idiomatic sayings translate rather differently from their Flemish and French equivalents:

- English   For next to nothing/for peanuts
  Flemish For an apple and an egg
  French   For a mouthful of bread
- English   You can't have your cake and eat it
  French   You can't have the butter and the money of the butter
- English   I won't beat about the bush
  French   I won't take four routes to get there
- English   It's nowhere near ready
  Flemish It's not near the door

WALLOON

Mô m'tièsse means 'My head aches'
[*mô* is 'hurt', *m'* is 'my' and *tièsse* (or *tchess*) is 'head'].

And so it does when I try to take in all the swirling varieties of Walloon dialect. Walloon is based on French but only in the most tenuous of fashions. And to talk of Walloon in the singular is not really appropriate—it can be subdivided into several dialects that barely resemble one another.

For example, in standard French, 'watch out' is *attention*. In some Walloon dialects, it's very similar: *atincion*. In Liège, a possible alternative is *astème*. In Binche, you could shout *arwête!*

While older people still speak Walloon, it is not taught in school. Although Walloon is mostly an oral language, there have been plays written in Walloon, and the Assimil series publishes a pocket Walloon phrase book with words in the Charleroi, Namur and Liège sub-dialects.

Website

The French language website:

      http://users.skynet.be/lorint/croejh/

has an extensive vocabulary and grammar of Walloon.

BRUXELLOIS

Bruxellois is the patois language of old Brussels, an entertaining mix of French and Flemish, with odd words of Spanish and Hebrew extraction thrown in. Bruxellois native speakers are typified by the old men that you find propping up bars around the Place du Jeu de Balle of a morning. Au Laboreur (a marvellous olde-style bar on the rue de Flandres) is another great place to hear snatches. Bruxellois turns of phrase have most locals in hysterics, and the population at large uses certain Bruxellois terms to add humour to a conversation. But as with using Cockney rhyming slang, the comic effect is only as good as your attempt to mimic the accent. Use copious *rkh* sounds where an *r* should do. Stress other consonants that lie dormant in French. And spice up your speech with a few linguistic malapropisms. *Ça dépend de ce que vous voulez dire* in correct French, would be *Ça depende de quoi ske tu veux dire* in Bruxellois.

Another way to get a Bruxellois twang is to use the suffix *-ke* (effectively a version of the Flemish *tje*, meaning 'little') to certain French words. For example, in French *une fille* is 'a girl', *ma fille* is 'my daughter', while (dangerously) *fille* said alone is 'prostitute'. In Bruxellois, adding the *-ke* suffix to the word takes away the sting; *filleke* is a friendly, jovial way of saying 'young lady'.

In Brussels' Marolles district, street signs are sometimes trilingual in French, Flemish and Bruxellois.

Some streets signs in the Marolles district now have trilingual road signs—French, Flemish, and Bruxellois. The difference is not always minor, e.g. Rue du Faucon (in French) = Valkstraat (in Flemish) = de Builestroet (in Bruxellois). Classic Bruxellois plays, *Bosmans et Coppenole* and *Le Mariage de Mademoiselle Beulemans* are still available on video. A teach-yourself guide to Bruxellois, *Le Bruxellois en 70 Leçons* caused considerable media interest when published in 1999.

Some Bruxellois Words and Phrases

Brol	stuff, things
Chârel	a genius
Chouke/Chikske	darling
Dikke Papzak	fatso
Echte Brusseleirs	real Bruxellois
Façade klasher	a classic insult, now used with humour. The term literally means 'bad painter' referring to Hitler and his lack of talent as an artist
Fieu	mate, old chap (from *mon vieux*)
Fieutje	my friend/mate
Godverdoem	bloody hell
Jeannette	gay/homosexual. Note *voeile jeannette* by contrast means slag/whore (female)
Schuun	attractive
Schuunmeike	cute babe (nice looking young woman)
Schuune brol	cool stuff
Skhieve lavbo	literally 'twisted wash-basin. A classic if archaic term of abuse.
Spinnekop	spider
Tich (tish)	penis

Tishke	literally 'little penis', but actually meaning 'young lad'
Tof	good, cool
Tout près	literally 'very near' in the French language. When appended to a Bruxellois phrase it's effectively meaningless. A bit like 'you know' or '...like', often added willy-nilly to sentences in English.
Zoug	someone who goes on and on at needless length
Zwanze	joke
Zwanzeur	joker
Zot	twit

For more Bruxellois gems read Roger Kervin de Marke ten Driessche's classic *Marollian fables: Les Fables de Pitje Schramouille* which is republished by Editions Labor.

BELGIAN GERMAN

Although German is spoken by a tiny minority of Belgians, specialist linguists have still managed to divide Belgian-German into two sub-dialects: Ripuarisch, spoken in Eupen and Mosel Franconian, in St Vith. Both tends to somewhat harden the throaty German *ch* sound towards an outright *k* and give the *i* sound a more Dutch *ij* twang.

An official German-language community is recognised in nine municipalities of the Ostkantonen (Eastern Cantons) area along the country's eastern border. It has limited legal powers, and autonomy in matters relating to culture, health, and education. Public services are in German and officials must be able to speak the language, although many signs are bilingual (with French). Classes in schools are conducted in the German medium but as there are no universities for the German-speaking population in Belgium, students who aren't bilingual in French or Flemish must proceed across the border for higher education.

NAMES
People's Names

Many Christian names have different forms in French, Flemish, and English. With people you meet, there's no need to attempt a translation. But with monarchs, historical figures, and especially saints (and thus church names), it can be useful to know each form. While some are very similar (Nicholas and Niklaas, Marie and Maria). some are more divergent. (*See the list below and in* Chapter 10: Fast Facts, *page 256.*) Traditionally, many Francophones were christened with three Christian names, of which the last was frequently Ghislain/Ghislaine— a superstitious mantra for good health. Note that Belgian women keep their original family names after marriage, although their children adopt the father's surname.

French	Flemish	English
Arnaud	Arend	Arnold
Baudouin	Boudewijn	Baldwin
Catherine	Katelijn	Catherine
Charles	Karel	Charles
Étienne	Steven	Steven
François	Frans	Francis
also as Tchantchès in Liège Walloon, and Susse/Sus/Suske in Bruxellois		
Gaspard	Kasper	Casper
Godefroy	Godfried	Godfrey
Georges	Joris, George	George
Géry	Gorik	
Gudule	Goedele	
Guillaume	Willem	William
Jacques	Jacob	James
Jean	Jan, Johannes, Hans	John
Jeanne	Johanna, Hanna	Jane/Joanna/Hanna
Laurent	Laurens	Lawrence

French	Flemish	English
Louis	Lodewijk	Louis/Ludwig
Philippe	Filip	Philip
also Flupke in Bruxellois slang		
Pierre	Pieter, Petrus	Peter
Yves	Ivo	

What's in a Name?

You might think that it's easy enough to guess by someone's surname, which language they speak. In fact it's almost impossible. Francophone families with Dutch-sounding names are common, as are Flemish family names with a distinctly French twang. The one thing that is fairly certain is that a 'de' in front of the surname indicates someone of 'breeding'. Such surnames in Belgium carry similar nuances as double-barrelled names in modern Britain—classy or snobby according to your perspective. Originally, they simply showed where a family came from; 'de' literally means 'of'. Hence, the derivation of the unfortunate name Death (de Ath) whose forbears may be traced back to the Hainaut town of Ath, besieged by Louis XIV in 1667.

Geopolitical Names

There's plenty to get confused about. Single geographical terms often represent an entity whose extent has varied substantially over time. Flanders once stretched well into what is now France. There's a Limburg Province in the Netherlands as well as one in Belgium. Liège, like Namur and Antwerp, is the name of a city as well as that of a province, and historically was an independent prince-bishopric. Luxembourg (or Luxemburg) might refer to the independent Grand Duchy or to the Belgian province.

Just as many foreigners don't appreciate the difference between the British Isles (the UK and Ireland), the United Kingdom (a nation state) and Great Britain (geographical term for the biggest island of the UK), so some people get mixed up with the terms Low Countries (a geographical term referring to the Netherlands and Belgium), Netherlands

This memorial to a great Brussels mayor is bilingual—
he's Charles Bulls in French and Karel Buls in Flemish.

(a nation state of the EU), and Holland (a province of the Netherlands, although often used colloquially to refer to the whole of the Netherlands).

Tourist offices have created an additional confusion by marketing the whole of Wallonia under the title Ardennes, though the latter is geographically limited to the hilly south-eastern corner of the region.

Place Names

Outside Brussels, road signs tend to use only the local language version of a name. This is fine for street signs but gets ludicrous for signs pointing to faraway places e.g. Flemish motorway signs for Paris and Lille in France point you to 'Parijs' and 'Rijsel' respectively. In Wallonia, signs directing you to the Hague and Aachen will show 'La Haye' and 'Aix-la-Chapelle' respectively. And that's nothing compared to the confusion between Belgian town names. There are simply dozens of alternative versions just waiting to catch you out. Classics include Mons (called Bergen in Flemish) and Jezus-Eik which Francophones somehow manage to translate as Notre-Dame-au-Bois. (*See* Chapter 10: Fast Facts, *page 256 for many more examples.*) And by the way, Uitrit is not the name of a town, but the term for 'exit'. You'll see this posted along motorways in Flanders, as well as pointing to the route out of towns.

NON-VERBAL COMMUNICATION
Gestures

Although not necessarily unique to Belgium, there are a few interesting gesticulations to watch out for.

(He's/she's) drunk	a loosely clenched fist, twisted swiftly about the nose. Accompanied by a manic grimace
(He's/she's) gay	make a loose fist with your left hand, then gently slap it with your right

Getting nervous!!	Hand held vertically, bring thumb and fingers together, rhythmically simulating a beating heart
You're talking too much	As in the UK, 'rabbiting on' is suggested by flapping the thumb up toward the other four fingers held horizontally simulating a chattering mouth-rather like Rod Hull's 'Emu' and is meant to be a sign to shut you up.
F*** off	Raising the right forearm jerkily against the left fist, or the similarly insulting 'one finger salute', are as potentially dangerous in Belgium as they are elsewhere. However, these are also used fairly casually as jokes between good friends—so think twice before getting angry.

Kissing

Greeting people is a social conundrum. Should you kiss their cheeks? If so, should you really go through with the full Belgian quota of three kisses. Which cheek first? I've put this question to a wide number of Belgians and the fact is that nobody seems to have hard and fast rules. Basically, do kiss the cheeks of close friends and relations, regardless of sex, and follow them for a lead as to the direction and kiss count.

Symbols

Just as Wales has its dragon and Ireland its shamrock, so Flanders is depicted by a lion and Wallonia by a rooster. The two creatures are frequently caricatured in cartoons, whether fighting or bound together by a restraining single crown. Brussels has its own symbol—a stylised yellow iris on a blue background which is said to have been the original inspiration for France's *fleur de lys* motif.

BUSINESS AND WORK

CHAPTER 9

'Americans live to work. We work to live.'
—Anonymous Belgian businessman over a very fine dinner

BELGIAN ATTITUDES TO WORK are something of a paradox. The country is, in many ways, delightfully uncommercial with a noticeable socialist lean to most governmental policy. Yet in their souls, Belgians are money-minded. The taunt 'He's no *commerçant*' was the worst thing you could say about a person in West Flanders, according to the hero's Grandpa in *The Sorrow of Belgium*. Whether to save a penny on the housekeeping, to cheat the tax man or simply to devise a moneymaking plan, most Belgians will rise to the challenge. However, when work interferes with eating a hearty dinner or offers only a marginal profit, then interest wanes very quickly. Well, why not let the Turkish or Moroccan fellow run the corner shop if he really wants to stay open after 6:30 pm?

Belgian employers generally offer relatively generous staff benefits and the average working week, 38 hours, is short compared to many other countries. Many bigger firms appear relatively inefficient but are still better than bureaucratic government organisations from which ordinary citizens have very low expectations of any kind of service.

PAY

'Positions vacant' notices in the Belgian press rarely state the salary available. You'll have to check. Like most Westerners, Belgians are not keen to disclose their income in conversation. But even if they do, they are likely to quote a monthly sum rather than an annual one. This is misleading because no full-time Belgian employee receives as little as 12 months' pay. Companies must give an extra 85 per cent of one month's salary as 'holiday pay', typically in early summer. Then at the end of December, most companies give another extra month's bonus—generous companies give two! Add to all this the luncheon vouchers, company health insurance top-ups and the relatively frequent award of a company car for people in middle management positions; no wonder the Belgians don't seem to be doing badly.

On the down side, taxes are pretty heavy. My wife has a relatively modest salary by local standards, but pays more than 50 per cent in taxes, social security and other assorted contributions.

BUSINESS ETIQUETTE

Business etiquette is not fundamentally different in Belgium than in other European nations. However, ideas on corporate gifts and tax dodging (see corruption, below) are comparatively *laissez faire*. While office staff and business-folk are expected to be reasonably smart, the standards are generally less formal than in the UK. Obviously each business sets its own standards. However, men are rarely required to wear full suits, and indeed might be considered slightly stiff for doing so. A jacket and non-matching but well-cut, semi-casual trousers is more common. Some offices don't even require ties. For women, slacks and a polo shirt are often sufficiently smart.

As in most countries, having a stock of name cards is usual for handing to contacts and customers. Don't forget to have these printed in two languages if doing business in both French- and Flemish-speaking areas. Remember that town names will usually be different in both languages, and street addresses in Brussels have Flemish and French forms.

WORKING ENVIRONMENT

Belgium has a strong socialist-leaning philosophy of labour-protection that ensures a certain sense of stability for employees. However, this can prove frustrating for foreign bosses. Those taking over a management posting in Belgium sometimes arrive imagining that they can swiftly downsize or reorganise an office or business. The reality is often a shock for those accustomed to more fluid labour markets as in the USA or Britain. While it is possible to fire staff, the procedure can be somewhat complex and time-consuming as well as potentially very expensive. The situation becomes all the more awkward when union representatives are involved.

Women are well represented in management and there's a relatively high standard of female equality in offices. Nonetheless, mildly flirtatious behaviour and comments between the sexes which might be classed 'sexist' in more 'politically correct' countries, are not generally considered as noteworthy unless they develop into genuine harassment.

SOCIALISING WITH CLIENTS AND COLLEAGUES

Corporate hospitality is alive and well in Belgium. Although the extravagance is diminishing as budgets are cut, it is still common to wine and dine potential clients at fine restaurants, and gift-giving is considered polite rather than corrupt, at least within certain boundaries. Business lunches are a common way of making discussions a little less formal.

Many larger companies have staff clubs, run occasional staff outings and might even arrange St Nicholas visits for their employee's children. A Christmas or New Year party is often organised. Although some staff do enjoy after-work drinks with colleagues, this tradition seems less common than in the UK and Belgians are generally more keen to scurry back to their comfortable homes.

BUREAUCRACY

Belgium has a thick layer of bureaucracy. And because of the multiple divisions in society between linguistic groups, communal and regional interests, and political factions, much gets duplicated.

In government jobs, there has traditionally been a high level of political interference. Again, there have been reforms but until recently, in most higher government positions, promotion relied upon your political affiliations. Ironically, that did not always mean that you were wise to join the biggest party of the ruling coalition. With postings shared amongst those with affiliations to each ruling partner, the ideal was to find who of the potential candidates were in which parties and join the party which seemed the least represented. Given the reforms, job promotion nowadays depends mainly on merit, but there is still a suspicion that for the highest posts, language balance and political affiliation remain important factors. Belgians have low expectations of their bureaucrats who are generally perceived to be lazy and unresponsive, whether or not that is actually the case.

UNIONISM

Unions in Belgium are primarily divided by political loyalty rather than by trade. There are thus three major union groupings, broadly, socialist (red), Christian (green) and less-aggressive liberal (blue). Bigger businesses are required to have a management-union committee for which a selection of union representatives is elected to represent the workers. This applies to all sectors, not just industrial labour. However, white collar employees are generally apathetic or wary—there's a middle-class disdain for unionism and union membership is quietly acknowledged to curtail any hopes of rapid promotion. On the other hand, union representatives are afforded a remarkable level of legal protection against redundancy if they can show that their dismissal had anything to do with their union activities. This even applies to those who stand for election but are not elected. In October 2005, Belgium suffered its first national strike for over a decade when the socialist unions stopped work for the day to protest controversial plans to reduce early retirement rights. The public transport system was paralysed, but much of the public supported the strike's aims.

UNEMPLOYMENT
The unemployed are paid a fairly generous allowance but, unlike in the UK, rent is not covered by the local council. Benefits are often paid indirectly through the unemployed person's trade union, and an annual 'holiday' is allowed during which time one doesn't have to show up to sign.

A surprising number of unemployed people are employed 'in black' (i.e. illegally) by businesses who thereby avoid a slew of social security obligations and can pay a lower salary to the employed 'unemployed' than to others who don't have the dole as an extra income. Attitudes toward this sort of activity seem to be surprisingly tolerant, except perhaps where the beneficiary is a 'foreigner'.

WORKING 'IN BLACK'
Anything that is 'in black' involves an element of tax avoidance. And in Belgium, the majority of the population see tax evasion as a light-hearted national sport rather than a crime. This applies particularly to the self-employed who are subject to a particularly withering fiscal barrage. By doing undeclared work, they can easily double their incomes. Customers and self-employed workmen (electricians, plumbers, etc.) are frequently in cahoots: "I don't need a receipt if you don't charge me VAT." A voucher scheme, briefly introduced in 1999, allowed you to purchase cheap credits toward various home improvement work at knock-down prices, assuming that you used reputable, tax-paying workmen who could cash the vouchers and who would declare the work to the authorities. Predictably, this proved very expensive and was rapidly scrapped.

CORRUPTION
One friend joked: "We like to think of ourselves as the small, sick boy of Europe. We're not as corrupt as Italy, but if we try a little harder we could be!" In 1988, a payment of over US$ 1.7 million from the Italian aircraft manufacturer Agusta made its way to the accounts of the governing socialist party. Hey presto!, the Belgian Army proceeded to purchase over 40 Agusta helicopters.

The 1990s also saw some pretty high-level scandals. Around a dozen ministers of the national government were sacked in various corruption cases. Most famously, Willy Claes (who had been Minister of Economics at the time) was finally pressured into resigning in 1995—a particularly newsworthy event as he had, by that stage, risen to the post of NATO Secretary General. Claes received a three-year suspended sentence.

Belgium is trying to shed its reputation as the most corrupt nation in northern Europe. However, the coalition-style government structure doesn't make radical reform at all easy. Since most of the upper bureaucracy is appointed according to political favour, a call from an MP can get rules bent, planning permission pushed through or jobs found for a nagging citizen in return for their votes and those of their grateful family. Certainly MPs all over the world meet and listen to their constituents' needs and concerns. But the Belgian MPs' *zitdag* (parliamentary surgeries) are, according to one local journalist, little more than deals for votes.

BELGIAN BUSINESSES

The archetypal Belgian industries are chocolate and beer, but of course the economy is really vastly more complex. Although no longer the world's second industrial power—a pinnacle achieved very briefly in the late 19th century—industrial companies like Electrabel, Bekaert, Beaulieu and Solvay remain major world players. Belgium has also marketed itself very successfully as a hub for international couriers and for financial institutions. DHL has its trans-European shipment centre here. Members of the management body of SWIFT are based near Brussels and MasterCard's European operations are run from Waterloo.

Antwerp has long been and remains the world centre for diamond cutting and trading (http://www.hrd.be). It also hosts Europe's biggest petroleum refinery and second biggest port.

CURRENCY AND MONEY

Most Belgians were relatively unperturbed to see their once stable currency subsumed within the Euro. Nonetheless, you'll still find that some older locals think in Belgian Francs ('BEF') especially when discussing salaries or house prices. Thanks to a historical quirk in exchange rates and inflation indices, the BEF used to be one of the world's most sensibly denominated currencies: the smallest unit you ever needed was 1 BEF, although ½ franc coins did exist.

Belgians are as paradoxical in their attitudes to money as in their business sense. It's considered sensibly practical that advertisements appear on state radio and TV (despite a licence fee) and sponsors even pay for certain communes' road signs. Many housewives and old ladies assiduously plough through the dozens of free magazines and supermarket flyers that clog up the mail, searching for bargains and coupons. Meanwhile the same individuals will have you believe that there are some stores that are just too 'low-class' to be seen in.

FAST FACTS

CHAPTER 10

'Churchill called Russia a riddle wrapped
in mystery inside an enigma.
Belgium's the same but with better beer.'
—Magnus Guppy,
hospital consultant, savant and Belgophile

Official Name
Kingdom of Belgium (English), Belgique (French), België (Flemish), Belgien (German)

Capital
Brussels

Flag
Three vertical bands of equal width in the colours (from left to right) black, yellow and red

National Anthem
La Brabançonne (The Song of Brabant)

Time
Greenwich Mean Time plus 1 hours (GMT +0100) but plus 2 hours (GMT +0200) from the last Sunday of April to the last Sunday of October). This is Central European time, the same as most of the EU, but one hour ahead of the UK.

Telephone Country Code
32

Area
30,519 sq km (11,780 sq miles)

Highest Point
Signal de Botrange (694 m / 2,276.9 ft)

Climate
Temperate with cool summers and mild winters

Natural Resources
Construction materials, carbonates and silica sand

Population
10,445,852 (January 2005)

Corruption Rank
Rated 19th out of 159 countries in Transparency International's 1995 Corruption Perceptions Index

Religion
Roman Catholic (75 per cent), Muslim (4 per cent). The make-up of the remaining 21 per cent is hard to define and varies greatly according to definitions.

Languages Spoken
Flemish (57 per cent), French (42 per cent), German (less than 1 per cent)

Average Lifespan
Men   74.8 years
Women   81.1 years.
Flemish people on average live 2.5 years longer than those in Wallonia.

Quality of Living Rating
Fifth highest in the world

Currency
Euro (€)

Gross Domestic Product (GDP)
US$ 316.2 billion (2004 est.)

Agricultural Products
Fruits, grain, sugar beets, tobacco, vegetables, beef, milk, pork and veal

Other Products
Beer, cut-diamonds, chocolate, glassware, mineral water

Industries
Basic metals, chemicals, engineering and metal products, glass, motor vehicle assembly, petroleum, beverages, food processing, textiles, transportation equipment and scientific instruments

Exports
Chemicals, diamonds, foodstuffs, beverages, pharmaceuticals, machinery and equipment, metals and oil products

Imports
Chemicals, diamonds, foodstuffs, oil products, machinery and equipment, pharmaceuticals, and transportation equipment

Airports
Estimated total of 43, of which 25 have paved runways. The main international airport is in Brussels

Electricity
220V/50Hz, plugs have either two (unearthed) or three (earthed) round pins

Videos
PAL system

Weights and Measures
Standard Metric System
1 km   =   0.62 miles
1 m   =   approximately 3.28 ft
1 kg   =   2.21 lbs
1 litre =   2.11 US pints = 1.76 British pints

Government System

Constitutional monarchy with two-house national parliament, but also with regional parliaments for three parts of the federation (Flanders, Wallonia and Brussels-Capital). Add to that a separate parliament for the linguistic communities, electoral arondisements, ten provinces and 589 highly autonomous 'communes', each with their own mayors. That's plenty to keep even the keenest politicos confused. See below for more details.

In Office	
King	Albert II (since 1993)
Prime Minister	Guy Verhofstadt (since 1999)

THE FEDERAL GOVERNMENT

On paper, the Belgian king (*see* Chapter 3: The Belgian People, *pages 34*) has greater power than most of Europe's constitutional monarchs. But in reality, he rarely uses his authority. Much more power lies with the national Federal

Parliament (Federale Kamers/Chambres Fédérales). This is divided into two parliamentary houses, nominally similar to those in the United States. The Senate (Senaat/Sénat) has 71 members, 40 of which are elected by the people every four years. Once elected, they get to choose the other 31 members. It's a curious system where linguistic concerns demand that certain quotas of senators come from certain language backgrounds or live in certain regions.

The House of Representatives (Kamer van Volksvertegen-woordigers/Chambre des Représentants) is elected entirely by the people, also on a four-year cycle. There are 18 ministers at national level including the Prime Minister and the Secretaries of State. There is a bewildering choice of political parties (over 40 for the 2003 elections) and public interest in politics isn't helped by the fact that many parties change names, split or combine every few years. The prime minister, typically but not always from the best-represented party, hammers out a working relationship between enough parties to create a majority coalition. The result is that ministers are frequently drawn from a variety of parties and don't necessarily share the same philosophy. In addition, there are special government commissioners charged with sorting out pressing issues of the day; at present, working on food safety, metropolitan policy (read unemployment), and 'administrative simplification'.

Below is a list of the main parties listed according to the approximate order of votes won in 2003. Those marked * are members of the far from cohesive governing coalition:

VLD*	Vlaamse Liberalen en Democraten Website: http://www.vld.be Flemish Liberals and Democrats. Prime Minister Verhofstadt's party.
sp.a*	Socialistische Partij-Anders Website: http://www.s-p-a.be Flemish Socialist/Social Democrat party, renamed August 2001

SPIRIT*	Sociaal, Progressief, Internationaal, Regionalistisch, Integraal-democratisch Toekomstgericht Website: http://www.meerspirit.be Left wing Flemish Liberals. Relatively small but formed an electoral partnership with sp.a
CD&V	Christen-Democratisch & Vlaams Website: http://www.cdenv.be Flemish Christian Democrats. Former CVP, long term ruling party of the 1980s and 1990s under ex-Prime Ministers Wilfred Martens and Jean-Luc Dehaene
PS*	Parti Socialiste Website: http://www.ps.be Francophone Socialist Party led by Elio di Rupo always seen wearing a trademark bow-tie. Much-teased, perhaps for his Poirot-esque appearance, Minister of Defence André Flahaut is also a PS member.
Vlaams Belang	Vlaams Belang Wesbite: http://www.vlaamsbelang.org Right wing Flemish Nationalists. In 2004, the former Vlaams Blok was declared to be a racist organisation. It promptly disbanded and reformed under a new name. Keeping them out of power is the main unifying feature in the present government.
MR*	Mouvement Reformateur Website: http://www. mouvementreformateur.be Didier Reynders' centre-right umbrella party combining PRL, FDF, MCC and PFF

CDH	Centre Démocrate Humaniste Website: http://www.psc.be Francophone Christian Democrats, known as PSC until May 2002. Led by Joëlle Miquet.
N-VA	Nieuw-Vlaamse Alliantie Website: http://www.n-va.be New Flemish Alliance: advocates what it calls 'humane Flemish-nationalism'. In fact, they're pretty radical.
Ecolo	Ecolo Website: http://www.ecolo.be Francophone Green party
GROEN	De Vlaamse Groenen Website: http://www.groen.be Flemish Green party, formerly Agalev.
FN	Front Nationale Right wing Francophone Nationalist party
NCD	Nieuwe Christen-Democratie Website: http://www.ncd.be New Flemish centre-right party, split from the CD&V but working with the VLD.

To make a little more sense of the system, the average Belgian voter tends to divide the parties along linguistic lines and then look for political pigeonholes: Catholic parties (CD&V and CDH), liberals (VLD, MR, NCD), or socialists (sp.a and PS). The Greens (Agalev and Ecolo) were included in the ruling coalition from 1999 but lost massively in the 2003 elections.

On TV news programmes, it's common to put a party icon beside a politician's subtitled name to give any viewer who's bothered the chance to see what party they're from. That includes even the prime minister.

As only parties gaining above a minimum threshold of the vote get to take seats in the house, electoral blocks are often formed between some smaller parties so that together they may have the necessary momentum. In 1999, the trio

FDF-PRL-MCC did this effectively (they later formed the MR), as did VU-VVD-ID21 group, elements of which later formed the N-VA.

There has been a disquieting rise in the electoral popularity of the far-right parties. Most notable is the Vlaams Belang which opinion polls now rate as the most popular party in Flanders. But there is also the xenophobic National Front which gained its first ever seat in parliament during 2003. These results should not necessarily be construed as a sign of rising fascism within Belgium. It's more a sign that the people are heartily fed up with a political status quo where little appears to get done. This was a message somewhat taken to heart in the mildly reformist 1999–2003 government. But even the popular, plucky stand against the second Iraq war by outspokenly straight-talking foreign minister Louis Michel, failed to gain electoral favour.

If anyone wanted to, they could look more closely at the policies of the Belgian political parties who post their manifestos and latest initiatives via their websites. But on the whole, people seem happier just grumbling and forgetting all about politics. Most Belgians vote, but only because it's a legal obligation. Those who don't vote are fined. This may explain the phenomenal number of spoilt and blank votes cast—over 364,000 (5.2 per cent) in 2003!

Regions and Linguistic Communities

Belgium is divided into both linguistic communities and Federal regions in a way that must be unique anywhere, especially for so small a country. The regions (Flanders, Wallonia and Brussels-Capital) are led by ministers, minister-presidents and regional parliaments, and are responsible for infrastructure, energy, water and tourism within their areas. The regions run their affairs almost as though they were separate countries. Although officially the national government remains responsible for all foreign policy, Flanders actually has its own representatives in many countries (see http://www.flanders.be) leading some observers to suggest that Flanders' 'great escape' from Belgium is already underway.

Confusingly, the country is also divided up into three Linguistic Communities. That's confusing because the linguistic communities cover similar but not the same areas as the regions. They are responsible for cultural matters, broadcasting, education and health. These also have the right to their own parliaments or councils, though the parliament of the Flemish-speaking community (Vlaamse Gemeenschap) has de facto merged with the parliament of Flanders region. The French-speaking Community (Communauté Française; htp://www.pcf.be) covers most but not all of Wallonia including French-speaking institutions in bilingual Brussels where it is based. The German-speaking Community (Deutschsprachige Gemeinschaft, htttp://www.dglive.be) covers roughly 70,000 people in Wallonia's eastern cantons around Eupen and has a council rather than a parliament. Elections for both the regional and community parliaments take place every five years.

Provinces and Arrondissements

Until federalisation, Belgium consisted of nine provinces loosely based on the ancient feudal duchies and counties. Four of these (Hainaut, Namur, Liège and Luxembourg) now form the bulk of Francophone Wallonia. Four more (Limburg, Antwerp plus East and West Flanders) make up most of Flanders. Brabant, the multilingual ninth province with Brussels at its heart, was split in the mid-1990s. Vlaams Brabant Province was added to the Flanders region, and Brabant Wallon to Wallonia. The last chunk of Brabant was left to become Brussels-Capital and is now a third region rather than a province.

Every province has a governor appointed by the king and a directly elected provincial council, but they have fairly minor importance compared to regions or communes (see below) and few Belgians seem to really notice they exist. Each province consists of between one and eight arrondisements, or electoral districts (although more than one representative will be elected for each). These don't have any administrative, organisational apparatus although certain legal functions are judged at arrondisement level. Much more power and public interest is wielded at the level of the 'commune' (town or borough municipalities) but even arrondisements can cause political controversy as they affect who votes for who. That's especially the case with Brussels. Bizarrely, although the capital is a region in its own right, that region is nonetheless WITHIN the arrondisement of Brussels-Halle-Vilvoorde encompassing all of eastern Vlaams Brabant. This anomaly allows the French-speaking communities on the Brussels periphery a chance to vote for non-Flemish candidates in elections despite living within Flanders. And this is an 'unfair' fact which infuriates Flemish nationalists. Redrawing the arrondisement more logically, however, would result in the effective disenfranchisment of a substantial Francophone population. Even though many odrinary Belgians aren't even interested and don't really understand what the fuss is all about, the result of discussions to solve the issue came close to splitting the country. So close that eventually both sides agreed to simply shut up. Is Belgium's knack of cunning compromises slipping? We will see when the whole subject returns in 2007.

The Commune (Gemeent/Commune)

The commune is the smallest organisational unit, whether it be a town, village or the equivalent of a city borough. In Belgium, the commune has considerable authority. It runs the schools, performs weddings and issues such hallowed documents as driver's licences. Until 2001, they even issued passports. However, the ease of stealing Belgian blank passports from barely guarded town halls made international news when the 2001 killers of Afghan leader Ahmad Shah Masoud were found to have thus provided themselves with apparent Belgian nationality. Indeed, newpapers reported that 19,050 passports were stolen in the 1990s, making Belgium what some called the global capital of identity fraud.

Belgium has 589 communes. There are 19 in Brussels alone, many of which have particularly grand town halls (Gemeentehuis/Maison Communale), notably St Gilles.

The mayor who leads a commune is called a *burgemeester/ bourgmestre* in Flemish/Belgian-French and has a surprising level of importance and power in comparison to the town or district councils in the UK. Mayors make self-conscious attempts to associate themselves with any event or promotion in the commune. High-profile mayors often become national or regional ministers at the same time. This is such a fact of life that there are rarely any complaints about individuals taking on too much. The public seems divided between the idea that a well-connected mayor will bring wealth to the town, and the contrary feeling that busy politicians are simply trying to get themselves rich. In fact, while many moonlighting mayors are wearing national hats, their actual day-to-day mayorial tasks are usually delegated to city aldermen.

FAMOUS BELGIANS

"Bet you can't name five famous Belgians," taunt friends who hear that I'm living in Euroland. Ironically, beyond tennis stars, the two Belgians that spring most rapidly to many minds aren't even real: Tintin, the quiffed cartoon boy and Hercule Poirot, Agatha Christie's hallmark detective, who was constantly grumbling that people think he's French.

However, you may find that you know more Belgians than you realise. The following are some notable examples. The great artists Anthony van Dyck, Peter Paul Rubens, Pieter Breughel and the 'Flemish primitives' who invented oil painting (*see* Chapter 7: Culture, Sport and Travel). James Ensor and surrealist Rene Magritte took Belgian art into the 20th century along with cartoonists like Hergé and great Art Nouveau architect Victor Horta. Musicians from Django Reinhardt to Plastic Bertrand to dEUS are/were all Belgian, as was the greatest ever 'French' singer Jacques Brel. Eddy Merckx (arguably the most famous cyclist ever) and Jacky Ickx (the motor sports champion) plastered Belgian 'ckx'es on to the sporting record books. Jean-Claude Van Damme is known to many as the 'Muscles from Brussels'. Fewer people know that Audrey Hepburn was also born there.

It's worth familiarising yourself with some of the famous and the lesser-known Belgian stars. Such knowledge is a really useful tool for fitting in and showing locals that you're interested in their culture. Many such celebrities are mentioned in the arts and sports sections of Chapter 7. For political, social and historical figures, see below.

Leaders and Religious Figures

OK, so Belgium doesn't jump to mind for flamboyant high-profile leaders. The infamous, bushy-bearded Leopold II was probably the most memorable, if not best loved, Belgian king. But Charles V, the greatest Hapsburg Holy Roman Emperor was born in Gent (*see* Chapter 2: Land and History, *page 16*) and several other historically significant leaders were born in what is now Belgium.

Few Brits realise that their English-Norman kings were so full of Belgian blood. In fact, William the Conqueror's mother Arletta was from Florennes (south of Charleroi) and his wife Mathilde was daughter of the count of Flanders (Baldwin V). The English crown might have had another strong dose of Belgian blood in the 16th century had the fake 'Richard IV' of England come to power. In 1495, a Walloon named Perkin Warbeck working as a merchant's servant in Ireland was 'discovered' to be one of the sons of England's Edward IV. In reality, those sons had actually been killed in the Tower of London; but whether blind, bribed or just potty, Margaret, Duchess of Burgundy, seemed to recognise Perkin as her nephew Richard. Eventually, with the help of scheming Scotland, Perkin attempted to invade England to claim his 'rightful throne' from Henry VII. He managed to take Cornwall while his Scots allies skirmished in Northumberland but in the end, the pretender was sent to the Tower of London just like the boy he'd imitated. The whole escapade was probably funded by Maximillian the Austro-Belgian Holy Roman Emperor.

Impress your friends by revealing that Clovis I (AD 465–511), the first major figure of the French Merovingian dynasty was born in Tournai. He created the first Frankish kingdom to cover all of Gaul (France) and his empire provided the eventual launching pad for 'King of Hearts' Charlemagne albeit with plenty of complexities in the interim. If you want to be a real smart arse, you could go on to mention that the first European 'king' of Jerusalem was Godfrey de Bouillon (1066–1099), the Belgian baron who bankrolled much of the dubious first Crusade by mortgaging his estates. Actually he was 'too modest' to use the title 'king' (preferring 'Guardian of the Holy Sepulcre') but not shy to lead the massacre of some 40,000 Muslims and Jews—that's what a pious man did in the 11th century after all. His brother Baldwin I (Baudouin I) kept Jerusalem 'Belgian' until 1118. And another Baudouin (Baldwin X of Flanders) was later to become the first crusader king of Byzantium (Istanbul). For the ultimate in Belgian trivia, reveal that Pope Adrian VI (1459–1523) was Flemish, born Adrian Florensz and previously a teacher at the then fairly new Leuven University where he educated the young Charles V in 1507. Or that the movie *Molokai* was based on the life of Belgian missionary Father Damien (1840-1889) who devoted his life to helping lepers in the Hawaiian Islands, eventually dying of the disease there.

Scientists, Inventors and Astronauts

If you've always thought that Greenland is about the size of Africa, it's probably Fleming Gerhard Kremer (1512–1594) that you have to blame. Better known as Gerardus Mercator, his Mercator cylindrical projection still remains more popular than the equal area Peters projection, which makes the world look inelegantly stretched.

Optimistically touted as Belgium's Leonardo Da Vinci, Simon Stevin (1548–1620) was the mathematician, physicist and great medieval all-rounder credited with devising the decimal system.

Georges Lemaître was the Belgian astronomer who proposed the idea of an 'evolving universe' though he remains overshadowed by his more famous friend Einstein.

If you visit the attractive town of Dinant, you'll find a rather odd looking topiary bush in the shape of a saxophone. It commemorates the locally born inventor of that instrument, Adolph Sax (1814–1894). Former US President Clinton popped by to play a tune in his honour.

Though utterly unknown beyond his homeland, many locals are proud of astronaut Dirk Frimout who was Belgium's first man in space. A second Belgian, Frank de Winne, was part of the 2002 mission to deliver a new 'escape craft' to the international space station, an extremely useful delivery as it turned out when the Challenger shuttle crashed leaving the space station crew short of a taxi to the pub.

PLACE NAMES
Variant Names of Regions

English	French	Flemish
Antwerp	Anvers	Antwerpen
Brussels-Capital	Bruxelles-Capitale	Brussels Hoofstedlijk Gewest
Flemish Brabant	Brabant Flamand	Vlaamse Brabant
Walloon Brabant	Brabant Wallon	Waals Brabant
East Flanders	Flandre Orientale	Oost Vlaanderen
West Flanders	Flandre Occidentale	West Vlaanderen
Hainaut	Hainaut	Hainaut
Limburg	Limbourg	Limburg
Liège	Liège	Luik
Luxembourg	Luxembourg	Luxemburg
Namur	Namur	Namen

Variant Names of Towns
Flemish Towns

Town	French Equivalent
Aalst	Alost
Antwerpen	Anvers
Borgloon	Looz
Brugge	Bruges
De Haan	Le Coq
De Panne	La Panne
Dendermonde	Termonde

Town	French Equivalent
Diksmuide	Dixmude
Gent	Gand (Ghent in English)
Halle	Hal
Ieper	Ypres
Mechelen	Malines
Jezus-Eik	Notre-Dame-au-Bois
Kortrijk	Courtrai
Leuven	Louvain
Lier	Lierre
Mesen	Messines
Oudenaarde	Audenarde
Roeselare	Roulers
Ronse	Renaix
Sint-Truiden	St-Trond
Veurne	Furnes
Tienen	Tirlemont
Tongeren	Tongres
Zoutleeuw	Léau

Francophone Towns

Town	Flemish Equivalent
Ath	Aat
Braine l'Alleud	Eigenbrakel (jokingly mispronounced as *Eigen braaksel* it would mean 'your own vomit')
Braine le Château	Kasteelbrakel
Braine-le-Comte	's Gravenbrakel
Enghien	Edingen
Huy	Hoeï
Mons	Bergen
Jodoigne	Geldenaken

Town	Flemish Equivalent
La Hulpe	Terhulpen
Liège	Luik (Lüttich in German)
Namur	Namen
Nivelles	Nijvel
Saintes	Sint Renelde
Soignies	Zinnik
Tournai	Doornik
Tubize	Tubeke
Waremme	Borgworm
Wavre	Waver

Many more villages have alternative names which have now been largely forgotten but appear on maps from the 1920s and earlier.

Rivers

Flemish	French
Ijzer	Yser
Leie	Lys
Maas	Meuse
Schelde	Escaut

Beyond Belgium

English	Flemish	French
Aachen	Aken	Aix-la-Chapelle
The Hague	Den Haag	La Haye
Lille	Rijsel	Lille
Lorraine	Lotharingen	Lorraine
Paris	Parijs	Paris
Gravelines	Grevelingen	Gravelines
Dunkirk	Duinkerke	Dunkerque

ACRONYMS AND OTHER BELGIAN CATCHPHRASES

AOC	Appellation d'Origine Controlée: mark awarded to a French wine from a small, carefully defined group of villages if it conforms to that area's specific stylistic and quality guidelines. These are stricter than for a *vin de pays*, which could come from anywhere within a much larger region.
Artois	Ancient county of north-western France, centred on Arras. Artois was passed to Burgundy in 1384 and thence, with Belgium, to Spain/Austria in 1493. It has been French again since occupation in 1640. However, Stella Artois remains a Belgian beer (brewed in Leuven).
a.u.b	Common abbreviation for 'please' in Flemish.
BEF	Commonly adopted abbreviation for Belgian francs, the former Belgian currency which was replaced by the Euro in January 2002.
begijnhof	Poorhouse cloister originally built as a retreat for religious women who didn't wish to to go the full distance and become nuns.
Belgae	Pre-Roman inhabitants of what is now Belgium.
Benelux	Belgium Netherlands Luxemburg. Customs union since 1948, and an economic union from 1960.

Beurs	Stock market; *bourse* in French and many other languages. While possibly derived from the Italian term 'bursa', there is a common belief that this word originates from the Van de Beurse family in whose house (still standing in Bruges), northern Europe's first mercantile exchange was hosted.
Brabançonne	The national anthem, named for the Brabançonne revolt of 1789. The final Flemish version of the words wasn't settled for over a century. Try asking a Belgian to sing it—few seem to know the words!
Bruxellois	The curious mixed French–Flemish language spoken by certain long-term residents of the capital.
collégiale	A collegiate church with its own chapter of canons but holding a religious status less than that of a cathedral
Demergothic	Architectural style of soaring, bulb-spired churches typical of Demer river towns.
EU	European Union. Brussels is its major bureaucratic hub.
foreigners	As used by Belgians, this is a generally pejorative term implying non-Europeans. Ironically, it might thus include Belgian citizens of Turkish or North African descent, yet exclude Americans, other Western Europeans, and even Japanese.

Huguenots	French Calvinists. Their support for the 16th century Dutch revolts proved insufficient to help deter Spanish interference. The term 'Huguenots' may have been derived from the surname of Besançon Hugues, the 16th century Calvinist mayor of Geneva who led the opposition to French annexation of Savoy.
luncheon vouchers	A common, legal tax fiddle to disguise part of an employee's salary. Although these vouchers can be used like cash in supermarkets (for food items) or restaurants, they don't count fiscally as 'pay' because they are officially 'purchased' by employees. Yet a typical € 5.55 voucher might only cost € 1.11! So by 'selling' them to staff, the company is actually paying over € 4 a day of extra salary tax free! Known as Cheques Repas/ Maaltijdcheques in French/Flemish.
N. D. de	Stands for 'Notre Dame de' which means 'Our Lady of...' in English. Churches are commonly thus prefixed. The Flemish equivalent is 'O.L.V.'
O.L.V op't	Onze Lieve Vrouw (see N.D. de above.)
OTSI	Office de Tourisme, Syndicat d'Initiative.Francophone citizens advice bureau and tourist office.
pintje	Flemish term for a standard 25 cl glass of draft beer.

police	Recently combined into a unified force, the police were formerly divided into commune level *politie/police* and the national *rijkswacht/gendarmerie*. The lack of communication between the two was legendary.
queuing	Despite some claims to the contrary, Belgians are not great at standing in line. If there's a clear queuing system, they'll stick fairly faithfully to it, and woe betide anyone who tries to push ahead of his/her turn in a shop. But where there can be any sense of ambiguity, the Belgian will be quick to use the excuse to get ahead, i.e. step aside for a moment and you'll lose your place.
Rode	From *rooien*, i.e. to clear forest. For some reason, this deforestation was often carried out in the name of a saint, hence the names of various towns, including St-Pieters Rode and St-Genesius-Rode.
RTBF	Radio Television Belge de la Communaute Francaise—the Francophone Belgian state TV and radio company
RTL	Radio TV Luxembourg
Sabena	The former Belgian national airline, founded in 1923 as Societé Anonyme Belge d'Exploitation de la Navigation Aérienne. It went bankrupt in 2001 and has been superseded by SN Brussels Airlines.
s.v.p	Common abbreviation for 'please' in French.

tipping	In restaurants, bars and taxis, service charges are always included so tipping is not expected (although taxi drivers try to claim otherwise). In a hairdresser's shop, one should tip everyone involved (separate people may cut, wash, perm etc.) except when the person serving you is the owner. In some theatres and cinemas, you're expected to tip the usherette 50 cents. The terms *pourboire inclus/fooi inbegrepen* translate as 'tip included'.
toilets	Men (*hommes/heren*), Women (*dames/damen*). While most cafés and hotels have toilets, department stores, exhibitions and many other places with public conveniences often have an old woman lurking at the entrance expecting 30 cents to use the facilities.
White Marches	A phenomenon of the late 1990s when whole communities marched in the streets to protest against the lack of action in the aftermath of a string of paedophile murder cases.
witches	Although Halloween is not a popular festival, there are witch marches in Nieuwpoort, Vielsalm and Beselare.
vin de table	Generic, cheap wine that doesn't qualify for AOC or even *vin de pays* status, and may be a blend of wines from unspecified vineyards.
Vlaams/ Vlaanderen	Flemish (language)/ Flanders in Flemish

VRT	Vlaams Radio-en Televisieomroep: the Flemish state TV and radio company
VTM	Vlaamse Televisie Maatschappij: Flemish private TV and radio company
VVV	Flemish citizens advice and tourist info office

CULTURE QUIZ

Time for a little fun. Below I describe eight possible situations in which you could conceivably find yourself. Choose the best available response or responses from the choices given. There are no prizes.

SITUATION 1

You're invited to the home of a married business Belgian colleague for a dinner party. Should you bring:

Ⓐ Chocolates.
Ⓑ Wine.
Ⓒ Flowers.
Ⓓ Nothing at all.

Comments

Any answer is OK except **Ⓓ**—a gift is almost always appropriate. Flowers are specially good for female colleagues or male colleagues' wives.

SITUATION 2

Late one evening, you're with some friends in a Belgian café and you've just ordered yourself a coffee. One of the half drunken regulars sidles up and asks you if you are Bob. Should you:

Ⓐ Exclaim, "How did you know?!"
Ⓑ Edge away—he's attempting a homosexual chat up line.
Ⓒ Agree and point out that you've got a long way to drive home.
Ⓓ Reply, "Robert to you, sir!"

Comments

While none of these may apply, the most appropriate answer is likely to be **Ⓒ** as Bob refers to the person in a group of drinkers who chooses not to drink alcohol in order to drive home safely. In reality, Bobs and Bobettes are rarer than they should be given the devil-may-care attitudes to drink-driving.

SITUATION 3

Around Christmastime, there's a knock at the door and there's a man claiming to be from the Post Office or Fire Brigade apparently selling a calendar. Do you:

Ⓐ Buy one.
Ⓑ Call the police.
Ⓒ Check his identification card and offer a small donation.
Ⓓ Complain that you're fed up with salesmen and tell him not to come round again.

Comments

Several of the services do send bona fide representatives to collect money for their employees' social clubs. While you're under no obligation to buy a calendar, a donation (i.e. **Ⓒ**) shows goodwill and just might be a good investment to stop letters going astray. However, do check the representative's identification documents as there are frequent cases of fakes.

SITUATION 4

You're visiting Leuven. You fancy a croissant filled with chocolate and have located a bakery that sells them. What is the most appropriate thing to say when the attendant comes to serve you?

ⓐ "Un pain au chocolat s'il vous plaît."
ⓑ "Een chokolate broodje alstublieft."
ⓒ "A chocolate croissant please."
ⓓ "Goede dag."

Comments

The best choice is **ⓓ**, i.e. saying hello before you actually ask for something! After you've said your greeting, then choose **ⓑ** as Leuven is a Flemish city. If you can't pronounce that then say **ⓒ** instead as it's probably wiser to speak English—French (i.e. **ⓐ**) is not at all appreciated in Leuven.

SITUATION 5

You're driving along the main road when a car squeals out of a side road to your right, turns left straight across your path, narrowly avoiding a crash. Do you:

ⓐ Make chase while shouting obscenities at the idiot.
ⓑ Write down the number plate of the offending car and try to find a witness.
ⓒ Grumble under your breath about Belgian road sense.
ⓓ Slow down and watch more carefully at subsequent junctions.

Comments

While **ⓒ** is a probable reaction, **ⓓ** is the only practical course of action as the *priorité à droite* rule means that legally it is you, not the driver of the other car, who was being reckless.

SITUATION 6

You've found a great vantage point where you can sit on a wall to watch a carnival procession. Suddenly, you're hit on the side of the head by an orange. You look around in time to see a man in a Tweedledum costume flinging another orange at your face. Do you:

Ⓐ Scream abuse to prevent him throwing another one.
Ⓑ Raise your middle finger in a clenched gesticulation meaning "one more".
Ⓒ Wave your arms to make yourself a more obvious target.
Ⓓ Catch the next orange and playfully lob it back at the thrower.

Comments

The only appropriate answer is **Ⓒ**. The throwing of oranges during carnivals, while occasionally a little over forceful, represents a gift of semi-religious significance. To throw it back (**Ⓓ**) is particularly bad manners. The one finger salute (**Ⓑ**) certainly doesn't mean "one more" and is gratuitously offensive. However, raising the first finger rather than the middle one is indeed a way that many people in the crowd appeal for more oranges to be thrown at them.

SITUATION 7

A Belgian acquaintance sums up typical Belgian food in a single word: *ballekes*. What does she mean?

Ⓐ She's adopting a mildly rude expletive. Such slightly coarse language, along with its implied modesty about the country's food, is typically Belgian.
Ⓑ She's using a Bruxellois term meaning 'rich' (i.e. referring to a dish traditionally only served at feasts and formal balls).
Ⓒ She means that the food seems remarkably similar to the cuisine of the Balkans.
Ⓓ She's describing a typical meatball dish.

Comments

The meaning of *ballekes* is indeed meatballs and they are typically Belgian. Answer **Ⓓ** is thus the nearest possibiliy. The other answers are patent nonsense.

SITUATION 8

Which of the following beers (Leffe, *framboise*, Jupiler, Kwak, Gordon's Highland Scotch) goes with which of the following glasses?

A Round-bottomed glass held upright in a wooden stand.

B A glass that tapers slightly from a wider top to a narrower base.

C A glass that resembles a thistle.

D An oversized wine glass with a heavy bowl and stem.

Comments

A with Kwak; **B** with Jupiler; **C** with Gordon's Highland Scotch; and **D** with Leffe. *Framboise* (raspberry beer) would usually be served in a champagne-style flute, i.e. none of the above.

DO'S AND DON'TS

DO'S

- Do ask questions that show Belgians that you're interested in their country. But watch out for joke answers. Belgian humour, like dry British sarcasm, is not necessarily signalled.
- Do restrain yourself if you have strong views on animal rights or the fur trade. Constant criticism of *foie gras* or hunting won't often win you friends.
- Do remember that the suicidal *priorité á droite* rule applies to foreigners too!
- Do telephone before making an impromptu visit to a Belgian home.
- Do be patient (but not to the extent that you get pushed out of queues).
- Do support the Red Devils (Belgium's national soccer team), but don't expect them to win too often.
- Do stay calm if someone makes what appears to be a politically incorrect statement.
- Do your shopping by Saturday as most shops are closed on Sundays.
- Do try ordering tap water in a restaurant; but only if you want to embarrass all your local friends!

DON'TS

- Don't call French speaking Belgians 'French'. They will not be flattered!
- Don't practise your French in Flanders! It would be much more tactful to speak English.
- Don't assume people speak Walloon because they live in Wallonia.
- Don't joke about apparently petty or comic displays of linguistic solidarity like De Gordel. They are serious.
- Don't imagine that even the most avowed nationalist would really prefer to join France or Holland.
- Don't trust pedestrian crossings without very good medical insurance.

- Don't assume drivers are sober. As one Belgian motorist put it, "If we weren't drunk, we'd be too scared to drive!"
- Don't miss the crazy carnivals, the bizarre pageants and the touchingly banal *braderies*.
- Don't admit to Belgian friends that you file your taxes properly. You'll be taken for a liar or a fool.

272

GLOSSARY

USEFUL WORDS AND PHRASES

English	French	Flemish
Hello	*Bonjour*	*Hallo*
Hi	*Salut*	*Dag*
How do you do	*Comment allez-vous*	*Hoe gaat het met U*
Very good thanks	*Très bien merci*	*Zeer goed, dank U*
OR LESS POLITELY		
How are you?	*Comment ça va?*	*Hoe gaat het?*
Fine thanks	*Ça va bien, merci*	*Goed, dank U*
How's it going?	*Ça va?*	*Hoe gaat het?*
OK	*Ça va*	*Alles goed*
Good day	*Bonjour / Bonne journée (said as a farewell)*	*Goed dag*
Good morning		*Goedemorgen*
Good afternoon	*Bon aprés midi*	*Goede-namiddag*
Good evening	*Bonsoir / Bonne soirée (said as a farewell)*	*Goede avond*
Good night	*Bonne nuit*	*Goede nacht*
Good bye	*Au revoir*	*Tot ziens*
Come back soon	*Reviens vite*	*Kom snel terug*
See you later	*A bientôt*	*Tot later*
Take care	*Fait gaffe (very colloquial)*	*Houd U goed*
Yes	*Oui*	*Ja*
No	*Non*	*Nee*
Maybe	*Peut-être*	*Misschien*
Please	*S'il vous plaît*	*Alstublieft*

English	French	Flemish
Thank you very much	*Merci beaucoup*	*Dank u wel*
Thanks	*Merci*	*Bedankt*
Excuse me	*Excusez-moi*	*Excuseer mij* or *sorry*
I'm sorry	*Je suis désolé(e)*	*Het spijt mij*
How much is that?	*Ça fait combien?*	*Hoeveel maakt dit?*
I	*Je/j'*	*Ik*
Me	*Moi*	*Mij*
My	*Mon/Ma*	*Mijn*
You (informal)	*Tu/Te*	*Jij*
You (formal)	*Vous*	*U*
Your (informal)	*Ton/Ta*	*Jouw*
Your (formal)	*Votre*	*Uw*
He	*Il*	*Hij*
Him	*Lui*	*Zijn*
His/hers	*Son/Sa*	*Haar*
She/her	*Elle*	*Zij*
It	*Il/Elle*	*Het*
Us	*Nous*	*Wij*
Our	*Notre*	*Ons/onze*
They	*Ils/Elles*	*Zij*
It's...	*C'est...*	*Dat is...*
Is it...?	*Est-ce que c'est...?*	*Is dat...?*
It isn't...	*Ce n'est pas....*	*Dat is niet...*
Delicious	*Delicieux*	*Lekker*
Good (food)	*Bon*	*Goed*
Good (other)	*Bien*	*Goed*
Beautiful	*Beau/Belle*	*Mooi*
Interesting	*Interesant(te)*	*Interessant (e)*
Strange	*Étrange*	*Vreemd(e)*

English	French	Flemish
Too big	*Trop grand(e)*	*Te groot*
Too small	*Trop petit(e)*	*Te klein*
Too expensive	*Trop cher(e)*	*Te duur*
Early	*Tôt*	*Vroeg(e)*
Late	*Tard*	*Laat(e)*
Fast	*Vite*	*Snel(le)*
Slow	*Lent*	*Traag (trage)*
Very	*Très*	*Erg*
Where is...?	*Où est...?*	*Waar is...?*
Which direction?	*Quelle direction?*	*Welke richting?*
Straight on	*Tout droit*	*Rechtdoor*
Left	*À gauche*	*Links*
Right	*À droite*	*Rechts*
(Not) far from here	*(Pas) loin d'ici*	*(Niet) ver van hier*
The post office	*La poste*	*Het postkantoor*
The town hall	*La maison communale*	*Het stadhuis*
The tourist office	*L'office de tourisme*	*Het toerismebureau*
The main square	*La grand place*	*De grote markt*
The station	*La gare*	*Het station*
The bus stop for...	*L'arrêt d'autobus vers...*	*... De bushalte*
Shops	*Magasins*	*Winkels*
Bakery	*Boulangerie*	*Bakkerij*
Cake shop	*Pâtisserie*	*Patisserie*
Butcher	*Boucherie*	*Slagerij*
Market	*Marché*	*Markt*
Bookshop	*Librairie*	*Boekenwinkel*
Library	*Bibliothèque*	*Bibliotheek*
Bank	*Banque*	*Bank*

English	French	Flemish
Supermarket	*Supermarché*	*Grootwarenhuis*
Pharmacy	*Pharmacie*	*Apotheek*
Toilet	*Toilette*	*Toilet*

NUMBERS

Numeral	French	Flemish
One	*Un/une*	*Een*
Two	*Deux*	*Twee*
Three	*Trois*	*Drie*
Four	*Quatre*	*Vier*
Five	*Cinq*	*Vijf*
Six	*Six*	*Zes*
Seven	*Sept*	*Zeven*
Eight	*Huit*	*Acht*
Nine	*Neuf*	*Negen*
Ten	*Dix*	*Tien*
Eleven	*Onze*	*Elf*
Twelve	*Douze*	*Twaalf*
Thirteen	*Treize*	*Dertien*
Fourteen	*Quatorze*	*Veertien*
Fifteen	*Quinze*	*Vijftien*
Sixteen	*Seize*	*Zestien*
Seventeen	*Dix-sept*	*Zeventien*
Eighteeen	*Dix-huit*	*Achttien*
Nineteen	*Dix-neuf*	*Negentien*
Twenty	*Vingt*	*Twintig*
Twenty-one	*Vingt-et-un*	*Eenentwintig*
Twenty-two	*Vingt-deux*	*Tweeëntwintig*
Twenty-three	*Vingt-trois*	*Drieëntwintig*
Thirty	*Trente*	*Dertig*
Forty	*Quarante*	*Veertig*

Numeral	French	Flemish
Fifty	*Cinquante*	*Vijftig*
Sixty	*Soixante*	*Zestig*
Seventy	*Septante **	*Zeventig*
Eighty	*Quatre-vingt*	*Tachtig*
Ninety	*Nonante **	*Negentig*
One hundred	*Cent*	*Honderd*
One hundred and one	*Cent-et-un/ Cent-et-une*	*Honderd en één*
One hundred and two	*Cent-deux*	*Honderd en twee*
Two hundred	*Deux cents*	*Twee honderd*
Three hundred	*Trois cents*	*Drie honderd*
One thousand	*Mille*	*Duizend*
Ten thousand	*Dix-mille*	*Tien duizend*
One hundred thousand	*Cent-mille*	*Honderd duizend*
One million	*Un million*	*Een miljoen*

* Only in Belgium

English	French	Flemish
What's the time?	*Quelle heure est-il?*	*Hoe laat is het?*
One o'clock	*Une heure*	*Eén uur*
Half past two	*Deux heures et demi*	*Half drie*
Quarter past four	*Quatre heures et quart*	*Kwart over vier*
7:20 am	*Sept heures vingt*	*Zeven uur twintig*
7:20 pm (19:20 hours)	*Dix-neuf heures vingt*	*Negentien uur*
Twenty to seven	*Sept heures moins vingt*	*Twintig voor zeven*

DAYS OF THE WEEK

English	French	Flemish
Monday	*Lundi*	*Maandag*
Tuesday	*Mardi*	*Dinsdag*
Wednesday	*Mecredi*	*Woensdag*
Thursday	*Jeudi*	*Donderdag*
Friday	*Vendredi*	*Vrijdag*
Saturday	*Samedi*	*Zaterdag*
Sunday	*Dimanche*	*Zondag*

MONTHS OF THE YEAR

English	French	Flemish
January	*Janvier*	*Januari*
February	*Février*	*Februari*
March	*Mars*	*Maart*
April	*Avril*	*April*
May	*Mai*	*Mei*
June	*Juin*	*Juni*
July	*Juillet*	*Juli*
August	*Août*	*Augustus*
September	*Septembre*	*September*
October	*Octobre*	*October*
November	*Novembre*	*November*
December	*Décembre*	*December*

RESOURCE GUIDE

- Telephone country code + 32
- International dial-out code 00
- Local calls Dial the complete number including city code even when you're in that town

Emergency Numbers
- Medical emergency 100
- Police 101
- Red Cross/24-hour ambulance 105
- Fire brigade 112
- Child Focus 110
  (European centre for missing children)
- Community Help Line (02) 648-4014
  (offering 24-hour help in English for problems of any kind)
- AIDS Helpline in English (02) 512-0505
  (7:00pm–9:00 pm only)

Directory Assistance
- Dial 1405 for assistance in English, but beware that the charge is € 2.20 for a maximum of two national/international queries. (Ouch!) If you can speak French/Flemish, call 1307/1207 instead for only € 1.12.
- SCOOT (http://www.scoot.be) is a commercial service finder—type in the product you want and the area you are in and they may give you a useful shop address (with a map to find it). Or maybe not.
  The following websites both conduct White and Yellow Pages directory searches:
- http://www.infobel.com/belgium/
- http://www.belgacom.be

USEFUL WEBSITES
Government Websites
- http://www.belgium.be

Belgian Search
- http://www.advalvas.be
- http://www.webwatch.be

Francophone Community
- http://www.cfwb.be

Flanders Online
- http://www.flanders.be

Wallonia Online
- http://www.wallonie.be

Brussels Capital Region
- http://www.bruxelles.irisnet.be

What's On Listings
- http://www.xpats.com
  (click Going Out then Agenda)
- http://www.idearts.com
  (Museums & Galleries in Wallonia—in French)
- http://www.cinebel.be
  (complete Cinema listings in French/Flemish)
- http://www.use-it.be
  (all you need for Antwerp and Gent)
- http://www.telemoustique.be
  (TV listings in French)
- http://www.demorgen.be/film/tvgids/index.html
  (TV listings in Flemish)
- http://www.iteevee.be
  (links to all Flemish TV channel sites)

Expatriate Information
- www.xPATs.com
- www.expatica.com/belgium

All Things Belgian
- www.frites.be

EMBASSIES IN BRUSSELS

- Australia
  Rue Guimard 6-8 Guimardstraat, B1040
  Tel: (02) 286-0500
- UK
  Rue d'Arlon 85 Aalenstraat, B1040
  Tel: (02) 287-6211
- USA
  Regentlaan 27 Boulevard du Régent, B1000
  Tel: (02) 508-2111
  Beware that heavy-handed security at this embassy means that visitors are not usually allowed to enter with any baggage. This can cause logistic problems as there are no baggage lockers available. Also beware that calls for visa information and appointments incur a € 15 call-charge.
- Other embassies are listed in the Brussels Yellow Pages telephone directory under 'Ambassades'.

MEDICINE

For official help with all things medical consult
- http://www.health.fgov.be

A helpful overview of medical procedures and an extensive hospital listing is available on
- http://www.xpats.com/cgi-bin/newcomer/guide.cgi?1020%A7103

For more about payments and reimbursements of medical expenses look at
- http://www.inami.be
- http://www.socialsecurity.be

For free AIDs tests visit the Centre Elisa, Rue d'Artois 46 Artiëstraat, Brussels, Tel: (02) 513-2651 (5:00 pm–8:00 pm, Tuedays or Thursdays; 11:00 am–2:00 pm, Wednesdays or Fridays)

Antwerp's ITG (Prince Leopold Hospital for Tropical Medicine, Nationalestraat 155, Tel: (03) 247-6666, http://www.itg.be)

is the place to head if you've picked up something rather peculiar on your exotic travels or if you want a non-standard immunisation, against lesser-known nasties like Siberian tick-born encephalitis.

For information on non-legal drugs, clinics, needle exchanges etc. consult
- http://www.ac-company.org/tips/en/belgen.htm

Major Hospitals
Antwerp
- Central/St Elizabet
  Leopoldstraat 26
  Tel: (03) 234-4111

Brussels
- St Pièrre/ULB
  Rue Haute 290 Hoogstraat
  Tel: (02) 535-3111
- Brugmann/ULB
  Three sites (in Laeken, Schaabeek and Jette)
  Website: http://www.chu-brugmann.be
  Unusual for its cannabis clinic since 2002.
- St Luc/UCL
  Ave Hippocrate 10 Hippocrateslaan
  Tel: (02) 764-1111
  Website: http://www.saintluc.be
- Erasme/ULB
  Route de Lennik 808 Lenniksebaan
  Tel: (02) 555-3111
  Website: http://www.hopitalerasme.be

Liège
- Centre Hospitalier Universitaire de Liège (CHU)
  Avenue de l'Hôpital
  Tel: (04) 366-7111
  Website: http://www.chuliege.be/

SCHOOLS

Useful information on schools appears in an annual schools' guide that comes free for subscribers of *The Bulletin* every April and in their twice yearly *Newcomer* guide. You can also visit:

http://www.xpats.com/cgi-bin/newcomer/
guide.cgi?1010%A7100

while

http://www.kuleuven.ac.be/soi/schoolbe.htm

has a vast selection of school web-links.

Do remember that where you choose to live will affect the language of the public schools that are available for your children.

For a full listing of Francophone primary schools in each commune, visit:

http://www.agers.cfwb.be/org/fondam/commune.asp

The website

http://www.restode.cfwb.be/org/index.htm

provides information on schools in the French community including details of special facility schools (in French).

For details on the compulsory education sector, visit the website (also in French):

http://www.agers.cfwb.be/ORG/ensoblig/sommaire.htm

Etudes, Toutes Directions produced annually by *Le Vif L'Express* is a useful Francophone booklet that helps with further education and career choices. Call (02) 640-8008 for a copy.

Information on Flemish schools is available at

http://www.ond.vlaanderen.be/

or at the smaller and less comprehensive English-language site

http://www.flanders.be/public/flanders/
education/index. asp

Language Schools

Numerous language schools are listed in *The Bulletin* and especially in its twice-yearly *Newcomer* directory. Also check:

http://www.xpats.com/cgi-bin/newcomer/
guide.cgi?1015%A7100.

As well as professional language schools, many local adult-education colleges offer excellent language courses, not just in French or Flemish (various levels), but also in a wide range of other tongues. Prices are generally very reasonable (around € 80 for a year's course studying around three hours per week). The main drawback is that all courses start in September and often require you to sign up several months before to ensure a place.

BOOKSHOPS

The biggest bookshop in Brussels is the cavernous French-owned FNAC on a special floor of the City2 shopping centre, off the rue Neuve. For books specifically in English the main Brussels choices are:

- Waterstones
  Boulevard Adolphe Max 71-75 Adolphe Maxlaan
  Tel: (02) 219-2708
  Website: http://www.waterstones.be/
- Sterling Books
  Fossé aux Loups 38 Wolvengracht
  Tel: (02) 223-6223
  Website: http://www.sterling-books.be
- The Reading Room
  503 Ave George Henri

  For travel books, try the Anticyclone des Açores (Rue Fosse aux Loups 34, Wolvengracht) which has a superb range in a variety of languages, or the much smaller Le 7ème Continent in Waterloo (Chaussée de Bruxelles 165, Passage Wellington 65, Waterloo; tel: (02) 353-0230; website: http://www.septiemecontinent.be/).

  For second-hand books and books at reduced prices (mainly Flemish but with a selection in English), try

De Slegte on the rue des Grands Carmes/Lievevrouwbroersstraat in Brussels or look into Evasions across the street at the corner with the rue du Midi/Zuidstraat (plenty of old guides to Brussels and Belgium, mostly in French). Rather like Hay-on-Wye in England, Redu in the Ardennes has become known as a 'book village' and has summer and Easter book fairs with shops staying open into the night. The Belgian equivalent of Amazon online bookshop is http://www.proxis. be which stocks books in English as well as French and Dutch. Their prices are typically somewhat higher than Amazon or Barnes & Noble, but this is offset by local postage rates and no fears of being hit for VAT charges by customs (via the post office).

NEWSPAPERS

De Standaard is the most stridently Flemish newspaper. *La Libre Belgique* (started during World War II as a secret underground newspaper) is a French-language daily with a perceived upper-class readership and a firmly 'keep-Belgium-united' stance.

De Morgen, *La Dernière Heure* and *Het Laatste Nieuws* are progressive-liberal newspapers, each with a relatively lowbrow populist tone. Curiously, considering the Belgian love of gossip, there are no real muckraking tabloid newspapers: "We don't have a culture for them," said one Belgian friend without a hint of irony.

Le Soir is a respected Francophone daily. It contains a useful cultural supplement on Wednesdays and has good online news archives at http://www.lesoir.com. Other regional newspapers include *Le Courrier et l'Escaut* in Tournai, *La Wallonie* in Liège and *Gazet van Antwerpen* in... guess where. *Vlan*, which appears in various local varieties, is a free advertisement listings newspaper which is useful if you're looking to buy or sell anything.

L'Echo and *De Financieel-Ekonomische Tijd* are the Francophone and Flemish business newspapers. Newspapers in English including *The Financial Times*, *The Times*, *Herald Tribune* and *The Wall Street Journal* are all reprinted locally.

Other British and American newspapers are available as imports.

Metro is a free newspaper given away on the Brussels metro and certain mainline trains. Available in French or Flemish, it has events and TV listings and gives website links for readers to follow up the news and sports stories reported. Its inspired 'Kiss and Ride' column allows love-struck passengers to admit their burning passions for fellow commuters with whom they may only have made brief wordless eye-contact across a crowded carriage. Some entries are quite poetic.

MAGAZINES

Le Vif L'Express and *Knack* are respectively the main Francophone and Flemish news weeklies. Both are respected for their independent political voices.

Télé Moustique is the Francophone Belgian equivalent of the British Radio Times, a TV guide that advertises itself as 'the magazine that bites' (its name translates as 'TV Mosquito'). It earned national respect for its investigative journalism by nibbling away at a series of paedophile and corruption cases and keeping the public focused on serious allegations when a bout of finger-pointing in 1997 appeared to taint half of the political elite. *Humo* is the Flemish-language equivalent. Considered a master of irony, its editor from 1969–2003, Guy Mortier is also a TV and radio personality. *Trends* is a Flemish business magazine.

Park Mail is a Francophone magazine given away at car parks. It's worth picking up for the amusing and sarcastic snipes at recent news events that you'll find on the first page. English-language news weeklies *Time*, *Newsweek* and *The Economist* are widely available while *The Bulletin* is the best source of Belgian news in English and has a comprehensive weekly events listing.

FURTHER READING

The selection here makes no claims to be comprehensive, but reflects what I have personally found to be most helpful and enlightening. Although sources in local languages tend to be even more useful, I have largely restricted the list to publications in English.

CULTURE: GETTING A FEEL

The best way to get a feel for a culture is to laugh sympathetically at its foibles rather than dissect it academically. If you don't have the time to do so in person, there are two particularly fine, lighthearted introductions to the Belgian people that do so for you:

Xenophobe's Guide to the Belgians. Anthony Mason. London: Oval Books (http://www.xenophobes.com), 1999. Updated 2004.

- Lots of genuine insights on the people and culture despite the jokey style. When I first read this little 64-page book, I wondered whether the author knew my wife and her family. I hadn't realised until then how typically Belgian they were!

A Tall Man in a Low Land. Harry Pearson. New York, NY: Little, Brown and Co, 1998.

- Pearson, a columnist and cycling fan, decides to take a long holiday in Belgium. What? A long holiday? In BELGIUM? "The concept was just too alien and difficult," he explains. "It was as if we had tried to explain the theory of special relativity to a 3-year-old." The resultant book is a brilliant series of well-informed swipes and chortles at everything from Walloon pet shops to racing pigeons to Flemish garden gnomes. Highly recommended, although non-British readers might struggle with some of his funniest analogies.

In the Belgian Chateau: The Spirit and Culture of a European Society in an Age of Change. Renée C Fox. Chicago: Ivan R Dee Inc, 1994.

- This book is an interesting attempt to look at the traditional class system within the Belgian context. However, it's hard to find and considered a little dated by some Belgian readers.

SETTLING IN

At the risk of repeating the fact a little too often, expatriates in Belgium will thank themselves for taking a subscription to the weekly magazine *The Bulletin*. Call (02) 373-9909 or fax (02) 375-9822 for subscription details. Subscribers receive the very useful magazine *Newcomer* twice yearly. It's packed with practical information about the way systems work here, and lists contacts for a variety of menial but important day-to-day needs. Another useful source is *Expats in Brussels*, an annual guide. A very useful annual mini-guide to all kinds of citizens rights and responsibilities is *Belgopocket* (http://belgopocket.belgium.be), available free from post offices in French or Flemish.

TRAVEL AND ACCOMMODATION GUIDES

In English, the *Blue Guide* is the best travel guide for its sheer weight of facts, places and historical detail, although it does not necessarily give practical advice for accommodation options and restaurants. The *Blue Guide* also has some very good town plans and has a fairly comprehensive colour atlas which is much more useful than a small country map. The *Michelin Green Guide* is likewise good but less detailed. Both the *Rough Guide* and the *Lonely Planet Guide to Belgium and Luxembourg* are reasonable enough for visiting major sites. Both have decent town maps, though these are worth supplementing with more comprehensive maps and accommodation pamphlets from local tourist offices. Neither really offers much on the smaller towns or lesser attractions.

As well as all-country books, there are several guides concentrating on Bruges, Brussels and Antwerp—

a particularly interesting choice is Derek Blyth's *Flemish Cities Explored* (London: Pallas Athene, 1996).

If you read French or Flemish, your choice is vastly wider; guide books and thematic picture books are written on pretty much any region, city or aspect of Belgium. For great B&B and hotel recommendations, try *Maisons d'Hôtes de Caractère/Karaktervolle Gastenkamers* or the very practical *Logis de Belgique*, a little sister volume to the great *Logis de France*. The *Ippa Guides* are excellent for their coverage on thematic interests (festivals, castles, abbeys, etc.) and have plenty of glorious photographs without skimping on detailed background information. However, the guides lack maps and have small indexes.

FOOD

For selecting restaurants, the excellent annual *Delta Guides* are incredibly thorough. Recipe books include the *Everybody Eats Well in Belgium Cookbook* by Ruth Van Waerebeek-Gonzalez (New York, NY: Workman Publishing, 1996). It has over 200 Belgian recipes from fancy fruit-meat counterpoints to good old meatballs in beer. The book offers ingredient alternatives for dishes where items like sorrel may be hard to find. Also worth a try is The *Belgo Cookbook* by Denis Blaise and Andre Pilsnier (New York, NY: Clarkson N Potter, 2000).

HISTORICAL

Histoire de Belgique is still the classic historical work, though written in the 1950s. Four volumes, in French.

History of the Low Countries. Ed. J C H Blom and E Lamberts. Trans. James C Kennedy. New York, NY: Berghahn Books, 1999.
- A well-illustrated collection of pieces by specialists in various fields, translated such that it manages to maintain a very readable consistency of style.

The Dutch Revolt. *Penguin Classic History* series. Geoffrey Parker. London: Penguin Books Ltd, 2002.
- One of those rare history books which manages to keep a sharp analytical focus yet remain as thrilling to read as

any good adventure novel. Gives a very broad feel for the background and history of the whole epoch as well as the two decades specifically described. As the author quickly makes explicit, the title is a misnomer—there was not one but three main revolts between 1566 and 1581.

The Low Countries in Early Modern Times. Ed. Herbert H Rowen. Hampshire, UK: Macmillan, 1973
- A specialist collection of translated source documents rather than a history book per se, focusing somewhat more on the Netherlands than on Belgium. But some fascinating snippets include Herman Ghijsen's 1663 analysis of the economic dangers that would result should France grab Flanders (which it did in 1667).

Medieval Flanders. David Nicholas. Boston, MA: Addison Wesley-Longman. 1992.
- A survey of Flemish life and times with interesting quotations from contemporary documents, of which many have not been previously translated into English. Readable enough, though aimed primarily at academic researchers.

Lion Rampant. Robert Woollcombe. Edinburgh: Black & White Publishing, 1994.
- Flemish nationalism considered.

BIOGRAPHICAL
The King Incorporated: Leopold the Second and the Congo. Neal Ascherson. London: Granta Publications, 2001.
- An intriguing attempt to understand King Leopold II without merely judging him as the monstrous dictator of the Congo. Meanwhile it gives you all you need to know about explorer Henry Morton Stanley's sex life, and the tearful fears that plagued it.

The Coburgs of Belgium. Thro Aronson,. London: Cassell, 1977.
- Written in 1968 but reprinted more recently, this book gives readers a glimpse of the lives of the Belgian kings

and those of their extraordinary extended family for the period until Baudouin's accession.

Paul Delvaux: Surrealizing the Nude. Essays in Art and Culture series. David Scott. London: Reaktion Books, 1997.
- Illustrated attempt to work out the importance of Delvaux to 20th century art and why he had to keep on painting his naked wife against classical landscapes.

HISTORICAL LITERATURE

If you read a single historical novel about Belgium, the obvious choice is Hugo Claus' epic *The Sorrow of Belgium* (New York, NY: Overlook Press/Tusk Ivories edition, 2003). It manages to handle the topics of Flemish nationalism and Nazi collaboration with great sensitivity, woven into a day-to-day tale of a teenage schoolboy during World War II. This book is a brave attempt at keeping all the characters ambivalent—no heroes, no baddies, just real people muddling through.

The Shovel and the Loom. Carl Friedman. New York, NY: Persea Books, 1999.
- A tale set in Antwerp's old Jewish quarter, about a family torn between trying to forget wartime horrors and to salvage memories. The movie *Left Luggage* starring Isabella Rossellini and Maximilian Schell was based on this book.

ABOUT THE AUTHOR

Mark Elliott first visited Brussels at the grand age of nine and blames the Atomium for a misguided childhood fascination with chemistry. Enlightened Belgian cousins revealed to him the charms of Kwak, *soukous* music and the Forêt de Soignes, yet he fled east. But after three years of squid and blues harmonica, Elliott left his temporarily adopted Japanese island exile, heading home for the UK. So far, he's only made it as far as Belgium where he's been living ever since with a very special woman who found him at a Turkmenistan camel market. Elliott has written several travel guidebooks, including *Asia Overland* (1998), *Azerbaijan with Georgia* (1999, 2001, 2004), *South-East Asia Graphic Guide* (2003, www.trailblazer-guides.com) and has contributed to numerous *Lonely Planet* guides.

INDEX

Titles in the CULTURESHOCK! series:

Argentina	Hawaii	Pakistan
Australia	Hong Kong	Paris
Austria	Hungary	Philippines
Bahrain	India	Portugal
Barcelona	Indonesia	San Francisco
Beijing	Iran	Saudi Arabia
Belgium	Ireland	Scotland
Bolivia	Israel	Sri Lanka
Borneo	Italy	Shanghai
Brazil	Jakarta	Singapore
Britain	Japan	South Africa
Cambodia	Korea	Spain
Canada	Laos	Sweden
Chicago	London	Switzerland
Chile	Malaysia	Syria
China	Mauritius	Taiwan
Costa Rica	Mexico	Thailand
Cuba	Morocco	Tokyo
Czech Republic	Moscow	Turkey
Denmark	Munich	Ukraine
Ecuador	Myanmar	United Arab
Egypt	Nepal	Emirates
Finland	Netherlands	USA
France	New York	Vancouver
Germany	New Zealand	Venezuela
Greece	Norway	Vietnam

For more information about any of these titles, please contact any of our Marshall Cavendish offices around the world (listed on page ii) or visit our website at:

www.marshallcavendish.com/genref